INVESTING IN OUR EDUCATION: LEADING, LEARNING, RESEARCHING AND THE DOCTORATE

INTERNATIONAL PERSPECTIVES ON HIGHER EDUCATION RESEARCH

Series Editor: Malcolm Tight

Recent Volumes:

INTERNATIONAL PERSPECTIVES ON HIGHER
EDUCATION RESEARCH   VOLUME 13

INVESTING IN OUR EDUCATION: LEADING, LEARNING, RESEARCHING AND THE DOCTORATE

EDITED BY

ALISON TAYSUM
University of Leicester, Leicester, UK

STEPHEN RAYNER
*Newman University, Birmingham, UK;
Monash University, Melbourne, Australia*

United Kingdom – North America – Japan
India – Malaysia – China

Emerald Group Publishing Limited
Howard House, Wagon Lane, Bingley BD16 1WA, UK

First edition 2014

British Library Cataloguing in Publication Data
A catalogue record for this book is available from the British Library

ISBN: 978-1-78441-132-9
ISSN: 1479-3628 (Series)

INVESTOR IN PEOPLE

CONTENTS

LIST OF CONTRIBUTORS

Richard Andrews	Anglia Ruskin University, Cambridge, UK
Justine Mercer	Centre for Education Studies, University of Warwick, Coventry, UK
Marlene Morrison	Oxford Brookes University, Oxford, UK
Richard Pring	University of Winchester, Winchester, UK
Stephen Rayner	School of Education, Newman University, Birmingham, UK; Monash University, Melbourne, Australia
Eugenie A. Samier	The British University in Dubai, Dubai, UAE
David Scott	Institute of Education, University of London, London, UK
Carolyn M. Shields	Wayne State University, Detroit, MI, USA
Charles L. Slater	Educational Leadership Department, College of Education, California State University, Long Beach, CA, USA
Emefa Takyi-Amoako	Oxford ATP International Education, Oxford, UK
Alison Taysum	School of Education, University of Leicester, Leicester, UK
Annette Thomas-Gregory	Faculty of Health, Social Care and Education, Anglia Ruskin University, Cambridge, UK
Yusef Waghid	Stellenbosch University, Stellenbosch, South Africa

INTRODUCTION: INVESTING IN OUR EDUCATION? LEADING, LEARNING, RESEARCHING AND THE DOCTORATE

Alison Taysum and Stephen Rayner

ABSTRACT

Purpose — *The purpose of this chapter is to introduce the role of the doctorate as an investment in education, and to consider whose education is being invested in, how and why. We examine the role of postgraduate research within the doctorate and how this may contribute to a self-improving profession, self-improving educational institutions and self-improving education systems.*

Methodology/approach — *The methodology is the representation of different chapters from authors that explore the key themes that we introduce in this chapter.*

Findings — *We present the three main findings from a British Educational Leadership, Management and Administration Doctoral Research Interest Group seminar series funded by the British Educational Leadership, Management and Administration Society (BELMAS). First*

Investing in our Education: Leading, Learning, Researching and the Doctorate
International Perspectives on Higher Education Research, Volume 13, 1–16
Copyright © 2014 by Emerald Group Publishing Limited
All rights of reproduction in any form reserved
ISSN: 1479-3628/doi:10.1108/S1479-362820140000013001

is the progression of a systemic basis for active educational research, engaged with the mobilization of learning-based and pedagogic knowledge leadership within doctoral scholarship, learning and pedagogy. Second is the continued examination of the internationalization of purpose, structure and function in doctoral study through evidence informed leadership. Third is the provision of opportunities to explore ways in which doctoral study may facilitate educational leaders to recognize 'minoritised' and marginalized communities, and disrupt dominant discourses that work within patterns of ecologies that 'pathologise' diversity and difference.

Originality/value — *Here, a clearly stated focus emerged during the seminar series, emphasizing how leaders engaging with doctoral learning have the opportunity to articulate generative transformative theories of human learning for a civic curriculum, and to apply this new knowledge to work for change for students' full economic, cultural and political participation in the society.*

Keywords: British Educational Leadership, Management and Administration Society; knowledge; learning; change; civic engagement; research

This book has emerged from a network called the British Educational Leadership, Management and Administration Society Doctoral Research Interest Group (BELMAS DRIG). As Stoll, Bolam, McMahaon, and Thomas (2006) and Rayner (2011) identify, international evidence reveals there is much potential in the use of networks to facilitate educational leadership, learning and change. The BELMAS DRIG network was developed as part of an attempt to introduce to a community of educational leadership practitioners, a research and development initiative comprising a strategy rooted in the idea of 'deliberated and focused research activity'. This involved the use of 'networking' to action for the mobilization of knowledge and its transfer by bringing individuals together to build collective capacity and progress better understanding in practising leadership, management, and administration of new knowledge framed by policy through the doctorate.

The aim of the BELMAS DRIG ties in with BELMAS (2014a, p. 1), which is a member organization, whose modus operandi is

> to maintain, promote, and extend public education by advancing the practice, teaching, study of and research into educational leadership, management and administration.

BELMAS aims to provide a distinctive, independent and critical voice in the pursuit of quality education through effective leadership and management. We are concerned with ideas and practice and the inter-relationship between the two. To do this BELMAS aims to:

- encourage and facilitate discussion and dissemination of ideas related to good practice
- encourage and facilitate collaboration between practitioners and academics within and across educational sectors
- encourage and facilitate reflective and research-based approaches to leadership and management
- encourage and facilitate networking
- represent nationally and internationally the importance of effective leadership and management for educational improvement

BELMAS's unique contribution is a capacity to bring together 'practitioners' and 'academics' as well as representatives from all sectors of education in a context in which no particular 'interest' is represented. BELMAS members are concerned with generating and debating ideas that make a difference and to discover, understand and disseminate good practice wherever it may occur.

In 'doing this' our effort is as Burgess, Sieminski, and Arthur (2006) suggest bringing together context, theory and practice. Our notion of 'leading scholarship' reflected in most of the chapters in this book is a key aspect of a wider approach to 'learning leadership' (see Rayner, 2009), which is we suggest, both about a way to provide professional learning for the formation of educational leaders as well as to reinforce and engender an essential quality in professional learning for educationists reflected in a continuing process of engagement with practitioner enquiry and doctoral level study that connects theory and practice (Shulman, Golde, Bueschel, & Garabedian, 2006). It is in every way an authentic rendering of the idea of research-led practice as well as research-informed leadership and management.

Doctorates include the Educational Doctorate (EdD) for those who seek to develop their leadership skills within the education profession, and the PhD for those wishing to develop as a career researcher. Taysum (2006) argues that a differentiating feature between the EdD and PhD is that the latter is examined only through the final thesis and the doctorate in education is assessed through module assignments and the final thesis, though latterly PhDs are becoming more modular in a potential attempt to standardize the doctoral experience. The PhD doctoral student often studies on their own and the professional or taught doctoral student shares a structured group learning context for most of their doctoral studies with professionals in the same field. Thus the EdD contains within its rubric the powerful potential to enable networks to be established from the outset, to both foster as well as focus upon the intellectual work associated with growing leadership, management and administration capacity within education systems shaped increasingly by globalized policy contexts (Ball, 2012).

EDUCATIONAL LEADERSHIP, MANAGEMENT AND ADMINISTRATION AND INTERNATIONAL DOCTORAL STUDY

Educational leadership focuses on the vision and values of an organization, however Gunter, Hall, and Bragg (2013) argue that the role of principal is too big for one person. After heavy investment into the notion of 'transformational leadership' compelling evidence identifies that such hero leadership needs problematizing (Leithwood & Levin, 2005) who argue that research about teacher leaders is usually reduced to hierarchical analyses of the lone leader causing effectiveness.

A more participatory approach to leadership has a flatter distribution of leadership. Oswad and Engelbrecht (2013) argue distributed leadership is an approach that requires a principal to balance confidence with humility. These characteristics, along with recognizing different team members' strengths and assigning tasks accordingly, are very important for a principal. Principals therefore need to provide opportunities for participation to enable teachers' voices to be heard. Preparation for effective distributed leadership appears to focus on ethics, values and pedagogical relationships (Taysum, 2012a). Day, Jacobson and Johansson (2011) affirm this and identify that a key aspect in preparing educational leaders for effective distributed leadership is to recognize members of the team's readiness for responsibilities and accountabilities. Moreover, Day (2009) agrees with Oswad and Engelbrecht that values are very important and principals need to develop leadership trust and trustworthiness for effective distributive leadership.

Education management on the other hand focuses on the systems that enable the strategies of the organization to meet the vision and values, to be performed (Ball, 2006). Educational administration arguably transcends the divide between leadership and management and Greenfield and Ribbins (1993, p. 2) defined the school principal as administrator:

> In a profession of administration based upon organizational science the task of the administrator is to bring people and organizations together in a fruitful and satisfying union. In so doing the work of the administrator carried the justification of the larger

social order since they work to link day-to-day activity in organizations to that social order. In schools and colleges the administrator may be Director, or Superintendent, principal or headteacher, department head or supervisor. Whatever their titles, their tasks are the same. They bring people and resources together so that the goals of the organization and presumably of an encompassing social order may be met.

The doctoral programme enables programme providers and students to work in partnership to explore leadership, management and administration and advance knowledge within international networks to build capacity. The BELMAS DRIG network is an internationalizing community, in which doctoral students and doctoral programme providers have crossed borders to participate in the network; this is both physically in face-to-face events, or virtually, where events are mediated via a website on the World Wide Web. International mobility – either physical or virtual – for those studying in and providing a doctorate is an authentic form of the internationalization of higher education and the knowledge economy (OECD, 2009). During doctoral studies, the international student, defined as one who has crossed borders with the specific intent to study, participates in the advancement of the field. The student is therefore able to take their knowledge, skills and understandings back to their nation state and local context along with the international networks that build capacity for both innovation and governance in different spheres (OECD, 2009). OECD (2009, p. 126) states:

> The share of foreign doctoral students in total enrolment differs widely across countries. Non-citizens represent more than 40% of the doctoral population in Switzerland, New Zealand and the United Kingdom, but less than 5% in Italy, and Korea. Shares of foreign and international doctoral students are between 25% and 40% in Canada, France, Belgium, Australia and the United States. In absolute numbers, the United States hosted the largest foreign doctoral population, with more than 92,000 students in 2006 from abroad, followed by the United Kingdom (38,000) and France (28,000).

Transnational higher education (TNHE) includes branch campuses that are attached to a main campus but are set up across borders and supported economically and/or culturally by a host organization of the host nation state. Western higher education institutions have set up branch campuses in the East, and more recently Eastern education institutions have been set up in the West (Haung, 2007). Quality assurance has been an important part of the massive international policy reform and changes to education systems that are impacting at every level of nation states' education systems. At the same time, there is a deepening austerity in education systems, which puts both an internal and externalizing pressure on higher education. These tensions might be represented as a continuum. At one end of the continuum is the maximization of reason (Furlong, 2012). At the other end is the contribution to economic growth. Perhaps the balance shifts at different times in a nation state's policies over time (Taysum, 2012b), but there is a need to maximize reason with a moral imperative whilst recognizing universities were responsible for £3.4 billion contribution to economic growth in 2011–2012 in the United Kingdom (HEFCE, 2013a, 2013b) with small and medium enterprises (SMEs) seeing an increase of activity of 11% through the advancement of specialist knowledge generated through research, or using facilities including computer-aided design (CAD).

AIMS, PURPOSES AND IMPACT OF THE DOCTORATE AS A PUBLIC GOOD

In the book, we explore the aims, purposes, and impact of the doctorate in terms of a public good that contributes to cultural, economic and political understandings and practice. We also explore the context of the doctorate, which is positioned within education systems that face massive global challenges. Indeed, Deem (2012) has suggested that the current UK government may want private-for-profit providers for non-Science, Technology, Engineering and Maths Postgraduate Research programmes. Such a move would arguably move towards privatizing higher education.

Within these complexities, the book considers how the doctorate enables partnerships to develop between practitioners (professional leaders) in higher education institutions and compulsory and post compulsory education systems, public organizations and the third sector. The ways in which the doctorate offers new and valid ways of enabling innovation, utility and building networks that strengthen leadership, management, and administration including governance capacity are also explored. The approach taken is to create and manage knowledge that embodies meaningful methods for assuring improvement, effectiveness, efficiency and equity in education systems. Taysum (2012a, 2013) argues that the doctorate offers the chance for leaders to spend enough time together for critical analysis and reflection leading to understanding the self, recognizing the other, and working for cultural alignment. However, for leaders to make an informed choice about whether doing a doctorate is the right thing for them, they need to understand if the doctorate is worth investing their resource [time and money] as well as the need for a commitment to make it worthwhile. The question emerges, why would an educational practitioner find time, resilience, and commitment to pursue a doctorate in professional learning?

There is in in all of the work contained in this collection a sense of an additional 'dividend' on offer for the practitioner engaged in doctoral study. It has in recent years become fashionable to use the idea of 'capital' in many different ways, ranging from its original meaning as a basis for monetary exchange and trade, to a number of different permutations on the way society enriches or impoverishes its population. Social capital, for example, has led to related ideas about restrictions, opportunities and 'encashing' both a social and/or personal set of resources in a membership of a number of different communities in individuals' work and life. Academic capital, derived from notions of human and/or cultural capital is a second example of the penetration of a monetarist vocabulary that is somewhat ironically accompanied by a wider neo-liberalism in management-speak that has permeated the zeitgeist in contemporary educational policy as it is articulated in the political establishment of the 'western world'. A doctoral community of practice affords authentic opportunity for new forms of critical leadership, which we would argue, ideally, should interrogate the zeitgeist. The need of a professional ethic, for example, is one that is increasingly exercising the business and management community since the collapse of the banking system in the last decade. It is also neatly encapsulated in the recent scandal rocking the Cooperative Bank in the UK. This same idea of personal learning combining with professional development and learning leadership, as argued by Rayner (2007, 2009), is fundamental to an effective educational leadership that has an inherent concern for facilitating the public good, enabling social justice and realizing the fundamental purposes tied to 'learning leadership' and 'professional' praxis.

In an educational setting, and with a view on 'professionalism' and 'learning', this reflects the belief identified by Lieberman and Friedrich (2010), who argue that US policy makers, and researchers call for teachers to become leaders in their institutions because of their knowledge of students, teaching and subject matter. However, they argue little research has focused on the purposes of postgraduate research in equipping professional educationalists to develop them as researchers, knowledge generators, data managers, networkers and leaders who can act as agents of change. Deem (2012) affirms there is a similar situation in the UK regarding a dearth of recent policy for postgraduate programmes. A report into higher education in England: Impact of the 2012 reforms (HEFCE, 2013a) also highlights the need for research to inform policy. The report focuses on the reforms that included the increase in fees students pay for higher education programmes. The report argues since 2010–2011 part-time postgraduate students numbers in England have fallen by 27%.

Moreover, the full extent of the impact of the government reforms will not be known until 2015 because that is when the first students to pay the higher fees and who may have higher levels of debt, will be registering on Postgraduate Research Programmes. The Report (HEFCE, 2013a, p. 11) states the reduction in numbers is of concern because:

> a vibrant postgraduate community is vital to the overall health of higher education in England and to our broader economy and society. However the impact of the Government's reforms on take up of postgraduate education will not be known until 2015 at the earliest.

The Report (HEFCE, 2013a, p. 12) states: 'research is needed to investigate what information prospective taught postgraduate students might need to help them make decisions about studying'. This is particularly important for this book because of the international mobility of doctoral students and growth of doctoral study. We need a call to policy makers which will re-focus attention, and ideally, lead to a recognition of the need to invest resources in part-time professional learning and the potentials embodied in doctoral education for present and future leadership, management, and administration of education.

Encouragingly, and at the same time in the United Kingdom, the Royal Society of Arts and the British Educational Research Association are working in partnership to examine the relationship between research and teacher education and Continuing Professional Development (British Educational Research Association – Royal Society of Arts, 2014). Their focus is on furthering understanding of the impact of research on improving quality within the education profession. In Finland, the role of research within the education system is already a hallmark of the Finnish education profession that enjoys autonomy and quality assurance of its standards as opposed to a regime of external inspectors. The research within the education profession includes the integration of theories, research methodologies and practice (Sahlberg, 2012). Sahlberg (2012) identifies three key principles of research. First, educational professionals need a deep knowledge of innovation linked to their discipline and how this can be learned. Second, a research-orientated disposition needs to be developed with what Sockett (2012) calls a critical approach to what counts as evidence for the claims of truth made, or in other words 'an epistemological presence'. Third, that teacher education and continuing professional development needs to be an object of study in and of itself.

The BELMAS DRIG is a community of practitioners which is research oriented and inquires into opportunities doctoral study offers in learning about substantive and methodological knowledge concerning leadership, management, and administration. The network also provides opportunities for individuals who provide doctoral programmes to link to, exchange, and progress understandings and practice of doctoral education within the global challenges presented by rapid international education reforms, and deepening austerity. We ask, should a University be concerned and involved with offering doctoral provision? And is there any purpose, relevance, or meaning in such a pursuit or provision of the wider field of Education in terms of its leadership, direction, future and the substance of what we will call here the 'educative endeavour'? Addressing these questions seeks to deliberately challenge yet mediate the so-called theory—practice divide in the field. The effort seeks to explore potential synergies between underpinning disciplines that can both inform and interact to generate and mobilize new knowledge in the field.

Most of the chapters in this edited collection emerge from international leading academics and/or researching practitioners who have contributed/participated in keynote presentations to a BELMAS funded seminar series that launched the BELMAS DRIG (Taysum, 2012c). The chapters focus upon aspects of the impact of the doctorate on educational organization, improvement, effectiveness, efficiency and equity in education. The main dimensions of the doctorate explored in this work are reflected in what we argue are key aspects of the doctoral learning experience: purposes of the doctorate, the pedagogies of the doctorate, and educational leaders' and leadership development. Further, the chapters in this edited collection reveal how doctoral study helps equip leaders to implement policy and develop strategies to steer their organizations towards improving policy provision and practice.

This book re-asserts the creative and functional possibilities of the doctorate as professional learning essential for building leadership capacity. Thus the doctorate informs educational processes, practices, growth and civic engagement for social justice, and is an important investment for the future of our education.

STRUCTURE OF THE BOOK

The book consists of three sections. The first section consists of the introductory chapter 'Introduction: Investing in Our Education, Leading, Learning, Research and the Doctorate', and the chapters titled: 'Academic and Professional Knowledge in the Professional Doctorate'; 'Doctoral Study in Challenging Times: Entrenching Banality or Revitalising Prospects for 'Wicked' Intellectual Work. The Case of Educational Administration'; Leadership: Skilled Manager or Virtuous Professional?'; 'New Directions for the Doctoral Thesis' and examines the purposes of the doctorate, the kinds of knowledge that connects with different purposes of the doctorate and how doctorates located within higher education institutions and other courses from non-degree awarding institutions contribute knowledge creation, and economic and cultural growth, or stagnation. The second section of the book consists of the chapters titled: 'Western Doctoral Programmes as Public Service, Cultural Diplomacy or Intellectual Imperialism? Expatriate Educational Leadership Teaching in the United Arab Emirates'; 'Can We Impact Leadership Practice through Teaching Democracy and Social Justice?'; 'The Education Doctorate (Ed. D) and Educational Leader Dispositions and Values in England and the United States' which examine the doctoral pedagogies. The final section of the book consists of the chapters 'Democratic Citizenship Education and Islamic Education: On Sceptical Doctoral Encounters'; 'Developing Nodes in Leading Networks of Knowledge for Leader and Leadership Development: Some African Students' Perspectives on Their Experience of Doctoral Education'; 'Investing in Our Education? Leading, Learning, Researching and the Doctorate'; 'Conclusions: The Doctoral Dividend; Leading, Learning, Researching' which reveal the impact of the doctorate for educational leaders, managers and administrators including their interventions to improve participatory processes, practices, exam results and destinations.

In this chapter, we introduce the book and its structure of three parts. In the chapter titled 'Academic and Professional Knowledge in the Professional Doctorate', David Scott makes the argument that pressures on Universities to introduce doctorates to connect with continuing professional development have had implications for knowledge structures. The leadership of knowledge generation and transformation is being co-constructed with educational professionals and the academy. Scott's chapter focuses on the implications of such reforms.

Marlene Morrison in the chapter titled 'Doctoral Study in Challenging Times: Entrenching Banality or Revitalising Prospects for 'Wicked' Intellectual Work. The Case of Educational Administration' explores the location of leadership development through doctoral study. Morrison considers whether the doctorate entrenches banality and de-intellectualizes leadership studies or provides spaces to revitalize theory, research and practice to co-construct authentic knowledge creation through networked leadership development programmes.

The theme of leadership development through the doctorate is further explored by Richard Pring in the chapter titled 'Leadership: Skilled Manager or Virtuous Professional?'. Pring examines the hegemonic discourses of targets, examination results and performativity encouraged by globalized league tables produced by the Programme for International Student Assessment. Pring argues for a moral imperative and ethical dimension to be at the centre of educational leadership practices and preparation. This is important because leaders have positions of power that have a significant impact on the culture of an organization. The culture of an organization can influence where students' school careers are positioned on a continuum with education of a student who finds their element (Robinson, 2013) at one end, and the training of a student for the labour market today, at the other end. How doctoral study engages with such moral issues is meaningful to international contexts because Nanda and Roche (2014) state that 75 million young people are unemployed around the world, yet 40% of employers cannot fill first-level jobs. There is a gap in the skills set, and perhaps what is missing is the development of moral human beings who are practised in problem solving initiatives that matter to them, rather than the training of a workforce to develop skills for jobs that may not exist in the future (Riddell, 2014).

Richard Andrews in the chapter titled 'New Directions for the Doctoral Thesis' looks at the different ways in which a doctoral thesis can be produced as a representation of new knowledge. Andrews further explores how new projects on the doctorate can challenge traditional knowledge production. Andrews makes the argument that traditional theses submitted for a doctorate may limit and narrow the kinds of doctoral research that may be possible when leading and participating in new social groups of knowledge-based communities. He also makes the argument that theses are traditionally read in particular cultures from left to right and that this serves as only one dominant way in which convention restricts the innovative creation of new knowledge.

Andrews also calls our attention to potential futures for doctoral work and the argument that totally digital submissions, dissertations that are part 'creative' component (e.g. a website, an art installation, an exhibition, a musical or theatre or dance performance, a film, a piece of software) and part critical commentary; dissertations that arise out of and capture the spirit of practice-based research; 'portfolio' submissions, may reveal new forms of knowledge generation and transformation that reveal both leadership capacity building and authentic contributions to the field. Andrews' compelling arguments are an important component of this book because they challenge Policy, Educational Leadership, Management, and Administration readers to consider alternative ways of conceptualizing what counts as a doctoral thesis submission.

Eugenie A. Samier in the chapter titled 'Western Doctoral Programmes as Public Service, Cultural Diplomacy or Intellectual Imperialism? Expatriate Educational Leadership Teaching in the United Arab Emirates' explores doctorate provision in the Western scholarly tradition in non-Western countries like the Arab and Muslim country of the United Arab Emirates. Samier focuses on this issue through three identities. The first is a view of teaching the Western curriculum as a Public Servant motivated by public service to the goals and aims of the country's development articulated by United Arab Emirates (UAE) rulers and its citizens. The second is a view of this as a Cultural Diplomat, representing the Western tradition and its scholarly achievements while respecting and in dialogue with other traditions. The third is a view of delivering a Western curriculum as an Intellectual Imperialist, aiming at a colonizing incorporation of the UAE into the Western academic world. Samier examines how these different identities, through three levels of experience – the existential, the pedagogic and the political – produce different attitudes, values and curriculum.

In the chapter titled 'Can We Impact Leadership Practice through Teaching Democracy and Social Justice?' presented by Carolyn M. Shields, the challenge laid down is one of more effectively ensuring that we teach a deep democracy, and sustain doctoral work that can make a difference in the social worlds from which students come to study Policy, Education, Leadership, Management, and Administration. Drawing on empirical evidence from doctoral programmes, Shields argues it is possible to change the beliefs and leadership practices of graduate students in ways that promote more deeply democratic understandings of, and approaches to, school leadership.

In the chapter titled 'The Education Doctorate (Ed.D.) and Educational Leader Dispositions and Values in England and the United States', Alison Taysum and Charles L. Slater present cases of an English principal and US curriculum leader's experiences of doctoral research. The evidence reveals that these professional educationalists were developing professionally before the doctoral programme and continued to develop afterwards. However, the doctoral programme developed multicultural dispositions and values and helped them to use thinking tools of criticality and reflection as they developed their doctoral thesis, which was identified as a signature pedagogy of the EdD. These changes were not confined to their personal development but equipped them to work for deep democracy in their school communities (Shields, 2013).

Working for deep democracy involves critiquing and reflecting upon inequitable practices and working for cultural alignment that enables greater individual achievement and a better life with shared values, behaviours, symbols and institutions that are in common with others (Shields, 2013). Shields makes the additional important point that work for deep democracy will be different in different contexts and therefore cannot be prescribed. Rather it requires transformative leadership or agents of change to embed a few common principles and values that connect individual accountability with social responsibility.

Yusef Waghid in the chapter titled 'Democratic Citizenship Education and Islamic Education: On Sceptical Doctoral Encounters' examines the role doctoral study plays on sceptical encounters with doctoral students with a sharp focus on two themes. The first is how democratic citizenship education is not always considered as commensurable with Islamic education. The second focuses on how Islamic education is aimed at producing 'good persons' whereas democratic citizenship education aims to engender responsible citizens. However, Yusef argues that the two concepts do not have to be considered as mutually exclusive and that cultivating good persons invariably involves producing responsible persons. Through encounters with three doctoral students, Yusef reveals how sceptical encounters along the lines of 'just action', 'deliberative engagement' and 'responsibility towards' connect, firstly, with liberal education and secondly, present possibilities for Islamic educators.

In the chapter titled 'Developing Nodes in Leading Networks of Knowledge for Leader and Leadership Development: Some African Students' Perspectives on their Experience of Doctoral Education', Emefa Takyi-Amoako explores the question, 'What does the Doctorate and its experience in the United Kingdom mean to the international student?' Over the years, UK universities have served as academic homes to many doctoral students from other parts of the world. Understanding what it means for an international student to obtain a Doctorate in the United Kingdom with regard to developing leadership capacity as nodes in networks is explored. Further, Emefa explores the implications of doctoral study for building governance systems as part of home nation states' strategies. Using data generated from in-depth interviews and a questionnaire, this chapter analyses the views of some international students (particularly those from Africa) with regard to doctoral study in the United Kingdom.

In the chapter titled 'Investing in Our Education? Leading, Learning, Researching and the Doctorate', Annette Thomas-Gregory and Justine Mercer discuss the interrelationships between different aspects of the middle manager's identity related to knowledge, research and practice. A fundamental proposition relates to a conviction that performance within any given role is intrinsically grounded upon the essential integrity of the individual. In other words, effective management is more about the person than the role. The chapter argues that the doctorate offers middle leaders the chance to engage with critical analysis and become reflective and reflexive practitioners who are comfortable with being uncomfortable. Successful management and leadership is claimed to be dependent upon a process of personal authenticity which is related to a complex inter-relationship between different skill sets that have emerged through a lengthy process of deep learning and experience that the doctorate helps to facilitate.

In the chapter titled 'Conclusions: The Doctoral Dividend; Leading, Learning, Researching', Stephen Rayner and Alison Taysum explore by way of a conclusion how the future for doctoral provision in the field of education should both be subject to and involve digging for a new doctoral dividend in professional learning for educational leaders and leadership! The themes previously identified and presented in this collection of work arguably represent a powerful statement as well as a platform upon which to build, involving engagement with new and important strands of the doctorate. We believe this in turn reflects and presents new knowledge regarding leading networks of knowledge that inhabit and suffuse the doctorate site [student experience, personal and professional learning and a doctoral pedagogy]. There is an exciting and full role for such networks to play in integrating knowledge, research and practice.

The BELMAS DRIG continues with calls to seminars found on the BELMAS website (BELMAS, 2014b). The network will build on the intellectual content in these chapters and develop with three new focused aims. The first is to progress a systemic basis for active educational research, engaged with the mobilization of learning-based and pedagogic knowledge leadership within doctoral scholarship, learning and pedagogy. The second is to continue to examine the internationalization of purpose, structure and function in doctoral study through evidence informed leadership. The third is to provide opportunities to explore ways in which doctoral study may facilitate educational leaders to recognize 'minoritised' and marginalized communities, and disrupt dominant discourses that work within patterns of ecologies that 'pathologise' diversity and difference. For the third aim, a clearly stated focus has emerged during the seminar series, emphasizing how leaders engaging with doctoral learning have the opportunity to articulate generative transformative theories of human learning for a civic curriculum, and to apply this new knowledge to work towards change for students' full economic, cultural and political participation in the society.

REFERENCES

Ball. (2006). *Education policy and social class.* London: Routledge and Taylor and Francis Group.

Ball, S. (2012). *Global Education Inc.: New policy networks and the neoliberal imaginary.* London: Routledge.

BELMAS. (2014a). *Development plan.* Sheffield: BELMAS.

BELMAS DRIG. (2014b). BELMAS DRIG website. Available at: http://www.belmasdrig.co.uk/BELMAS_DRIG/Home.html. Downloaded 10th May 2014.

British Educational Research Association – Royal Society of Arts. (2014). Research and the teaching profession. In *Building capacity for a self improving education system.* London: British Educational Research Association.

Burgess, H., Sieminski, S., & Arthur, L. (2006). *Achieving your doctorate in education.* London: Sage.

Day, C. (2009). Building and sustaining successful principalship in England: The importance of trust. *Journal of Education Administration, 47*(6), 719–730.

Day, C., Jacobson, S., & Johansson, O. (2011). Leading organisational learning and capacity building. In R. Ylimaki & S. Jabobson (Eds.), *US and cross-national policies, practices and preparation: Implications for successful instructional leadership, organisational learining, and culturally responsive practices* (pp. 29–50). London: Springer-Kluwer.

Deem, R. (2012). The twenty-first-century university: Dilemmas of leadership and organizational future. In A. Nelson & I. Wei (Eds.), *The Global University.* New York, NY: Palgrave Macmillan.

Furlong, J. (2012). *Education – An anatomy of the discipline: Rescuing the university project?* London: Routledge.

Greenfield, T., & Ribbins, P. (1993). *Greenfield on education administration. Towards a humane craft.* New York, NY: Routledge.

Gunter, H., Hall, D., & Bragg, J. (2013). Distributed leadership: A study in knowledge production. *Educational management administration and leadership, 41*(5), 555–580.

Haung, F. (2007). Internationalization of higher education in the developing and emerging countries: A focus on transnational higher education in Asia. *Journal of Studies in International Education, 11*(3–4), 421–432.

HEFCE. (2013a). A report into higher education in England: Impact of the 2012 reforms. Retrieved from http://www.hefce.ac.uk/about/intro/abouthighereducationinengland/impact/. Accessed on 10th October 2014.

HEFCE. (2013b). *UK universities contribute to economic growth.* Retrieved from http://www.hefce.ac.uk/news/newsarchive/2013/news81928.html. Accessed on May 10, 2014.

Leithwood, K., & Levin, B. (2005). *Assessing school leader programme effects on pupil learning.* DfES Research Report RR662. Nottingham: DfES.

Lieberman, A., & Friedrich, L. (2010). *How teachers become leaders learning from practice and research*. New York, NY: Teachers College Press.

Nanda, P., & Roche, E. (2014). *Jobs go abegging as unemployment rises globally. Live mint and the Wall Street Journal*. Retrieved from http://www.livemint.com/Companies/jG9Nh3BxnARJnhHmn5EBNI/Jobs-go-abegging-as-unemployment-rises-globally.html. Accessed on April 10, 2014.

OECD. (2009). International mobility of doctoral students. In OECD, *OECD Science, Technology and Industry Scoreboard 2009*. OECD Publishing. doi:10.1787/sti_score board-2009-53-en

Oswad, M., & Engelbrecht, P. (2013). Leadership in disadvantaged primary schools. *Educational Management, Administration and Leadership, 41*(5), 620–639.

Rayner, S.(2007). *Managing special and inclusive education*. London: Sage.

Rayner, S. (2009). Educational diversity and learning leadership: A proposition, some principles and a model of inclusive leadership? *Educational Review, 61*(4), 433–447.

Rayner, S. (2011). Researching style: Epistemology, paradigm shifts and research interest groups. Learning and Individual Differences, *21*(2), 255–262.

Riddell, M. (2014). Britain is educating its children for jobs that soon won't exist. *The Telegraph*. Retrieved from http://dralfoldman.com/2014/01/22/britain-is-educating-its-children-for-jobs-that-soon-wont-exist-telegraph/. Accessed on September 10, 2014.

Robinson, K. (2013). *The element: How finding your passion changes everything*. London: Penguin Books.

Sahlberg, P. (2012). *Finnish lessons. What can the world learn from educational change in Finland?* New York, NY: Teachers College Press.

Shields, C. (2013). Leading creatively in high poverty schools: A case for transformative leadership. *European Conference for Educational Research*, Istanbul, September.

Shulman, L., Golde, M., Bueschel, A., & Garabedian, K. (2006). 'Reclaiming education's doctorates: A critique and a proposal. *Educational Researcher* (American Educational Research Association), 35(3), 26.

Sockett, H. (2012). *Knowledge and virtue in teaching and learning*. London: Routledge.

Stoll, L., Bolam, R., McMahaon, A., & Thomas, S. (2006). Professional learning communities: A review of the literature. *Journal of Educational Change, 7*, 221–258.

Taysum, A. (2006). *The learning journeys of educational leaders doing the EdD*. Unpublished Thesis. University of Birmingham.

Taysum, A. (2012a). *Evidence informed leadership in education*. London: Continuum.

Taysum, A. (2012b). A critical historiographical analysis of England's educational policies from 1944 to 2011. *Italian Journal of Sociology of Education. 4*(1), 54–87. Retrieved from http://www.ijse.eu/vol-4-no-1-2012-learning-from-international-educational-policies-to-move-towards-sustainable-living-for-all/. Accessed on May 18, 2014.

Taysum, A. (2012c). BELMAS Doctoral Research Interest Group evaluation report. BELMAS Doctoral Research Interest Group Website. Retrieved from http://www.belmasdrig.co.uk/BELMAS_DRIG/Home.html. Accessed on April 14, 2014.

Taysum, A. (2013). 'Educational Leaders' doctoral research that informed strategies to steer their organizations towards cultural alignment' in *Educational Management, Administration, and Leadership* (first published on October 1). doi:10.1177/1741143 213496660

ACADEMIC AND PROFESSIONAL KNOWLEDGE IN THE PROFESSIONAL DOCTORATE

David Scott

ABSTRACT

This is a conceptual paper. I argue that knowledge-construction, or learning in a profession, has changed with the introduction of professional doctorates, though the divide between these new forms of doctoral study and the older and more established forms such as the PhD are now not as wide as they once were. In particular, three elements of the knowledge-construction process are implicated here. The first of these is a move towards learning environments which prioritise situated-theoretical applications of the theory-practice relationship at the expense of technical-empiricist, technical-rational, multi-methodological and multi-discursive variants. The second is movement towards different sites of learning, so that instead of the knowledge-construction process taking place exclusively in universities or institutes of higher education, the workplace is now central to the construction of learning environments. And the third is the development of new types of knowledge-construction, and these are now acting to reframe relationships between the professions and the state. This has resulted in forms of deprofessionalisation, with

Investing in our Education: Leading, Learning, Researching and the Doctorate
International Perspectives on Higher Education Research, Volume 13, 17–30
ISSN: 1479-3628/doi:10.1108/S1479-362820140000013000

some professions in the United Kingdom and other parts of the world
experiencing significant losses of autonomy and independence in relation
to ownership of their specialized bodies of knowledge and skills, control
of the means for credentialising these bodies of knowledge, and renego-
tiated professional mandates, leading to restrictions on their capacity to
determine for themselves these specialized bodies of knowledge and those
learning environments in which practitioners acquire them.

Keywords: Learning environments; professional doctorates; the PhD;
knowledge-construction; professionalization; the professions

Freidson (2001), amongst others, suggested that a profession is characterized by a specialized body of knowledge and skills, a means for credentializing this body of knowledge, usually by a university or institute of higher
education, and a degree of independence from government, which allows it
to determine for itself what this specialized body of knowledge is and those
learning environments in which practitioners acquire it (cf. Etzioni, 1969;
Millerson, 1964; Saks, 1995). This independence from the state has been
described as its professional mandate and this refers to the degree or
amount of freedom from state control that it has negotiated with the relevant government (cf. Whitty, 2001).

The past 20 years in the United Kingdom have seen major changes to
the university sector, such as the feminization of the student body, the
bureaucratization of university administration and academic practice, an
increase in the numbers of participants in higher education, and the closer
role universities now play in the development of professional knowledge.
Higher education is thus being brought into a closer relationship with
the workplace. In the wake of these changes has come a growing political
interest in postgraduate and doctoral education with, inevitably, concerns
being expressed by policy-makers over the quality and standards of awards.
It is in this context that the rapid growth in the numbers of professional
and practice-based doctorates is giving rise to significant questions about
the nature and purposes of doctoral education and the relationship between
these more recent doctorates and the traditional PhD.

It would, however, be misleading to suggest that these developments in
doctoral study round the world have resulted in the creation of professional
doctorates alone. Along with the rapid growth in this new form of doctoral

study has gone the reinvention and reconfiguration of the PhD (Allen, Smyth, & Wahlstrom, 2002) itself. The PhD (certainly in the United Kingdom and also in some other parts of the world) is now beginning to embrace a significant taught element, with the consequence that its teaching and learning apparatus is beginning to resemble the type of doctoral study (i.e. the professional doctorate) to which it gave rise. However, it is still possible to distinguish between the two forms of doctoral study, and these differences refer to the stepped nature of study on the professional doctorate, the introduction of formal assessment processes throughout the degree, and the way the programme of study is focused directly on professional practice of one type or another. The student's subsequent thesis is shorter than the PhD, with the average length being 50,000 words.

The professions themselves are remodelling their practices with consequences for the type of special relationship with the government they are able to negotiate; many have increased their qualification requirements; and for some of them, such as clinical psychologists, this has meant a move towards doctoral programmes for initial qualification. The requirements for greater accountability of their professional practice and a rapidly deteriorating financial environment have led to changes in the orientation of the degree, to its modus operandi and to the important relationship between academic and professional knowledge, in addition to a reconceptualization of its theory-to-practice relation. The doctoral degree in the United Kingdom, and in some other parts of the world, is therefore no longer just an academic qualification, but also a professional, and in some cases a vocational qualification.

These factors have contributed to the widespread development of professional doctorates in the United Kingdom, and this has followed in close order their developments in the United States and Australia. Professional and practice-based doctorates were introduced in the United Kingdom during the 1990s mainly to provide a higher qualification for already experienced practitioners in a range of fields, for example, the DEng for qualified engineers, the DBA for senior business managers and the EdD for senior education professionals. In Australia, two generations of professional doctorates have been identified (cf. Maxwell, 2003). The first conforms to a model of coursework plus thesis and is dominated by academic interests. The second is characterized by a shift in orientation of both the site and the nature of knowledge-production (Seddon, 2000), so that academic interests coexist with workplace concerns.

Moreover, the university itself is increasingly being influenced by policy-driven interventions of the state, new forms of communication, its marginalization from the centre of the knowledge industry, and by crises in disciplinarity and professionalism. The introduction of professional doctorates in the United Kingdom signals a move by both the university and the professions to reconfigure what is considered appropriate research and practice forms of knowledge. A tension therefore exists between theory-orientated and practice-based forms of knowledge and this has implications for pedagogy at doctoral level, assessment of products, legitimation, and more generally the relationship between higher education and the continuing development of serving professionals. A number of different models have been developed for the provision of such programmes, and universities have adopted a range of flexible learning approaches, which emphasize active roles for students and interactive and collegial processes throughout the teaching and learning programmes.

ACADEMIC AND PROFESSIONAL KNOWLEDGE

A key area of concern for those universities which have developed or are developing educational doctorates is the relationship between academic and professional or practitioner knowledge. There are five possible ways of understanding this relationship: technical-empiricist, technical-rational, multi-methodological, situated-theoretical and multi-discursive, with proponents of each of them having a different view about how educational theory is constructed and how it relates to educational practice.

The first of these has been termed the 'scientistic' or *technical-empiricist* approach (Habermas, 1987). Scientific description is understood as the only possible way of understanding the world and it refers to 'science's belief in itself; that is, the conviction that we can no longer understand science as one form of possible knowledge, but rather must identify knowledge with science' (*ibid.*, 4). All the other forms of knowledge, including practitioner knowledge, are considered to be inferior or mistaken versions of it. What this also suggests is that it is possible to identify a correct method for collecting data about educational activities, and if this method is properly applied, then this will inevitably lead to the construction of objective, value-free and authoritative knowledge. Furthermore, though there are subtle differences between natural and social scientific knowledge, these differences are not distinctive enough to warrant the designation of two different approaches or sets of methods. There is one correct approach and one set of methods. This monistic approach, with its associated reductionist and essentialist elements, has been critiqued extensively, and even described as the fundamental error of Western philosophy (cf. Bhaskar, 2010).

Practitioners therefore need to set to one side their own considered and experience-based ways of conducting themselves at work because these are partial, incomplete and subjective; by contrast they need to incorporate into their practice scientific knowledge which transcends the local and the particular. Practitioner knowledge is therefore considered to be inferior and incomplete because it is context-dependent, problem-solving, contingent, non-generalizable and is judged not by objective criteria but by whether it contributes to the achievement of short-term goals and problems encountered in situ.

This type of knowledge is underpinned by particular understandings of epistemology and ontology. Hacking (1981), for example, suggests that the theory-practice relation implicit in this version of scientific knowledge conforms to the following principles: there is a real world being described which does not depend on how it is understood or articulated. Furthermore, there is a uniquely best way of describing it, which is not dependent on history or society. Scientific theories are different from the other types of beliefs. Science works by building on previous ideas and theories; indeed, it works towards an ultimate goal, which is a proper understanding of the natural and social worlds. Scientists in their everyday practice make a clear distinction between observational and theoretical statements. Hypotheses and theories are tested deductively using observations and experiments, and linguistic terms have fixed meanings and concepts are defined precisely. In short, similar methods are appropriate to the discovery of truths about both the natural and social worlds.

No single philosophy has embraced all of these. For example, Popper (1976) rejected the distinction made between observational and theoretical statements. However, within this model, an assumption is being made that the objective knowledge which is produced about educational activities and institutions binds the practitioner in certain ways; those ways being the following of rules which can be deduced from that knowledge. Practitioner knowledge therefore is inferior because it has incorrectly conceived foundations.

The second perspective, which we might want to describe as *technical-rationality*, conforms to this model in that it understands the relationship between theoretical and practice-based knowledge in a similar way. What is different is that the researcher constructs the original knowledge differently. Instead of conforming to the principles which underpin the scientific model described above, researchers work from different foundational principles.

These may comprise a different conception of the relationship between ontology and epistemology, or a different understanding of the relationship between the knower and what it is that they seek to know, or a different way of conceptualizing objectivity (for example, choosing between epistemic, ontological, positional, extrinsic, methodological or warranted forms of objectivity; cf. Scott, 2010). In short, those who adopt, even provisionally, a positivist/empiricist view of the world are going to understand their brief as researchers in a different way from those who are implicitly or explicitly positioned within an interpretive or hermeneutic framework, whether by themselves or other people. However, they share the conviction that knowledge produced by outsiders, or practitioners behaving as outsiders, is superior to the knowledge produced by practitioners working in situ.

The implication for practitioners undertaking academic study is that they should divest themselves of their prior incorrect and incomplete knowledge and adopt precepts based on the objective study of educational activities. Scott and Usher (2010, p. 26) describe this model as:

> ... the solving of technical problems through rational decision-making based on practical knowledge. It is the means to achieve ends where the assumption is that ends to which practice is directed can always be predefined and are always knowable. The condition of practice is the learning of a body of theoretical knowledge, and practice therefore becomes the application of this body of knowledge in repeated and predictable ways to achieve predefined ends.

This is a view which is concerned with determining a measure of technical efficiency which will necessarily lead to the achievement of predetermined ends and these are separate from the determination of means per se.

A third way of understanding the relationship between theoretical and practice-based knowledge is a *multi-method* or *eclectic* approach. Again, there are epistemological and ontological foundations of this view of knowledge. Researchers would deny that there is a correct way of seeing the world but would argue for a plurality of perspectives. There is no one correct method, only a series of methods which groups of researchers have developed and which have greater or lesser credibility depending on the way those groups are constructed and the influence they have in society. The educational texts which they produce are stories about the world, which in the process of their telling and re-telling, re-stock or re-story the world itself. They have credence because enough practitioners see them as a useful resource for the solving of practical problems they encounter in their everyday working lives.

Whether or not the practitioner works to the prescriptive framework of the researcher, and implicit within any research text is a set of prescriptions about how the practitioner should behave, will depend on the fit between the values and frameworks held, respectively, by the theorist and the practitioner. The theorist can produce broadly accurate knowledge of educational settings, but the practitioner then adapts and amends it in the light of the contingencies of their own work practices. However, in all essential respects, the practitioner still follows the prescriptive framework developed by the external researcher.

A fourth way of understanding the relationship between theoretical and practice-based knowledge is to see practice as the source of educational theory. Walsh (1993, p. 43) argues that the *situated-theoretical* relationship which concerns us here, 'turns on the perception that deliberated, thoughtful, practice is not just the target, but is the major source (perhaps the specifying source) of educational theory'. He goes on to suggest that 'there is now a growing confidence within these new fields that their kind of theorizing, relating closely and dialectically with practice, is actually the core of educational studies and not just the endpoint of a system for adopting and delivering outside theories' (*ibid.*, 43). This takes another step away from the technical-rationality position described above. This is because it suggests that there may not be a role at all for external theorists, because they operate outside practice. This perspective understands practice as deliberative action concerned with the making of appropriate decisions about practical problems in situ. However, we should not conclude from this that there is no role for theory at all. What is being reconceptualized is the idea of theory itself.

Proponents of this viewpoint reject the notion of means-ends implicit in the technical-rational model and argue that practitioner knowledge prohibits the making of appropriate technical decisions about applying precepts developed by others. Practitioner knowledge is not just about the identification and application of pre-defined ends, it is also about the designation of ends in the light of deliberative activity about practice. As Usher and Bryant (2011, p. 127) suggest, practice situations are 'characterized by a complexity and uncertainty which resist routinization'. Such knowledge is and can never be propositional, but always involves continuous cycles of deliberation and action which cannot be transformed in the process into generalizable accounts of educational activities. This closely ties together theory and practice; informal theory central to practice is, as Usher and Bryant (2011, p. 128) suggest, 'situated theory both entering into and emerging from practice'.

The fifth position which it is possible to take and which we might want to describe as *multi-discursive*, is an extension of situated-theoretical knowledge, in that the theorist and the practitioner are actually engaged in different activities. Walsh (1993, p. 44), for instance, suggests that there are four mutually supporting but distinctive kinds of discourses:

> deliberation in the strict sense of weighing alternatives and prescribing action in the concrete here and now ... evaluation, also concrete, and at once closely related to deliberation and semi-independent of it ... science, which has a much less direct relationship to practice ... and utopianism, being the form of discourse in which ideal visions and abstract principles are formulated and argued over.

Discourse, he defines, as a sustained and disciplined form of enquiry, discussion and exposition that is logically unique (*ibid.*, 53). If we accept this argument, we are also accepting the idea that the practitioner and the theorist are engaged in different activities and therefore that they will operate with different criteria as to what constitutes knowledge.

Choosing between these different accounts of the theory-practice relationship is problematic because it is not possible to derive a role for the outside theorist and a role for the practitioner from an a priori examination of the concept of education, on its own. In other words, how these matters are considered and what conclusions are drawn about the most appropriate relationship between theory and practice is a question of value. It involves deliberation and argument about the purposes of the educational enterprise and such deliberation is located within power structures which provide the essential contexts for action.

THE PROFESSIONALIZATION AND BUREAUCRATIZATION OF THE DOCTORATE

What it does mean, however, is that the theory-practice or academic-professional relationship and the solution to the problem that is implicit within it (expressed above as a choice between five options: technical-empiricist, technical-rational, multi-methodological, situated-theoretical and multi-discursive) have implications for how we understand and develop doctoral programmes of study. It also has implications for those professionalization processes (cf. Whitty, 2001), undertaken by the professions, where the occupational body (whether professional, semi-professional or quasi-professional) seeks professional status and influence and the rewards that accompany it. Professionalization can therefore be understood as a move by members of occupations to extend their power and influence, to support their particular epistemology of practice and to secure for themselves the means for their continued existence. One part of this strategy is the development of a professional doctorate so that recognition of achievement by a university both accredits learning for the individual, and bestows status on the profession to which the individual belongs, with the intention of creating stronger forms of insulation within the occupational division of labour. However, this means that the profession is subject to a form of regulation by an external body (the university), which in turn is regulated by the state.

In the United Kingdom and elsewhere recently there have been moves to standardize and bureaucratize the procedures and processes of the doctoral experience. In part, this is because policy-makers, concerned as they are with the quality of the degree and operating through empiricist/positivist epistemic frameworks, equate quality with completion and set targets for institutions in relation to these completions (cf. UK Council for Graduate Education, 2002). However, the result is, as Cowan (1997, p. 196) suggests, 'an increasing bureaucratisation within doctoral programmes; of pedagogic sequence; of pedagogic relations, through memoranda; and of knowledge, into training methods'. Alongside this increasing bureaucratization, there has been an emphasis on the creation of instrumental forms of knowledge, and a desire to make doctoral programmes and doctoral completion more relevant to the perceived needs of the economy and in particular professional practice. This has been driven both by universities operating within the market and thus competing for a limited number of potential students (developing a vocational element for doctoral study widens the potential pool of applicants), the desire by the professions to give higher status (endorsement by universities) to both their forms of professional development and in some cases licensing-to-practice arrangements, and by governments determined to establish close connections between disciplinary forms of knowledge and economic productivity.

Freidson (2001), as we suggested earlier, identified three characteristics of professions: a specialized body of knowledge, skills and dispositions, a way of credentializing this body of knowledge, usually by a university or institute of higher education, and a degree of independence from government, which allows it to determine this specialized body of knowledge and those learning environments in which practitioners acquire it. He characterized these learning environments in three ways: craft-based, technician-focused and professionally orientated. Professional doctorates are of the last type, and he suggested that this professional training inevitably takes place in specialized schools or university faculties. He went on to argue that the university faculty, as a part of the profession:

> do not merely recruit, train and certify students. What gives them and their profession of which they are a part the capacity to preserve and even expand their jurisdiction is the fact that in addition to teaching, their faculties can devote themselves to systematizing, refining, and expanding the body of knowledge and skill over which the profession claims jurisdiction. (*ibid.*, p. 96)

This model of advanced professional training needs to be modified with the introduction and development of professional doctorates. This is in part because a different type of knowledge is being developed which has different characteristics: the site of knowledge development is now the workplace and this assumes a pivotal role in the learning environment; theory-to-practice and indeed practice-to-theory relations have changed; and curriculum arrangements are now different with consequences for pedagogic approaches and strategies, relations between knowledge domains, knowledge/skill/dispositional orientations, knowledge framing, progression and pacing modes, relations between teachers and students, relations between types of learners, spatial arrangements, temporal arrangements, types of formative assessment and feedback processes, and the criteria used for evaluating these arrangements (cf. Scott, 2008).

We have already suggested that the type of knowledge developed on professional doctorate programmes is different in the various occupations. Further to this, the capacity of the faculty to erect a labour market shelter round their professional doctorate through controlling the supply of recruits to higher levels of the profession is limited. The promotional and status benefits of higher professional degrees, such as professional doctorates, are complex and differ considerably between different professional groups. On the one hand, a profession such as clinical psychology in the United Kingdom (and increasingly other types of psychology professions) requires a professional doctorate qualification for entry, and increasingly rewards senior practitioners who have undertaken professional doctorates; on the other hand, in the field of education, the acquisition of a higher professional degree such as the EdD rarely has direct promotional or status advantages. Indeed with regard to some professions, governments have sought to bypass university-accredited professional qualifications and create their own. This is exemplified in the United Kingdom by head teachers in schools who are now required to gain a qualification which is accredited and taught outside the university sector. Finally, professional training is both pre-service and in-service, and though Freidson's model fits better with the former rather than the latter, is still misconceived in that it implies a servicing arrangement by universities for the profession. University academics certainly at doctoral level have their own agendas, so their contribution to learning should not be understood as merely facilitative. Their view of the profession, and of what is appropriate professional knowledge, is likely to influence the professional development practice, which is their prime concern.

SITES OF KNOWLEDGE-PRODUCTION

Three interdependent sites of knowledge-construction can be identified: the research site where knowledge is initially developed; the pedagogic site at which members of the profession acquire that knowledge and the workplace site where this knowledge is applied, though knowledge development, acquisition and application are not exclusively located at these three sites. These sites are interdependent in that workplace knowledge provides the context in which particular forms of pedagogy are enacted and influences what those forms might be; and in turn feeds back into the research site. In a similar way, the pedagogic site has a dialectical relationship with the research site, which is always evolving in response to the development of new knowledge or the development of new pedagogic forms or the development of new workplace practices. However, the state intervenes to a greater or lesser extent at all three sites, and this determines the degree of autonomy allowed for that profession. Furthermore, because these sites operate in different ways in different professions or occupations, it is possible to designate knowledge development as regional to indicate the different forms of knowledge as they impact on the workplace.

Though knowledge may be formed in a particular way at the research site and influences the messages delivered at the pedagogic site, in turn, knowledge reconfiguration at this site also occurs as a result of internal and external factors which include interventions by the state. A knowledge base of a profession may therefore comprise a weak horizontal structure, with a proliferation of forms of knowledge; however, interventions by the state may mean that one of those forms is given a privileged status over the other. For example, Scott, Lunt, Brown, and Thorne (2004) identified four modes of knowledge developed on professional doctorate courses. The first of these is disciplinarity, where the practice setting is understood as the source for reflection, but not the arena in which that theorizing takes place.

Technical-rationality, on the other hand, prioritises outsider knowledge over practice-based knowledge, with the result that the practitioner is required to implement protocols and practices developed elsewhere. Dispositionality comprises the teaching of certain skills and dispositions, such as a capacity to reflect and in turn meta-reflect about practice, which allows the practitioner to develop their understanding of what they do in the workplace. The fourth mode of knowledge is criticality, and here the student-practitioner reflects critically on the discourses, modes and ways of working of the institution of which they are a member, with the intention of changing the way it works.

The state has in recent times redefined its role in relation to the professions, and in certain circumstances will channel its considerable power to favour forms of technical-rationality at the expense of disciplinary, dispositional or critical forms of knowledge. For example, the state in the United Kingdom has reallocated government funds for in-service training from universities (through the Higher Education Funding Councils) to quasi-governmental agencies and placed strict limits on the type of course that can be accredited for professional development. This further blurs the distinction between discretionary and mechanical specialization (cf. Freidson, 2001), where these are understood as work being organized in the first case to enhance and in the second case to limit the degree to which discretion is appropriate if the task is to be performed successfully.

Tensions between the three sites mean that in practice these modes of knowledge are compromised in various ways. This is achieved through processes of adaptation and colonization, so that hybrid forms of knowledge are developed. For example, a discipline may have evolved so that it is understood as a practical activity with clear and explicit relations to the practice setting. One of the consequences of this is that weak boundaries are established between the academy and the practice setting. The Engineering Doctorate in the United Kingdom more closely aligns itself with this model. On the other hand, some forms of integration are more problematic, and tensions exist between these different modes of knowledge. A particular mode of knowledge may be so powerful, and may be supported by the state, that it subsumes other modes of knowledge. By examining the development of professional doctorates as influential, though not exclusively so, in the formation of specialized bodies of knowledge, it then becomes possible to understand both the different ways such formative processes take place and the nature of those specialized bodies of knowledge which are the end-result.

CONCLUDING THOUGHTS

In this chapter, I have suggested that knowledge-construction, or learning in a profession, has changed with the introduction of professional doctorates, though the division between these new forms of doctoral study and the older and more established forms such as the PhD is now not as wide as they once were. In particular, three elements of the knowledge-construction process are implicated here. The first of these is a move towards learning environments which prioritize situated-theoretical applications of the theory-practice relationship at the expense of technical-empiricist, technical-rational, multi-methodological and multi-discursive variants. The second is movement towards different sites of learning, so that instead of the knowledge-construction process taking place exclusively in universities or institutes of higher education, the workplace is now central to the construction of learning environments, both literally and relationally. This has implications for the construction of its specialized body of knowledge and skills by the profession (whether full, semi- or quasi-), ownership of which marks out the degree and type of professionalism that it can claim for itself, the way practitioners acquire it and the subsequent professional mandate for that profession which is negotiated with the state.

Finally, the types of knowledge-construction which are now an essential part of the doctoral experience (though different in the various doctorates that we have made reference to) are acting to frame and reframe relationships between the professions and the state. This has resulted in forms of deprofessionalization, with some professions in the United Kingdom and other parts of the world experiencing significant losses of autonomy and independence in relation to ownership of their specialized bodies of knowledge and skills, control of the means for credentializing these bodies of knowledge, and renegotiated professional mandates, leading to restrictions on their capacity to determine for themselves these specialized bodies of knowledge and those learning environments in which practitioners acquire them.

REFERENCES

Allen, C., Smyth, E., & Wahlstrom, M. (2002). Responding to the field and to the academy: Ontario's evolving PhD. *Higher Education Research and Development, 21*(2), 203–214.

Bhaskar, R. (2010). *Reclaiming reality*. London: Routledge.

Cowan, R. (1997).Comparative perspectives on the British PhD. In N. Graves, & V. Varma (Eds.), *Working for a doctorate: A guide for the humanities and social sciences*. London: Routledge.

Etzioni, A. (1969). *The semi-professions and their organization: Teachers, nurses, social workers*. London: Collier-Macmillan Ltd.

Freidson, E. (2001). *Professionalism: The third logic*. Chicago, IL: The University of Chicago Press.

Habermas, J. (1987). *Knowledge and human interests*. Cambridge: Polity Press.

Hacking, I. (1981). Introduction. In I. Hacking (Ed.), *Scientific revolutions*. Oxford: Oxford University Press.

Maxwell, T. W. (2003). From first to second generation professional doctorate. *Studies in Higher Education, 28*(3), 279–291.

Millerson, G. (1964). *The qualifying associations: A study in professionalisation*. London: Routledge.

Popper, K. (1976). The logic of the social sciences. In T. Adorno, H. Albert, R. Dahrendorf, J. Habermas, H. Pilot, & K. Popper (Eds.), *The positivist dispute in German sociology*. London: Heinemann.

Saks, M. (1995). *Professions and the public interest: Medical power, altruism and alternative medicine*. London: Routledge.

Scott, D. (2008). *Critical essays on major curriculum theorists*. London: Routledge.

Scott, D. (2010). *Education, epistemology and critical realism*. London: Routledge.

Scott, D., Lunt, I., Brown, A., & Thorne, L. (2004). *Professional doctorates: Integrating professional and academic knowledge*. London: Open University Press.

Scott, D., & Usher, R. (2010). *Researching education: Data, methods and theory in educational research*. London: Bloomsbury.

Seddon, T. (2000). What is doctoral in doctoral education? Paper presented at the 3rd International Professional Doctorates Conference, Doctoral Education and Professional Practice: The Next Generation? Armidale, 10–12 September.

UK Council for Graduate Education. (2002). *Report on professional doctorates*. Dudley: UKCGE.

Usher, R., & Bryant, I. (2011). *Adult education as theory, practice and research*. London: Routledge.

Walsh, P. (1993). *Education and meaning: Philosophy in practice*. London: Cassell.

Whitty, G. (2001). Teacher professionalism in new times. In D. Gleeson & C. Husbands (Eds.), *The performing school: Managing, teaching and learning in a performance culture*. London: Routledge Falmer.

DOCTORAL STUDY IN CHALLENGING TIMES: ENTRENCHING BANALITY OR REVITALISING PROSPECTS FOR 'WICKED' INTELLECTUAL WORK. THE CASE OF EDUCATIONAL ADMINISTRATION[☆]

Marlene Morrison

ABSTRACT

Purpose – *This chapter provides a retrospective and prospective exploration of some of the challenges faced by doctoral education, specifically as they relate to advanced studies of educational administration (EA).*

☆ A generic term is used here to refer to the advanced study of educational administration, management and leadership.

Investing in our Education: Leading, Learning, Researching and the Doctorate
International Perspectives on Higher Education Research, Volume 13, 31–57
Copyright © 2014 by Emerald Group Publishing Limited
All rights of reproduction in any form reserved
ISSN: 1479-3628/doi:10.1108/S1479-362820140000013002

Methodology – *It applies a critical stance to the current status of knowledge in the 'leadership field' and the intellectual underpinnings that inform the studies available as reference for doctoral students.*

Findings – *Nested within wider changing conditions for university and doctoral education, it is argued that the published field as currently constituted suffers from both banal and 'non-wicked' leadership orthodoxies that might lead to doctoral stagnation.*

Practical implications – *Reasons are suggested and prospects considered for revitalising scholarship for the upcoming generation of EA alumni, scholars and practitioners.*

Keywords: Doctoral education; research; educational administration; sociological critique; intellectual prospects

INTRODUCTION

This chapter is offered as a thought piece to encourage theoretically framed discussion and debate about the current status of doctoral knowledge (EdD and PhD) and the intellectual work that informs and enriches it. Many specific considerations are drawn autobiographically from my experience as PhD and EdD thesis and university programme examiner, director and supervisor and as a sociologist of education. This exposes the chapter to accusations of particularism that readers will need to take into account as they read. It is not possible to cover the entire field of publications; therefore, selection bias is inevitable. Some explorations might be considered provocative; the intentions are that it might expand directions as well as encourage new scholars and provide scholarship for the advanced study of educational administration (EA).

The author recognises the work by colleagues who have already been engaged deeply with such issues, not always in relation to doctoral education. This includes those who claim an epistemological legitimacy derived from the mutuality of higher education-based research interests and professional 'knowing', not least among practitioners and students who also value intellectual leadership work to stimulate theory, research and practice. Practitioners might also include those more inclined to engage with higher education institutions (HEI) through doctoral studies; this, it is argued, makes the need for a heightened awareness of what might constitute a doctoral study, specifically in EA, even more necessary. As will be suggested, some mutual interests raise challenges that need to be made explicit.

WICKED AND BANAL

Underpinning the chapter is a call for a reconceptualisation of the theories, research and practices of EA as 'wicked issues' (following Blackman et al., 2006; Trowler, 2010). The term 'wicked' is used here to refer to studies of EA in which 'effective leadership' does not necessarily relate clearly or simplistically to education problem solving; rather, it reports on scholarship (some more visible and powerful than others) that might be used to reassess intellectual and practical 'problems' of and 'solutions' for leaders and leadership (Briggs, 2007). It is argued that reassessments contrast with many published sources in which the tendency is for 'leaders' and 'leadership' to be cited as core problems of and, frequently, algorithmic solutions for effective education (Day et al., 2009, 2010; Leithwood, Day, Sammons, Harris, & Hopkins, 2006; Sammons, 1999).

The term 'banality' in this chapter title is used in two senses; *first*, as a form of 'triteness' that is applied to the purposes, processes, content and outcomes of EA as published and upon which doctoral students might depend. In many respects, the 'banal' represents and focuses EA as 'non-wicked', and includes repetitive discourses and models, to the point where the 'domain assumptions' (following Gouldner, 1970) can become hackneyed or even 'delusionary' (Lumby & English, 2011).

Second, banality is associated with 'normalisation' (Trowler, 2010, p. 2) of dominant leadership discourses which remain relatively stable whilst, simultaneously, adjectival descriptors for leadership multiply (Morrison, 2009, p. 65). As importantly, potential researches urgently require attention by existing and aspiring EA scholars remain unrecognised or 'silenced' (Lumby, 2013, p. 590). In this sense, publications can exude 'tameness' (Trowler, 2010, p. 1), a reversal of investigations about EA as 'wicked issues'. When this occurs, consensus is assumed, leadership traits and behaviours are understood tacitly, and their significance to educational problem solving reduced to rational evaluations and/or application of single solutions (*ibid.*, p. 1). Here, the EA field, it is argued, is complicit in the 'educationalization' (Bridges, 2008) of problems that are deemed to have (mainly) school-centric solutions. Ball's (1995) warning about the use of 'tacit theory' is apposite. When preoccupations about EA are assumed:

> ... the absence of [explicit] theory ['we' 'know' leaders have primal significance for orga-
> nisations, networks, teachers, pupils, heads, teams ...] leaves the researcher prey to the
> unexamined, unreflexive preoccupations and dangerously naïve ontological and episte-
> mological a *prioris*. (pp. 265−266)

Because the 'significance' of leadership has become a global phenomenon, and 'leader' and 'leadership' applied to many educational actors, the need for astute cultural awareness to confront the potential for banality is heightened. Rizvi and Lingard (2009) argued that internationalisation has often amounted to little more than the 'vernacularisation' of dominant generic leadership behaviours to fit a wide range of contexts. Antonyms for banality would, therefore, refer doctoral students to the relationship between EA policy, research, theory and practice in terms of 'originality', 'extra-ordinariness', 'challenge', 'criticality' and 'unpredictability' and might enable researchers to surface issues to assist them in making decisions about the following: research questions that are or might become researchable in the field of EA; the conceptual frameworks needed to make 'innovative' sense of the date they collect and to reassess the consequences that flow from the selection of some epistemological and methodological frameworks rather than others.

NESTING EA

The following discussion is nested within recent developments in university and doctoral education. EA students frequently inhabit doctoral and professional spheres simultaneously; as leaders and/or would-be leaders they study themselves and those they might influence, and references are to developments in university education (see the chapter 'Academic and Professional Knowledge in the Professional Doctorate'). Concerns about EA studies relate to growing lacunae (also discussed by Gunter, 2012a; Lumby, 2013; Lumby & English, 2011; Samier, 2008a; Shields, 2012) in theoretical development, methodology (Foskett, Lumby, & Fuller, 2005; Lumby & Morrison, 2010) and restricted critical activity. This is reflected in repetitive pulls towards theories of transformational and distributed leadership despite periodic pleas for a more and better theoretical engagement (Bush, 2010, pp. 266−270). It also includes a reluctance to engage with or challenge 'dark' (Lumby & English, 2011; Samier, 2008b; Samier & Lumby, 2010) or 'destructive' (Reeves & Knell, 2009; Schaubroeck, Lam, & Cha, 2007) lea-dership. Despite burgeoning interests in ethical leadership, intensifying tech-nicisation increasingly absorbs moral (ising) technologies about leader selves and styles (Morrison & Ecclestone, 2011). Critical social researchers are also implicated when they inhabit, and may, indeed, thrive in a separate parallel universe of antagonism towards policy reform (Ball, 2007) that, regardless of intention, is left relatively untouched in some forms of leader-ship research and leadership training programmes.

Confronting such issues poses challenges for doctoral programme plan-ners, and supervisors, and not least for doctoral students who may have already been subject to the 'leadership speak' (Gunter, 2012a) that features in many leadership development courses, including headship training programmes in England, that, until recently, were mandatory (and led by the former National College of School Leadership). The next section sum-marises the recent developments in university education.

EA AND UNIVERSITY EDUCATION

What constitutes university education has changed markedly over 30 years, although more so in some disciplines and universities than others; it is char-acterised by an expansion in provision and students, an increased competi-tion for students, resources and research funding (Holligan, Wilson, & Humes, 2011), a rise of a controlling managerial and administrative elite (Ollsen, Codd, & O'Neill, 2004) and by an almost absolutist belief that com-petition increases quality. In England, this is underpinned in the Browne Report (Independent Govt. Review, 2010) and its subsequent White Paper (Department for Business, Innovation and Skills [DfBIS], 2011).

Developments are viewed either as essential to the pursuit of excellence in higher education or, more negatively, to the destructive of its core pur-poses. In England, Fred Inglis, Professor of Cultural History, University of Warwick (2011), scathed in his condemnation not only of the reports and the strength of the external government forces they represent, but also equally about 'the enemies within' (p. 38) who, he argues, are beginning to 'dictate the limits and direction of the universities' distinctive products', namely, research graduates and, it follows, postgraduates and whose 'only function' is reduced to 'benefit[ing] the "economy" — a term left, as usual in unexampled opacity'. In relation to the public sector, more broadly, the rise of 'a new accountability culture' is one in which 'quality has become a powerful new metaphor for new forms of managerial control' (Ollsen et al., 2004, p. 191).

Holligan et al. (2011) have researched on other aspects of changing university cultures in England and Scotland and, it follows, the contexts in which doctoral education might ensue. Educational departments are of special interest, not least because doctorates centring EA are mostly located there. (Increasingly, University Business Schools and Departments of Health and Social Care are also featured.) Education departments are notable because, historically, research identities of staff and students have been shaped by teaching as well as or more than by research. This is not to underestimate other inter-university and inter-department variations, which extend to what does and should constitute the kinds of education research to be undertaken, whether by doctoral students or staff, and to staff opportunities for conducting research. Hazelkorn (2005, pp. 59−60), in Holligan et al. (2011, pp. 714−715) refers to 'basic', 'applied' and 'strategic' research. 'Basic' accords with 'the creation of knowledge for its own sake' in line with early 19th century liberal education; 'applied' to more vocationally orientated education (e.g. an early feature of many English post-1992 universities) and 'strategic' as research more directly linked with governmental priorities. Whilst earlier government reports in England (Department for Education and Skills [DfES], 2003), for example, called for more diversity in research outputs, in reality, the emphasis on previous research assessment exercises and frameworks is still firmly aligned 'with the traditions of basic research of the highest quality' (Holligan et al., 2011, p. 715) as evidenced in publications from highly rated peer review journals, albeit with greater emphasis on demonstrations of practical impact.

Post-1992 HE institutions have been vulnerable to research exclusion especially when staffs face heavy teaching and administrative workloads. A 'split focusing' (Holligan et al., 2011) between teaching and research, it is suggested, then, will have rather different repercussions for those involved in postgraduate education in different kinds of universities or, indeed, departments. It is interesting to consider, for example, the consequences − positive and negative − for EA students supervised 'by the most successful researchers' who have 'become circulating elites' among research-intensive universities (p. 716) and those supervised in less research-intensive universities, where staff with limited published research experience (perhaps because they were recruited for reasons of professional expertise rather than publishing acumen) are simultaneously teaching and supervising students on, as Holligan et al describe, 'Masters' degrees and the professional doctorate in education (EdD) with a commitment to impacting on

professional practice and school improvement' (p. 717). For such departments, the existence of alternative providers, for example, the National
College for Teaching and Leadership (an executive agency of the
Department of Education, formerly the National College for the
Leadership of Schools and Children's Services, previously the National
College of School Leadership), and other universities and/or private providers, places additional competitive pressures on programme planners to
consider whether the education they offer is distinctive or emulative of
other agencies, not least government training.

For some universities in England and Scotland, decisions have already
been made to focus their offer on full-time international students (Holligan
et al., 2011). In part, this relates to ongoing pressures to generate income;
many international students pay up to two-thirds more for courses than
their domestic European Union (EU) counterparts. This raises questions
about which education systems, domestic or international, or both, benefit
most from HEI's attempts to juggle 'quality' concerns with income generation. Moreover, implications for scholarship might be various. In the case
of EA, for example, the touting of effective leadership as a core factor in
improving schools has become a global phenomenon. This raises questions
about the extent to which university departments will be willing/have
the capacity to engage its international students in culturally nuanced yet
critically focused ('wicked'?) studies about leadership, not least when leadership orthodoxies that refer to frameworks/standards approaches, for
example, may have drawn international students towards British-based HE
experiences.

THE ACADEME

Barnett (1997) has discussed the changing role of university academics in
the production and circulation of knowledge, and, it follows, their interactions with research students supervised by them. In a confidently 'modern'
world, he argued, academics 'took it for granted that there was a world to
know' (p. 151) and that their main role was to 'produce methodologies for
knowing the world in more secure ways' (op. cit.). In late modernity (or
early postmodernity), academics 'lost their monopoly over the production
of high status knowledge' (p. 150). For many others outside, academe has
become 'practising epistemologists' (op. cit.). This is profoundly the case in
EA where intellectual work has been undertaken at various interfaces

between sponsors, practitioners and the academe. For academics, at least three new roles have been ensued: firstly, as 'problem solvers in the grand style' where academics offer solutions to given problems; secondly, as 'endorsers' of state policies where problems and solutions are determined in advance, and academics infill the detail, providing evaluations and performance indicators to plug gaps and 'ensure' predetermined outcomes. Or, thirdly, they become post-modernist 'cultural voyeurs' who 'eschew all grand narratives' (p. 153). Barnett argued that in all three instances, critical consciousness is present but in limited forms. For 'problem solvers', academics might be able to refashion problems 'critically' so that others might see them innovatively. For 'endorsers', narrowly circumscribed critical thinking occurs when new kinds of manager, roles and responsibilities are insisted upon. Endorsers' 'allegiance to surveillance techniques and concerns for bottom-line outcomes are given' (op. cit.) and inward-looking critique mainly absent. 'Cultural voyeurs' may be 'thoroughly' critical, but, for Barnett, problems lie with their 'total undermining of all forms of knowledge' (p. 154) to the extent that they deny or underestimate the strength of existing ideologies and of the relation between knowledge and power. Examples of all approaches are discernible in EA and among academics who supervise doctoral students, albeit in contexts of an evolving dominance of 'functional knowledge production' involving frameworks for leadership that have been endorsed by successive governments in the United Kingdom and have focused upon leaders' primacy in relation to 'effective' organisations (Gunter, 2012a, p. 47).

For Barnett, 'being critical' no longer implies a retreat to university spaces but demands engagement with the wider world through critical action derived from critical knowledge created by academics, professional communities and students, an approach to which the chapter returns. Yet, for Stronach (2004, p. 17), 'no other era [of the academy] has worn its academic freedom more lightly, nor given it away more readily', referring to 'well-known legions of carefully conformist educational researchers bent on doing the government's will, even if grudgingly' (op. cit.). In response, he calls for acts of 'civil courage' (following Svedberg, 1999) by those who inhabit academe (ibid.).

Such developments do not exist in isolation. Knowledge production and those with the power to determine what is to be produced, what should be known and learnt, and by whom, have serious implications for both HEI students and staff alike. This penetrates into all areas of university experience, not least doctoral education. This is considered next.

DOCTORAL EDUCATION

In doctoral education, trends replicate those found in other education sectors and achievement levels with direct and indirect attempts by governments to standardise the processes of and outputs arising from university doctorates, notably financial inducements and penalties in relation to poor completion rates, inadequate supervisions and the incorporation of completions into institutional audits such as research assessment/excellence frameworks. Regulation includes generic skills for doctoral education (Quality Assurance Agency, 2001) against which HE institutions are held accountable; these include skills set timelines for students and supervisors, sometimes referred to as 'personal development planning' and, more importantly, as pre-specified transfer points. The latter requires evidence that students have completed mandatory activities, related broadly to a generic skills base that all doctoral students are deemed to require (for employment, communication, entrepreneurship ...) as well as having achieved progress levels judged acceptable in the generation of a thesis.

As Scott and Morrison (2010) consider, the introduction of diverse doctorate types is more than a consequence of universities meeting increased demand. It also reflects pressures to modify the doctoral experience. Scott and Morrison note how various reports (QAA, 1999; the Dearing Report, 1997; the Harris Report, 1996; The Winfield Enquiry, 1987) expressed concerns about quality, the narrow and specialised nature of enquiries undertaken by students, the restricted disciplinary orientation of degrees, the individualised and thus non-collaborative nature of pedagogies employed, the non-transferability of acquired skills and an academic emphasis with little relevance to economic needs. Although some concerns reflect inadequacies, others reflect ideological disagreements about the nature of knowledge and a desire to impose a non-disciplinary or interdisciplinary structure. Recent doctoral reforms are profound, insofar as they have threatened (in many cases, successfully, if Barnett's, 1997 analysis is accurate) hitherto enclosed knowledge structures, whether department or discipline based, in UK universities.

Cowan (1997, p. 184) describes the history of the PhD as the 'bureaucratisation of originality' – that the original and largely individual search for a universalising and trans-cultural knowledge has been circumscribed by bureaucratic procedures that have reconstituted the type of knowledge produced. As highlighted previously, this extends through doctoral 'pedagogic sequence ... pedagogic relations [and] knowledge, into training methods'

(p. 196) and is accompanied by more emphasis on instrumental knowledge, not least for particular professional practices (ESRC, 2001; Scott & Morrison, 2010). The PhD (Allen, Smyth, & Wahlstrom, 2002) which now includes a significant taught element, is thereby coming to resemble pedagogically the type of doctoral study (the professional doctorate) that it gave rise to.

Implications extend to the substantive content of doctoral programmes (Boud & Lee, 2009; Lee & Darby, 2012; Scott, Brown, Lunt, & Thorne, 2009), the resources used, how and why. Doctoral pedagogies and curricula are deeply implicated. In EA, for example, future research is needed not only to assess the substantive, theoretical and methodological content of advanced EA study but also to compare provision with numerous other 'leadership' providers. Research has been conducted on EA content in Australian universities (Bates & Eacott, 2008). At least one commentator, Gronn (2008), considers findings 'dispiriting' (p. 182). Positively, he notes the decline in the use of Anglo-American textbooks, less positively, 'the dominance of the theme of change', specifically organisational. He explains:

> 'Change' which is much used is devoid of any particular referent or context and is simply 'out there' − is emblematic of what has become an era of fast knowledge, in which students ... increasingly heavily reliant on the Internet need not even visit libraries ... and can engage minimally with knowledge in the traditional discipline sense ... This ... tells us something of what markets do to knowledge: they reduce it to the lowest common denominator. (pp. 182–183)

Furthermore, he notes that whilst two decades ago a prospective student might select from 'a smorgasbord of offerings' from universities representing different approaches to EA, by 2008, 'such variety and diversity ha[d] all but disappeared' (p. 183).

'AN EASY DOCTORATE'?

In a recent Foreword to an internationally focused text, McWilliam (2012, pp. xvii−xviii) notes two overall trends, the first evidenced statistically and the second subject to more speculation than evidence. The first is towards the increased desirability, popularity and status of a doctorate in global employment markets where the importance of the knowledge economy is reiterated and competition for professional employment 'fierce'. The second relates to a 'suspicion', whether imagined or real, that some doctorates may be 'suspect' in 'over-promising' whilst 'under-delivering' on issues of 'quality, relevance, and rigour' (xviii). Lee and Darby (2012, chapter 1) highlight some of the fears that underpin this concern. Whilst the notion of an 'easy doctorate' ought to be 'an oxymoron', they declare current educative pressures towards avoiding difficulty and complexity, following Carr (2010, p. 117), may increase when servicing the doctoral student becomes servicing the customer; the impetus towards time-controlled doctoral completions supports the use of simplistic research methods and/or when Internet resources can (but do not necessarily have to) produce work that is fragmented, broad based and/or lacking intellectual depth. Reference is also to a more generic tendency to retreat from difficulty, drawing on Foley (2010, p. 113), who argued that in 'an age of absurdity'

> Difficulty has become repugnant because it denies entitlement, disenchants potential, limits mobility and flexibility, delays gratification, distracts from distraction, and demands responsibility, commitment, attention and thought.

Currently, and with widespread variations by discipline, the highly specialised academic identity implicit in the idea of doctoral education as initiation into a discipline is being replaced, paradoxically, perhaps, with both standardisation and orthodoxy, and fragmentation and variation. In EA, the potential for tension and overlap between what might constitute the 'stuff' of leadership development/training courses and that of doctoral study remains considerable (but not unique to EA) and is accentuated when doctoral education increasingly combines orientations towards study as training as well as education.

Despite global trends, there is limited evidence (Scott et al., 2009) that the acquisition of a doctorate in Education has *direct* promotional or status benefits. Indeed, in EA, notably in the United Kingdom and Unites States (English, 2012), successive governments have sought to bypass university-based leadership studies and have been relatively successful in accrediting their own, most frequently training/development based, and where some HEIs have contributed towards delivery. In HE, it is suggested that a professional doctorate contributes towards professional practice, whereas a PhD contributes to the knowledge base of discipline. However, Scott and Morrison (2010) argued that such perspectives both exaggerate and misconstrue the distinction; some PhDs contribute to practice and some EdDs contribute to discipline. The reasons for confusion are not difficult to discern, especially in Education where fragmentation deriving from inter-disciplinary as well as multi-disciplinary bases proliferates, and where, in some sections of EA, some forms of knowledge production have accelerated, not least that which separates the work of policy-driven 'on-message' (favoured) from 'off-message' (less favoured) researchers and of the latter from practitioners (Gunter, 2012a, p. 31).

Learning is central to creating and sustaining doctoral identities and, for students, is complex and potentially rich (Hinchcliffe & Jolly, 2011), not least when students are presented with a mass of information, ideas and schema from different sources. Such a view, argued Scott and Morrison (2010), is very different from training models currently endorsed by governments in which the learning metaphor is that of acquiring a set of behaviours, called skills, which once acquired, enables the student to perform a set of actions which have been designated as the norm for the workplace, whether in the academy or the profession. As Scott and Morrison (2010) suggested, the juxtaposition between instrumentality and criticality is now precariously positioned in doctorates, not least in EA.

EDUCATIONAL ADMINISTRATION (EA)

In the processes of educational reform in the United Kingdom, and amidst what Ball (2007, p. 2) described as 'the slogans, recipes, incantations, and self-evidences' about education's role, 'leadership capacity building' (p. 7) is championed as 'a heartland project' (Morrison, 2009, p. 66). In the leadership field, knowledge producers are in an increasing demand against a backdrop of regulation about what is researchable, how such research might be funded, why and to which ends (pp. 66–67). Gunter (2012a, pp. 37–51) pointed out that, in the United Kingdom, governments have tended to favour research/evaluations conducive to 'functional knowledge production'. She notes how education researchers have been complicit in the mediation of policy into practice where the emphasis is on 'the school as a unitary organisation, where people trained to show the right behaviours and skills can enable effectiveness ... based on ... listings that translate complexity into easy-to-apply models of good practice' (p. 40). In the education modernising project, primacy has been given to the starting point of a single leader; to leadership that is then distributed 'inclusively' within organisations that are also viewed as 'rational' (p. 47). The latter is interwoven with references to values, morality and transformation, and reinforced by leadership training that increasingly focuses inwards on leaders either as emotionally resilient or in need of training to acquire it, not least to enforce government policy (Allen, 2009; Goleman, Boyatziz, & McKee, 2002;

Harris, 2004). In EA, critical responses to emotional resilience regimes remain relatively uncommon (but see Morrison & Ecclestone, 2011). A related modelling of coaching and mentoring has burgeoned (Clutterbuck, 2004; Creasey & Paterson, 2005; Whitmore, 2002) and is increasingly a core recommendation in research/evaluations about training and/or the experiences of new and aspiring school heads (Earley et al., 2011; London Challenge, 2011; Silver, Lochmiller, Copland, & Tripps, 2009).

Theories of transformational and/or distributed leadership remain largely dominant; simultaneously, leadership descriptor lists, frameworks and standards proliferate alongside much deeper calls for leaders to become and remain 'moral educators' (Starratt, 2004). In 2009, Morrison (p. 65) listed 53 adjectival descriptors. All become part of 'leadership lore' (Rayner, 2008), although, in detail, they vary little from descriptions of transformational and distributed leadership or their anti-theses. For doctoral students, there may be tension while working with academic staff who have become adept (if grudgingly, according to Stronach, 2004, p. 17) in moving between published government-sponsored research evaluations about 'what works' (Gunter and Rayner, 2006, p. 38) and the more complex discourses of academic journals. According to Macfarlane (2012, p. 40), 'Sponsorism ... when someone's research is designed to fit the agenda of funding bodies ... now looks like a modern day virtue'. Many published EA studies share such trends, with epistemological and methodological challenges for students as they move simultaneously between orthodoxies that seem sacrosanct, and alternative perspectives.

Published challenges to orthodoxy provide important epistemological alternatives. Lumby (2013), for example, charted out the historical transformation of distributed leadership theory from 'a tool to better understand the ecology of leadership to a widely prescribed practice' (p. 581), which 'involve[s] multiplying taxonomies of methods of distributing leadership (Harris, 2009; MacBeath, 2009)'. It has evoked a range of reactions, sharing both 'the ring of something revitalising and inclusive' and a 'questioning of the purpose and impact' of a 'distributed leadership industry' (op. cit.). According to Lumby, when theory moves from being 'a lens for research' to 'outright advocacy' (p. 583), not only are theories of power largely ignored but also, as importantly, the predominance of distributed leadership lore becomes, in itself, an act of power, in which the dominance of specific views tends to obliterate others, even when it is evidenced that distributed leadership contains contradictions which foreground inclusion but practise hierarchical control. This reveals not only 'the naivety of distributed leadership claims' (p. 589) but also its exposure to published evidence, often ignored, that 'renders discriminatory practice' invisible, not least because distributed theory encourages 'all to think that equality is given' (pp. 589–590), avoiding 'engagement with the implications of more heterogeneity in leadership'. Lumby's arguments draw this chapter back towards its opening comments about banality. If her analysis holds good, then distributed leadership

> is *not* 'little more' than rhetoric (Hartley, 2010, p. 279); it is far more insidious ....The persistence of unequal and unjust systems is located in *banal,* everyday choices not to think critically, to be comfortable with current majority choices ... In its avoidance of issues of power, distributed leadership is a profoundly political phenomenon, replete with the uses and abuses of power. (Lumby, 2013, p. 592, emphases added)

Attention is drawn to this publication, not least because it appears to crystallise current challenges for doctoral students who need to engage in deep reading from a range of intellectual perspectives (rather than with shallow bullet-point references aimed at focusing the minds of otherwise busy professionals) not only to enhance their learning and writing but also to inform professional practices. In a recent EdD session organised by this author, doctoral students were encouraged to reflect on dominant theories of transformation and distribution, drawing on Lumby (2013) and others to apply complex theoretical lens. Positively, it provoked deep intellectual discussion and challenge for professional students steeped in the rhetoric of distributed leadership, going some way to act on Foley's (2010, p. 113) plea that study does not avoid 'wicked' issues or 'the distraction' of 'distraction'. As importantly, the session exemplified the intellectual effort required to reveal what remains largely invisible (Hartley, 2010; Hatcher, 2005), notwithstanding the earlier mappings of the leadership field (Ribbins & Gunter, 2003a, 2003b).

LEADERSHIP FOR LEARNING AND SOCIAL JUSTICE

According to Ribbins (2006, p. 113) 'effective leaders ... need a good grasp of history'. Bates (2007, p. 137) considered that EA has *always* had a 'disreputable history', tracking its development from the early 20th century to the beginning of the 21st in which it has

> been concerned with efficiency, accountability, and control ... Despite damning criticisms such as Raymond Callahan's *Education and the Cult of Efficiency* (1962) and Arthur Wise's *Legislated Learning: the Bureaucratization of the American Classroom*

(1979) the pursuit of the science of educational administration continued unhindered by any educational, social, or ethical concerns. (pp. 137—138)

Citing early attempts by Greenfield (1975) to 'redefine educational administration as a normative, cultural process concerned with the management of knowledge, culture and life chances' (p. 138), he argued that the field has continued to ignore criticisms and opportunities and remains as committed to 'performativity' (Ball, 2001) as previously.

Elsewhere, Ribbins and Gunter (2003a, 2003b) drew upon 'socio-empirical' approaches (Ribbins, 2006, pp. 118—119) to map 'the origins, evolution, and nature' of the EA knowledge domain. Revealing eight knowledge provinces: the conceptual, critical, humanistic, evaluative, instrumental, descriptive, axiological and aesthetic (pp. 119—120), Ribbins suggested that there *have* been a range of 'countervailing positions' to those predicated on performativity. Morrison (2009, pp. 4—5) argued that these include field members who h .ve sought to make

more inclusive the links between leadership and learning ...(Lingard, Hayes, Mills, & Christie, 2003)... and of both to social justice and issues of power (Shields, 2006; Starratt, 1996)... whether through the lens of diversity (Lumby & Coleman, 2007) or radical race and gender theories. (Blackmore, 1999, 2006)

Nonetheless, it is also suggested that:

Their intellectual strengths have frequently been ... absorbed into and absorbed by powerful hegemonic discourses of advanced capitalism (Avis, 2007) or dismissed by some exhausted and disgruntled practitioners seeking 'bullet-point' fixes to improve leadership or learning or both, or just to survive. (Morrison, 2009, p. 5)

For doctoral students seeking links between leadership and learning, the field is multi-faceted and complex, as is the relationship between leadership and student learning. Starratt (2007) challenged scholars to resist 'make-believe learning' (p. 165) that includes enforced assessment and pedagogic routines; such resistance, he argues, has been absent mainly from published EA literatures (p. 182). With exceptions (Bottery, 2004; Starratt, 2004), some leadership scholars have tended to avoid getting too much involved in issues of critical approaches to learning and its relation to social justice, either assuming an 'obvious' consensus about its importance and/or preferring to confine themselves to questions of individual morality that can be included in standards and lists for leaders, and/or absorbable into organisational mission statements. Morrison (2009, p. 11) noted how

> asking leaders to consider different philosophical positions, especially in relation to
> equality and diversity, is still relatively uncommon; ... instead the preferred emphasis ....
> is on ensuring a moral consensus among staff ... or relates to a confidence to act
> ethically ... over time.

Yet, the intricate relationship between education, learning and social justice has a long history (Freire, 1970); Larson and Murthada (2002, p. 202) argued, for example, that Freire's work, whilst used widely in curriculum theory, has been 'largely overlooked' by 'leadership theorists' (p. 146). More recently, in the United States, Shields (2012) made renewed links between what she described as 'transformative leadership' (in which critical consciousness and action are explicit) and social justice in a changing world.

It is in the conversion of critical thought to practical action that, in my experience, doctoral students have found it more challenging to discern in published literatures. In this respect, Anderson's (2009) work on advocacy leadership and Apple's (2012) response to the question *Can Education Change Society?* have been helpful, if mainly (although not entirely) US-focused. Others have turned to Amartya Sen's Capabilities Approach (Bates, 2007; Morrison, Lumby, & Sood, 2006) to examine what it has to offer EA scholars and students in relation to learning and social justice. With exceptions (Lingard et al., 2003), empirical research investigations fall behind theoretical exposition. Identified by Apple (Gunter, 2012b, p. 5) are the various tasks needed to 'interrupt ... dominant interests' (op. cit.). For scholars and students, these include

> bearing witness to what is going on, and so practising the politics of recognition; point-
> ing to spaces for opportunities to take action, finding contradictions within those
> spaces ...[and]... modelling the excellent critical researcher, teacher, and activist. (*ibid.*)

Such activities have the potential to provide alternative intellectual theories and tools to reassess professional and doctoral identities, as well as professional practices. The use of the term 'tool' seems apposite, not least when critical theory also needs to be subject to critique. According to Ball (2006, p. 64) whilst its appeal to 'beleaguered academics in an increasingly slippery world' might be considerable, there are attendant dangers. Where 'theory lays it dead hand upon the creativity of the mind ...[it can become]... no more than a mantric reaffirmation of belief rather than a tool for exploration and thinking otherwise' (*ibid.*).

Where leadership theories operate from various dispositions, there are enhanced opportunities for students to reassess links between epistemology, methodology and method. In EA, this becomes more urgent. Despite periodic methodological reflections about the state and status of the field (Foskett et al., 2005; Lumby & Morrison, 2010; Morrison & Lumby, 2009), research designs remain mainly small-scale and outcomes increasingly predictable. Such trends are explored next.

METHODOLOGY AND METHOD

In doctoral studies of education, the completion of an empirical research investigation is a (some would argue *the*) key component. In the United Kingdom, it is this feature of thesis that receives major attention, not least in the *viva voce* examination. Increasingly, EA doctoral students may look in vain for published researches that move beyond the use of the small-scale and the interview, and mainly with leaders. Writing in 2005, Gorard's challenge to the field was 'to demonstrate convincingly what practical difference educational leadership ma[de] to anything other than itself' (p. 156). Here, some reflections are offered about how and why this has happened and links to banality.

At least five phenomena are discernible. The *first* is built on a cumulative approach to evidence building; for example, as per Leithwood et al. (2006), effective school leadership was/remains second only to the quality of teaching and learning in the classroom as an indicator of a successful school. Much of the research before and after has been to confirm this to be the case and demonstrate how and why this happens. With many research organisations, rather than pupil learning-centred, the approach has extended beyond schools. Most explanations rest within dominant paradigms of transformational and distributed leadership that are transported internationally where similar researches take place. The predominant research tool has been the interview, whether face-to-face, on-line, survey or group based. The underpinning basis for data collection is one of perception and self-reports by leaders or would-be leaders.

Secondly, and relatedly, there has been a proliferation of sponsored research on headship/leadership preparation and early headship; both are integral to government-sponsored 'leadership capacity building' (Ball, 2007, p. 7). Here, research frequently comprises evaluations of government-sponsored initiatives to train new and emerging leaders, and there has been a heavy reliance on interview self-report by participants (Crawford & Cowie, 2012; Crawford & Earley, 2011; Earley et al., 2011; Pont, Nusche, & Hopkins, 2008). Time-scales often mean that there is minimal evidence of long-term impact.

A *third* phenomenon relates to the homogenisation of discourse across projects that take place in many countries, begin with the same starting assumptions and give primacy to the role of the leader. These tend to reduce prospects for findings that contradict those starting points. Cumulatively, then, a number of challenges seem evident so far – a tendency towards methodological reductivism and the primacy of self-report, the short-term and the small-scale, and a view of scaled-up international research as the total of the small-scale added together.

The *fourth* phenomenon relates to a continuing emphasis on the positive effects of leadership. The field's persistent reluctance to engage with or confront the 'dark side' of leadership (Lumby & English, 2011; Samier, 2008a, 2008b) is notable. Where research exists, it tends to feature among the concerns of the business world/faculties rather than education (Reeves & Knell, 2009; Schaubroeck et al., 2007).

A *fifth* phenomenon links to critical policy research and scholarship; whilst both have burgeoned (Anderson, 2009; Apple, 2012; Gunter, 2012a), they tend to sit alongside dominant orthodoxies rather than present penetrating challenges to them. There are attendant dangers when critical theorists are accused of being 'self-referential' or a field that 'speaks to itself' (Gunter, 2012b, p. 5) unless it addresses 'real life problems' (*ibid.*). Elsewhere, MacFarlane (2012, p. 40) was less generous in his critique of critical commentators, considering that challenges are more than communication or practical issues. Instead, he referred to a declining cadre of scholars prepared to take 'intellectual risks', arguing that some academic scholars act within 'a culture of complicity ... playing the game of academic capitalism'... in relation to some aspects of their research but hoping 'to be left alone' (*ibid.*) to engage in other interpretations of their work.

INTERVIEW OVERLOAD

Whilst, at best, the proliferation of interview research gives richness when dialogue encourages leaders to describe vicarious education experience, as in life history approaches (Floyd, 2012) and/or as 'co-researchers' (Ribbins & Sherratt, 1999), it

> may have done little to counter tendencies to 'canonise' or 'romanticize' leaders (Gronn, 2007), interview research described on occasions as 'an incantation for the bewitchment of the led' (Hodgkinson, 1983, p. 228 quoted by Gronn, 2007, p. 197). (Morrison, 2009, p. 73)

The consequences of treating interview research as non-problematic (Lumby & Morrison, 2010) can be profound. In face-to-face and interview surveys in schools where distributed leadership, for example, dominates normative thinking, interview data are likely to align with the latter, and the investigative potential for exposing 'latent experiences' (Lumby, 2013, p. 592) among researchers and practitioners, who have more to gain by non-exposure, remains limited.

Yet, some recent additions to the methodological literature (Briggs, Coleman, & Morrison, 2012) do present a much wider selection of approaches to critically assist engaged scholars and practitioners in making revitalised links between epistemology, methodology and method and give more respect for research voices other than leaders. This may enhance prospects for engaging in advanced studies where outcomes may be less predictable or repetitive. Students might also select from expanding disciplinary approaches (Lumby & English, 2011; Samier & Lumby, 2010), especially important when there is a declining cadre of new scholars to reinterpret the field.

Bridges (2008, p. 461) referred to the 'educationalisation' of social and economic problems as 'the tendency to look to educational institutions [schools … colleges, and increasingly universities] to resolve pressing social problems'. The term has evoked to refer to a displacement of the more radical and economic attention to underlying structures of social and educational injustice, with solutions typically vested in educational institutions. In brief, the tendency for EA studies to be the means for activating 'evidence-based' solutions to government-initiated problems and policies remains strong. Resistance through methodological as well as epistemological innovation and originality provides alternative possibilities for students.

SUMMARY

This chapter has endeavoured to resist the binaries of leadership compliance and resistance 'in managerialist times' that has been documented elsewhere (Thrupp & Wilmott, 2003). Instead, it debates a growing tendency for EA to exude banality by stagnating intellectually whilst publications proliferate numerically. Such trends are magnified in doctoral studies, where the nurturing of scholarship is delicately balanced between instrumentality and criticality and where many leadership studies wallow in approaches that lack a sense of 'wickedity' (Rittel & Webber, 1973) favouring 'solutions' in the absence of widespread structural change. Published EA projects and leadership development evaluations continue to emanate largely from the starting points of individual leaders. In summary, the trends are towards emaciated forms of leadership study. And whatever its intentions, even critical policy scholarship has, to date, been unable to counter fully the supremacy of 'the leadership premium' (Barber, Whelan, & Clark, 2010), although some scholars (a number of whom are cited in this chapter) persist in their efforts to develop research-centred theoretical and practical engagement by giving fulsome attention to 'wicked' issues.

Advanced studies of EA continue against a backdrop of methodological stagnation, trends exacerbated by challenges in gaining *access* to research in the absence of 'rubber stamping' by and financial support from primary sponsors. Yet, many areas remain relatively untouched by research. In relation to the leadership of universities, for example, regular attempts to restructure staff and resources in ways that persistently fail, yet are repeated, are ripe for further research, not least in examining how and why the 'delusional' (Lumby & English, 2011) is converted into compulsive—obsessive leader behaviours that are rarely investigated intellectually. For example, instinctively 'we' know that changing the colours of the logo at the University of Bloggsville or renaming an institution the University of Bloggsville rather than Bloggsville University will not improve doctoral learning experiences. Even the suggestion is risible; yet, such views are currently taken seriously by managerial elites and are transmitted to followers as sound management orthodoxy. Lumby and English (2011, p. 101) contended that it is the systems in which both large-scale and small-scale organisations operate which induce what they describe as 'pathological behaviours' akin metaphorically to a kind of 'lunacy'.

This is not to deny that leaders have been subjected to relentless accountability pressures that, when resisted can result in the kind of principal baiting, described by Gronn (2008, p. 177) as 'a blood sport'. Rather, it is to contend that victimisation is not the entire story about leaders, leadership knowledge, and action and that disingenuity is open to critical scrutiny, not least through doctoral engagement with such issues. Lumby and English (2011, pp. 103—104) also reminded us that it is not only the policy makers who practise delusion but principals also, it would appear, are increasingly encouraged by specific genres of leader development, to see themselves as working benignly and selflessly 'in the best interests of all students' (p. 103), even in the face of 'overwhelming research evidence' (Lumby & English, 2011; Lumby & Morrison, 2006) to the contrary. Even fewer scholars have gone as far as considering the forms of 'passive evil' constituted in some forms of EA which, according to Samier (2008a, 2008b, p. 2) 'emphasises the failure to respond to the everyday cruelties and moral lapses within the ranks of administration'. Elsewhere, Wilkinson (2008) is concerned about the ethical, practical and socially unjust consequences that continue to flow from what Gronn (2008, p. 183) describes as the mainly 'white, Anglo-Celtic, middle class, male assumptions still mainly dominating the field' (Gronn, 2008, p. 183).

REVITALISING SCHOLARSHIP

This chapter has confronted tendencies towards banality and non-wickedity in EA studies, some of which are exacerbated as a consequence of recent changes to universities and doctoral education. There is an attempt here to surface 'invisibility' in order to expand the knowledge creation capacity of EA scholars and to problematise what is frequently assumed to be the links between leaders, leadership, learning and social justice.

I hope I have also begun to argue the case for a new EA research agenda and accompanying this, a reinvigoration of methodology and method. Following Apple (2010), this involves recognising the 'privileges' (and indeed responsibilities) scholars have 'to open up the spaces for universities ... for those who are not there, [and] ... do not have a voice in that space' (pp. 15−18, in Davies, Popescu, & Gunter, 2011, p. 49). For field members, this behoves us to rethink and make links to children, teachers, students, families and the 'disadvantaged' (*ibid.*).

Optimistically, the potential for EA studies is big and exciting, if fraught with challenges when new forms of educational governance proliferate. Ball (2011, pp. 50−52) looks towards to new research that examines the tensions between the rise of the 'entrepreneurial head' and the 'corporate' or 'chain' head who is appointed by a sponsor. Elsewhere, Morrison and Arthur (2013) and Morrison and Glenny (2011) have begun to examine the implications of inter-professional education and practices for the theories and conduct of EA. Such optimism remains guarded. For doctoral researchers, the potential for innovative research can be thwarted in climates where business logic prevails and makes access to core educational actors and the reporting of ensuing research more complex (Ball, 2011). Skills to understand new financial and political environments will become essential for the advanced scholar (*ibid.*). Anderson (2009) records how, in the North American context, some doctoral candidates in the EA field, notably school leaders, may be increasingly reluctant to draw upon 'the warts and all' approaches of ethnography, for example, because of potential risks to their professional careers and the 'standards' of their schools if 'exposure' follows.

New 'stewards' (following Golde & Walker, 2006) are urgently needed to re-envision the future. Successful doctoral students are among those to whom the vigour, quality, professionalism and integrity of EA will need to be entrusted. This suggests that students' recognition of and exposure to a full panoply of discourses and practical challenges, including the 'banal' and the 'wicked', is even more necessary. For those moved to critical action, what seems essential is not the 'emotional resilience' to cope with or propagate 'delusion' but rather the 'resilience' to resist and be empowered by such resistance towards reflective practice.

REFERENCES

Allen, C., Smyth, E., & Wahlstrom, M. (2002). Responding to the field and to the academy: Ontario's evolving PhD. *Higher Education Research and Development, 21*(2), 203–214.

Allen, W. (2009). *The heart of the head. The emotional dimension of school leadership.* Nottingham: National College for the Leadership of Schools and Children's Services (NCLSCS).

Anderson, G. L. (2009). *Advocacy leadership: Towards a post-reform agenda in education.* New York, NY: Routledge.

Apple, M. (2010). *Global crises, social justice, and education.* London: Routledge.

Apple, M. (2012). *Can education change society?* London: Routledge.

Avis, J. (2007). *Education, policy, and social justice.* London: Continuum.

Ball, S. J. (1995). Intellectuals or technicians? The urgent role of theory in educational studies. *British Journal of Educational Studies, 43*, 255–271.

Ball, S. J. (2001). Performativities and fabrications in the education economy. In D. Gleeson & C. Husbands (Eds.), *The performing school: Managing, teaching, and learning in a performance culture* (pp. 210–226). London: RoutledgeFalmer.

Ball, S. J. (2006). *Education policy and social class: The selected works of Stephen J. Ball.* London: Taylor and Francis.

Ball, S. J. (2007). *Education plc: Understanding private sector participation in public sector education.* London: Routledge.

Ball, S. J. (2011). A new research agenda for education leadership and policy. *Management in Education, 25*(2), 50–52.

Barber, M., Whelan, F., & Clark, M. (2010). *Capturing the leadership premium: How the world's top school systems are building leadership capacity for the future.* A report by McKinsey and Company conducted in association with the NCSL, Nottingham.

Barnett, R. (1997). *Higher education: A critical business.* Buckingham: SRHE and Open University Press.

Bates, R. (2007). Developing capabilities and the management of trust. In M. Walker & E. Unterhalter (Eds.), *Amartya Sen's capabilities approach and social justice in education* (pp. 137–156). England: Palgrave Macmillan.

Bates, R., & Eacott, S. (2008). Teaching educational leadership and administration in Australia. *Journal of Educational Administration and History, 40*(2), 149–160.

Blackman, T., Harrington, A., Elliott, E., Greene, A., Hunter, B., Marks, L., ... Williams, G. (2006). Performance assessment and wicked problems: The case of health inequalities. *Public Policy and Administration, 21*(2), 66–80.

Blackmore, J. (1999). *Troubling women: Feminism, leadership and educational change.* Buckingham: Open University Press.

Blackmore, J. (2006). Social justice and the study of leadership in education: A feminist history. *Journal of Educational Administration and History, 38*(2), 185–200.

Bottery, M. (2004). *The challenges of educational leadership. Values in a globalized age.* London: Paul Chapman Publishing.

Boud, D. & Lee, A. (Eds.). (2009). *Changing practices of doctoral education.* England: Routledge.

Bridges, D. (2008). Educationalization: On the appropriateness of asking educational institutions to solve educational problems. *Educational Theory, 58*(4), 461–474.

Briggs, A. R. J., Coleman, M., & Morrison, M. (Eds.). (2012). *Research* methods in educational leadership and management (3rd ed.). England: Sage.

Briggs, L. (2007). *Tackling wicked problems: A public policy perspective.* Barton ACT: Australian Public Service Commission.

Bush, T. (2010). Editorial. Special issue on education leadership theory. *Educational Management Administration and Leadership, 38*(3), 266–270.

Callahan, R. (1962). *Education and the cult of efficiency.* Chicago, IL: University of Chicago Press.

Carr, N. (2010). *The shallows: How the internet is changing the way we think, read, and remember.* London: Atlantic Books.

Clutterbuck, D. (2004). *Everyone needs a mentor.* Wimbledon: CIPD.

Cowan, R. (1997). Comparative perspectives on the British PhD. In N. Graves & V. Varma (Eds.), *Working for a doctorate: A guide for the humanities and social sciences.* London: Routledge.

Crawford, M., & Cowie, M. (2012). Bridging theory and practice in headship preparation: Interpreting experience and challenging assumptions. *Educational Management Administration and Leadership, 40*(2), 175–187.

Crawford, M., & Earley, P. (2011). Personalised learning? Lessons from the pilot NPQH in England. *Educational Review, 63*(1), 105–118.

Creasey, J., & Paterson, F. (2005). *Leading coaching in schools.* Nottingham: NCSL.

Davies, P. M., Popescu, A.-C., & Gunter, H. M. (2011). Critical approaches to education policy and leadership. *Management in Education, 25*(2), 47–49.

Day, C., Sammons, P., Hopkins, D., Harris, A., Leithwood, K., Gu, Q., & Brown, E. (2010). *10 strong claims about school leadership.* Nottingham: NCSL.

Day, C., Sammons, P., Hopkins, D., Harris, A., Leithwood, K., Gu, Q., ... Kingston, A. (2009). *The impact of school leadership on pupil outcomes.* London: DCSF/NCSL.

Dearing Report. (1997). *The national committee of enquiry in higher education.* London: HMSO.

Department for Business, Innovation and Skills. (2011, June). Higher education students at the heart of the system. Paper presented by the Secretary of State for the DfBIS, London.

Department for Education and Skills. (2003). *The future of higher education*. Norwich: The Stationery Office.

Earley, P., Nelson, R., Higham, R., Bubb, S., Porritt, V., & Coates, M. (2011). *Experience of new head teachers in cities – A report for the National College*. Retrieved from http://ncsl.org.uk/experiences-of-new-headteachers-in-cities-full-report.pdf

Economic and Social Research Council. (2001). *Postgraduate training guidelines*. Retrieved from www.esrc.ac.uk/esrccontent/postgradfunding/postgraduatetrainingguidelines2001.asp

English, F. (2012). Bourdieu's misrecognition: Why educational leadership standards will not reform schools or leadership. *Journal of Educational Administration and History*, *44*(2), 155–170.

Floyd, A. (2012). Narrative and the life history approach. In A. Briggs, M. Coleman, & M. Morrison (Eds.), *Research methods in educational leadership and management* (3rd ed., pp. 223–235). London: Sage.

Foley, M. (2010). *The age of absurdity: Why modern life makes it hard to be happy*. London: Simon and Schuster.

Foskett, N., Lumby, J., & Fuller, B. (2005). Evolution or extinction? Reflections on the future of research in educational leadership and management. *Educational Management Administration and Leadership*, *33*(2), 245–253.

Freire, P. (1970). *Pedagogy of the oppressed*. New York, NY: Seabury.

Golde, C. M. & Walker, G. E. (Eds.). (2006). *Envisaging the future of doctoral education. preparing stewards of the discipline. Carnegie essays on the doctorate*. Stanford, CA: The Carnegie Foundation for the Advancement of Teaching.

Goleman, D., Boyatziz, R. E., & McKee, A. (2002). *Primal leadership: Realizing the power of emotional intelligence*. Boston, MA: Harvard Business School Press.

Gorard, S. (2005). Current contexts for research in education leadership and management. *Educational Management Administration and Leadership*, *33*(2), 155–164.

Gouldner, A. (1970). *The coming crisis of western sociology*. New York, NY: Avon.

Greenfield, T. (1975). Theory about organization: A new perspective and its implications for schools. In M. Hughes (Ed.), *Administering education: International challenges*. London: Athlone Press.

Gronn, P. (2007). Interviewing leaders: Penetrating the romance. In A. Briggs & M. Coleman (Eds.), *Research methods in educational leadership and management* (2nd ed., pp. 189–204). London: Sage.

Gronn, P. (2008). The state of Denmark. *Journal of Educational Administration and History*, *40*(2), 173–186.

Gunter, H. (2012a). *Leadership and the reform of education*. Bristol: Policy Press.

Gunter, H. (2012b). Why we 'knead' theory. *Management in Education*, *27*(1), 4–6.

Gunter, H., & Rayner, S. (2006). The researcher, research, and policy in England. *International Studies in Educational Administration*, *34*(3), 37–50.

Harris, A. (2009). Distributed leadership and knowledge creation. In K. Leithwood, B. Mascall, & T. Strauss (Eds.), *Distributed leadership according to the evidence* (pp. 253–266). London: Routledge.

Harris, B. (2004). Leading by heart. *School Leadership and Management*, *24*(4), 391–404.

Harris Report. (1996). *Review of postgraduate education*. Bristol: HEFCE, CVCP.

Hartley, D. (2010). Paradigms: How far does research in distributed leadership 'stretch'? *Educational Management Administration and Leadership*, *38*(3), 271–285.

Hatcher, R. (2005). The distribution of leadership and power in schools. *British Journal of the Sociology of Education, 26*(2), 253–267.

Hazelkorn, E. (2005). *University research management: Developing research in new institutions.* Paris: OECD.

Hinchcliffe, G. W., & Jolly, A. (2011). Graduate identity and employability. *British Educational Research Journal, 37*(4), 563–584.

Hodgkinson, C. (1983). *The philosophy of leadership.* Oxford: Blackwell.

Holligan, C., Wilson, M., & Humes, W. (2011). Research cultures in English and Scottish university education departments: An exploratory study of academic staff perceptions. *British Educational Research Journal, 37*(4), 713–734.

Independent Review. (2010). *Securing a sustainable future for HE in the UK: An independent review of higher education funding and student finance.* Retrieved from http://www.independent.gov.uk/browne-report. Accessed on October 17, 2011.

Inglis, F. (2011). Economical with the actualite. *Times Higher Educational Supplement, 6*(October), 36–41.

Larson, C., & Murthada, K. (2002). Leadership for social justice. In J. Murphy (Ed.), The educational leadership challenge: Redefining leadership for the 21st century. Chicago, IL: University of Chicago Press.

Lee, A., & Darby, S. (Eds.). (2012). *Reshaping doctoral education. International approaches and pedagogies.* Abingdon: Routledge.

Leithwood, K., Day, C., Sammons, P., Harris, A., & Hopkins, D. (2006). *Seven strong claims about school leadership.* Nottingham: NCSL.

Lingard, B., Hayes, D., Mills, M., & Christie, P. (2003). *Leading learning. Making hope practical.* Buckingham: Open University Press.

London Challenge. (2011). *Lessons learned from London.* London: London Challenge.

Lumby, J. (2013). Distributed leadership: The uses and abuses of power. *Educational Management Administration and Leadership, 41*(4), 581–597.

Lumby, J., & Coleman, M. (2007). *Leadership and diversity. Challenging Theory and Practice in Education.* London: Sage.

Lumby, J., & English, F. (2011). *Leadership as lunacy. And other metaphors for educational leadership.* Thousand Oaks, CA: Corwin Press.

Lumby, J., & Morrison, M. (2006). Partnership, conflict, and gaming. *Journal of Education Policy, 21*(3), 323–341.

Lumby, J., & Morrison, M. (2009). Youth perspectives: Schooling, capabilities and human rights. *International Journal of Inclusive Education, 13*(6), 581–596.

Lumby, J., & Morrison, M. (2010). Leadership and diversity: Theory and research. *School Leadership and Management, 30*(1), 3–17.

MacBeath, J. (2009). Distributed leadership: Paradigms, policy, and paradox. In K. Leithwood, B. Mascall, & T. Strauss (Eds.), *Distributed leadership according to the evidence* (pp. 223–252). London: Routledge.

Macfarlane, B. (2012). I'm an academic and I want to be proud of it. *A commentary for the Times Higher Education Supplement, 4–10*(October), 36–40.

McWilliam, E. (2012). Foreword. In A. Lee & S. Darby (Eds.), *Reshaping doctoral education. International approaches and pedagogies.* Abingdon: Routledge.

Morrison, M. (2009). *Leadership and learning. Matters of social justice.* Charlotte, NC: Information Age Publishing (IAP).

Morrison, M., & Arthur, L. (2013). Leadership for inter-service practice: Collaborative leadership lost in translation? *Educational Management Administration and Leadership*, *41*(2), 179–198.

Morrison, M., & Ecclestone, K. (2011). Getting emotional: Recent trends in the development of school leaders. A critical exploration. *School Leadership and Management*, *31*(3), 199–214.

Morrison, M., & Glenny, G. (2011). Collaborative inter-professional policy and practice: In search of evidence. *Journal of Education Policy*, *27*(3), 367–386.

Morrison, M., & Lumby, J. (2009). Is leadership observable? Qualitative orientations to leadership for diversity. A case from FE. *Ethnography and Education*, *4*(1), 65–82.

Morrison, M., Lumby, J., & Sood, K. (2006). Diversity and diversity management. Messages from recent research. *Education Management Administration and Leadership*, *34*(3), 277–295.

Ollsen, M., Codd, J., & O'Neill, A. M. (2004). *Education policy: Globalization, citizenship, democracy*. London: Sage.

Pont, B., Nusche, D., & Hopkins, D. (2008). *Improving school leadership*. Paris: OECD.

Quality Assurance Agency (QAA). (1999). *Code of practice for the assurance of academic quality and standards in higher education: Postgraduate programmes*. London: QAA.

Quality Assurance Agency. (2001). *The national qualifications framework for higher education qualifications in England, Wales and Northern Ireland*. London: QAA.

Rayner, S. (2008). Complexity, diversity, and management: Some reflexions on folklore and learning leadership. *Management in Education*, *19*(5), pp. 22–28.

Reeves, R., & Knell, J. (2009). Your mini MBA. *Management Today, March*, 60–64.

Ribbins, P. (2006). History and the study of administration and leadership in education. *Journal of Educational Administration and History*, *38*(2), 113–124.

Ribbins, P., & Gunter, H. (2003a). Mapping leadership studies in education. *Educational Management and Administration*, *30*(4), 359–387.

Ribbins, P., & Gunter, H. (2003b). Leadership studies in education. Maps for EPPI reviews. In L. Anderson & N. Bennett (Eds.), *Evidence informed policy and practice in educational leadership*. London: Paul Chapman Publishing.

Ribbins, P., & Sherratt, B. (1999). Managing the secondary school in the 1990s: A new view of headship. In M. Strain, B. Dennison, J. Ouston, & V. Hall (Eds.), *Policy, leadership, and professional knowledge*. England: Paul Chapman Publishing.

Rittel, H. W. L., & Webber, M. M. (1973). Dilemmas in a general theory of planning. *Policy Sciences*, *4*, 155–165.

Rizvi, F., & Lingard, B. (2009). *Globalizing education policy*. England: Routledge.

Samier, E. (2008a). On the Kitschification of educational administration: An aesthetic critique of theory and practice in the field. *International Studies in Educational Administration*, *36*(3), 3–18.

Samier, E. (2008b). The problem of passive evil in educational administration: The moral implications of doing nothing. *International Studies in Educational Administration*, *36*(1), 2–21.

Samier, E., & Lumby, J. (2010). Alienation, servility, and amorality: Relating Gogol's portrayal of bureaupathology to an accountability era. *Educational Management Administration and Leadership*, *38*(3), 360–373.

Sammons, P. (1999). *School effectiveness: Coming of age in the twenty first century*. Lisse, The Netherlands: Swets and Zeitlinger Publishers.

Schaubroeck, J., Lam, S. S. K., & Cha, S. E. (2007). Transformational leadership: Team values and the impact of leader behaviour on team performance. *Journal of Applied Psychology, 92,* 1020–1030.

Scott, D., Brown, A., Lunt, I., & Thorne, L. (2009). Specialised knowledge in the UK professions: Relations between the state, the university, and the workplace. In D. Boud & A. Lees (Eds.), *Changing practices of doctoral education* (pp. 143–156). England: Routledge.

Scott, D., & Morrison, M. (2010). New sites and agents for doctoral education in the UK: Making and taking doctoral identities. *International Work-based Learning E-Journal, 1*(2), 1–20.

Shields, C. (2006). Creating spaces for values-based conversations; the role of school leaders in the 21st century. *International Studies in Educational Administration, 34*(2), 62–81.

Shields, C. (2012). *Transformative leadership in education: Equitable change in an uncertain and complex world.* England: Routledge.

Silver, M., Lochmiller, C. R., Copland, M. A., & Tripps, A. M. (2009). Supporting new school leaders: Findings from a university-based leadership coaching program for new administrators. *Tutoring and Mentoring: Partners in Learning, 17*(3), 215–232.

Starratt, R. (1996). *Transforming educational administration.* New York, NY: McGraw Hill.

Starratt, R. (2004). *Ethical leadership.* San Francisco, CA: Joss-Bassey for John Wiley.

Starratt, R. (2007). Leading a community of learners: Learning to be moral by engaging in the morality of learning. *Educational Management Administration and Leadership, 35*(2), 165–184.

Stronach, I. (2004). Ending educational research, countering dystopian futures. In J. Satterthwaite, E. Atkinson, & W. Martin (Eds.), *The disciplining of education. New languages of resistance and reform.* Stoke on Trent: Trentham Books.

Svedberg, R. (1999). Civil courage (Zivil courage): The case of Knut Wicksell. *Theory and Society, 28,* 501–528.

Thrupp, M., & Wilmott, R. (2003). *Educational management in managerial times. Beyond the textual apologists.* Maidenhead: Open University Press.

Trowler, P. (2010). Wicked issues in situating theory in close-up research. Higher education close ups 5. Paper presented at the HECU5 conference, University of Lancaster: Lancaster, UK. Retrieved from http://www.lancaster.ac.uk/fss/events/hecu5.docs. Trowler.pdf. Accessed on December 24, 2013.

Whitmore, J. (2002). *Coaching for performance: Growing people, performance, and purpose.* London: Nicholas Brealey Publishing.

Wilkinson, J. (2008). Good intentions are not enough: A critical examination of diversity and educational leadership scholarship. *Journal of Educational Administration and History, 40*(2), 101–112.

Winfield Enquiry. (1987). *The social science PhD: The ESRC enquiry on submission rates.* London: Economic and Social Research Council.

Wise, A. (1979). *Legislated learning: The bureaucratization of the American classroom.* Berkeley, CA: University of California Press.

LEADERSHIP: SKILLED MANAGER OR VIRTUOUS PROFESSIONAL?

Richard Pring

ABSTRACT

Purpose — *This chapter looks critically at the changed language of education due to the adoption in the last two or three decades of a 'business model' for improving education. It briefly traces the history of these changes which have rarely been brought to the attention of the public.*

Methodology — *This chapter delves more deeply beneath this language in order to explore the unacknowledged philosophical assumptions — referring to Wittgenstein's aim which was to help people to pass from a piece of disguised nonsense to the recognition of it being patent nonsense.*

Findings — *This points out how, given the managerial language, this distorts our understanding of what it means to educate — there is an inappropriate 'logic of action'.*

Originality — *The ethical dimension to educational leadership gets distorted or ignored. There is a need therefore to examine more carefully what is meant by an 'educational practice' — otherwise leadership*

Investing in our Education: Leading, Learning, Researching and the Doctorate
International Perspectives on Higher Education Research, Volume 13, 59–73
Copyright © 2014 by Emerald Group Publishing Limited
ISSN: 1479-3628/doi:10.1108/S1479-362820140000013003

coursed might be good at teaching 'effectiveness' in teaching to the test, but have little to do with education.

Keywords: Language of management; performativity; logic of action; educational practice; ethics; teaching to the test

INTRODUCTION: A BIT OF HISTORY

Head teachers and those with specific responsibilities in school have only comparatively recently been referred to as 'managers' (or indeed as 'chief executives'), in need of courses in management skills. The 'management staff' of the London comprehensive school to which I was first appointed in 1965 consisted of one person, the head teacher's secretary. Schools were 'managed' by the Local Education Authorities. A head teacher was precisely that, expected to lead on the professional activities within the school.

This changed radically with the 1988 Education Act, a major innovation of which was the 'local management of schools'. The financial responsibility for running the school would now be in the hands of the respective governing bodies and exercised through the head teacher. The non-teaching staff of the school swelled considerably as financial and other responsibilities were transferred from the LEA. Being a head teacher required the management skills for running rather large businesses, with increased accountability in terms of the targets set for schools 'from above', and of the growing demand for 'performance related pay', very precise data was needed for such accountability and judgments. Much later, as chairman of the personnel committee of the governing body of a comprehensive school, I had to help the head teacher to identify the three objectives for improvement in the forthcoming year, on the basis of which an increase in salary would be recommended. At the end of each such year, the Ofsted inspector would arrive to check that the objectives had been met.

This increasing emphasis on explicit management procedures and structures was by no means confined to the teaching profession. There has emerged in the last few decades radical changes in the management of public services and thus of the professionals running those services (universities, the health service, the probation service, social work and so on). The result is burgeoning bureaucracies which themselves need to be managed, and thus the need for the management skills and know-how which go much beyond the professional knowledge required for good teaching, medical care, etc.

As an illustration, one might be referred to the change in language and practices in universities, following the 'efficiency review' of the Jarratt Commission, established by the Committee of Vice-Chancellors in 1984.

> The crucial issue is how a university achieves the maximum value for money consistent with its objectives. (2.12)

> Each department should maintain a profile of 'indicators of performance' to include standing costs of space, utilities (telephones, etc), market share of applications, class sizes, staff workloads, graduation rates and classes of degrees. (3.33)

> A range of performance indicators should be developed, covering both inputs and outputs and designed for use both within individual universities and for making comparisons between institutions. (5.4)

> The headships of departments ... ideally should be both a manager and an academic leader. (4.27)

The shift in the control of schools, eventually by government (e.g., in the creation of a National Curriculum), and in the management of public services, which emerged in the 1980s, was explained in a series of Government White Papers from HM Treasury and the Cabinet Office: *Modern Public Services in Britain: Investing in Reform* (1988, Cm. 4011); *Public Services for the Future: Modernisation, Reform, Accountability* (1998, Cm. 4181); *The Government's Measures of Success: Outputs and Performance Analyses,* 1999; *Modernising Government* (1999, Cm. 4310).

One important consequence of these White Papers (and thus of the 'modernisation' of public services) was what was referred to as 'public service agreements'. These were agreements over funding from HM Treasury, first to Departments of State in terms of overall targets, which were then 'cascaded down' in more precise forms, to the institutions which were the responsibilities of the respective Departments. In education, that was spelt out partly in terms of the proportion of students at different schools achieving so many GCSEs at different grade levels. But that gradually emerges as a way of rewarding teachers through 'performance related pay'. There is, then, a sharp division (which previously did not exist) between the ends or aims of education (established in precise outcomes) and the means of 'delivering' those outcomes, namely the pedagogical skills which the teachers are experts in.

It is important to be aware of this. Too often the increase in the dominance of management language and structures in schools and universities is not seen within this wider context of the reform of public services as a whole and of the consequent 'public service agreements', nor within the philosophical influences which underpinned those reforms, to which I now turn.

THEORY BEHIND THE CHANGES

The theoretical underpinning of these changes (which had slowly developed in education since the introduction of 'local management of schools' in 1988) became more explicit (at least for the writer of this paper) at a seminar in Oxford in the mid-1990s, which was led by the then Permanent Secretary at the DfEE. He promoted what he referred to as the 'quality circle', in which we were to think much more in business terms. This required first the explicit statement of educational *aims*. From these one derives precise *objectives* or *targets*. To achieve these objectives one needs to select the *content* and *teaching methods* which could be shown empirically to attain those targets. (Successful teaching is a science.) Then follows *assessment* — the measurement of what has been achieved in relation to those objectives. Finally, there is an *evaluation* of the whole process. If the assessment showed that the targets had not been hit, then either the targets were not the right ones or the means of hitting them (content or teaching methods) were ineffective. Hence, in the light of the evaluation, there is *revision*, and the virtuous circle is even more virtuous and the process can start again. At roughly the same time, there was a series of seminars at St. John's College, Oxford, on what was referred to by Mark Freedman as 're-inventing government' (see Faulkner, Freedland, & Fisher, 1999). These reforms of the management of public services so that they would be run on much the same way as private businesses, were spelt out by civil servants and other architects of the reforms.

That attempt to 're-invent government' led to the invitation of two Americans, Odden and Kelley, by David Blunkett, when he was the Secretary of State for Education and Skills (DfES). Their book was entitled *Paying Teachers for What they Know and Can Do* (1997), which influenced the 'performance management' of teachers, as that came to be perceived by government (performance thresholds, fast-track teachers, inspection programmes to ensure 'value for money' and greater focus in initial training upon practical skill for achieving nationally set standards of competence).

Odden and Kelley argued that the traditional way of paying and rewarding teachers is outdated. A more business-oriented model is required. As they argued:

> The tax-paying public, the business community, and policy makers still pressure the education system to produce results and to link pay – even school finance structures, more broadly – to performance.

This pressure arises from the felt need to 'raise standards', to 'improve productivity' in relation to these standards, to make teachers 'more effective' and to hold teachers accountable for their professional work. To enable this to happen, there needed to be much greater precision in what teachers were expected to achieve, sometimes referred to as 'productivity targets'. There needed to be clear statements of 'standards' against which the 'competence of teachers' might be judged. All this adds up to a new vision for the profession.

In that vision, there was a direct link between the 'target' (or 'measured performance') of the learner, on the one hand, and the 'performance' of the teacher, on the other. But what is meant by 'performance'? It generally refers to those 'behaviours' which can be observed and measured. They are the targets which the target-setters (the civil servants reflecting the wishes of the politicians) decide upon and 'cascade down' to 'chains of academies' or local authorities, thence to the schools, thence to the teachers. They require a 'standardisation' of what is to be produced. The government, at intervals, announces the performances required of teachers in terms of the performances required of pupils (measured in examination grades at different stages of their schooling) or in percentage increase in student performance.

The 'new vision' promoted by Odden and Kelly included 'improving leadership' through extended pay scales which rewarded 'strong and effective leaders', namely, head teachers, members of their management teams and advanced skills teachers. Fixed-term contracts would link rewards to the achievement of agreed objectives.

In similar vein, the Department for Education and Employment produced a further consultation document (Hay/McBer, 2000), at the cost of £3 million (worth now approximately £6 million) on what makes an effective teacher 'within a framework of professional development'.

The vision of Hay-McBer and of Odden and Kelly, as shown above, assumes a distinctive language through which to describe, assess and evaluate an 'educational practice' and thus professional engagement within it – the language of 'targets', 'performances' (expressed behaviourally), 'performance indicators', 'audits' of those performances, teachers as effective 'deliverers of those targets', learners as 'customers', or 'clients'. Such a language provides a different way of understanding learning and thereby of teaching. There is a metaphorical drawing upon the language of the business world – except it soon no longer was metaphorical. Professional judgement and development take on different meanings. Previous standards of professional judgement are replaced by externally imposed standards. And so, teachers and their 'managers' perceive what they are doing differently.

This requires a close examination of what it means for teachers to be acting professionally. It requires a questioning of whether the language of management is a true reflection of that professionalism. Is it a case of the mind being bewitched by the misuse of words? Wittgenstein said that:

> my aim is: to teach you to pass from a piece of disguised nonsense to something that is patent nonsense. (1:464)

That is what the remainder of this chapter tries to do by

- pointing to the unfortunate consequences of this language of management;
- showing why the 'logic of action' is at odds with an 'educational practice';
- pointing to the centrality of ethics to educational leadership, something absent from the language of 'performativity'.

UNSEEN CONSEQUENCES

Campbell's law stipulates that:

> the more any quantitative social indicator is used for social decision-making, the more subject it will be to corruption pressures and the more apt it will be to distort and corrupt the social processes it was intended to monitor. (quoted in Berliner & Nichols, 2007)

Campbell warned us of the inevitable problems associated with undue weight and emphasis on a single indicator for monitoring complex social phenomena. In effect, he warned us about the high-stakes testing programmes.

The result is a 'teaching to the test', fully explained and illustrated in Warwick Mansell's book in 2007, *Education by Numbers*: the tyranny of testing. So much hangs on the results of tests at 7, 11, 14 and then with

GCSEs and A Levels, that there is much evidence of 'teaching to the test'. Examination boards produce text books which give the sort of answers needed to pass their own examinations. For example, Edexcel produced in 2006 a new GCSE mathematics course, accompanied by a textbook 'so that you can be sure of a complete match to the new ... specifications'. And this is now typical across different examination boards – specifying precisely what the examinees have to write to meet the specifications which in turn meet the demands of the marking system.

When Capita successfully competed to gain the contract to improve the 'outputs' as measured on tests, advisers were appointed to oversee the government's drive to improve standards. The *Invitation to Negotiate* in conformity with the Public Service Agreement targets, stated:

> The ultimate objective of the National Strategy is to make improvements in the practice of teaching and learning in the classroom, and through these improvements to raise the pupils' attainments as measured by national curriculum tests. The central purpose of the contract [is] increasing the [test] attainment of pupils. (DES, 2003)

Typical comments from teacher, quoted by Mansell, were

- from a London school curriculum 14–18 coordinators with reference to Year 9:

> Most schools seem to be doing two to three mock tests per child before the real thing. Year 9 is totally dominated by test preparation. (Mansell, p. 58)

- from another teacher:

> I don't feel my Year 9 have learnt anything of value this term. I have done practice reading papers, writing papers, targeted writing for writing papers, and put immense pressure on them. (Mansell, p. 59)

But how far can such practices be pursued before this becomes cheating? In December 2011, examiners for the Welsh Joint Examination Board were suspended over the secret advice they gave to teachers on their courses. One had been recorded as saying:

> We're cheating. We are telling you the cycle of [of the compulsory question].
>
> Probably the regulator will tell us off. (Daily Telegraph, December 2011).

The highly respected Smith Report on mathematics raised

> serious concerns about the frequency of assessment of material in GCE AS and A Level Mathematics. This is felt by many respondents to hinder the developments of learning

and understanding of mathematics at this level. It is the consensus view that far too much time is devoted to examinations and preparing for examinations – 'teaching to the test' – and that this is at the expense of the understanding of the subject itself. (Smith Report, 2004)

There is much evidence to show that the pursuit of specific targets on the basis of their being the 'standards' has resulted in higher scores but less education. That should become clear when we elaborate what is meant by an 'educational practice'. But the fundamental flaw lies in the identification of educational standards with the attainment of targets. What might be useful *indicators* of knowledge and understanding are not the same as knowledge and understanding, as the Smith Report argued. One can be trained to come out with an answer to a well-prepared question without a real understanding of the underlying concepts or theories. The effective manager might be able to attain these high scores, but he or she may not be an educational leader.

AN EDUCATIONAL PRACTICE

More important, however, than the unseen consequences is the deeper erosion of what is meant by an 'educational practice' and of the professional role of the teacher as the leader in such a practice. What increasingly is being seen is excellent management of behaviour. But is it excellent leadership of education?

To understand the nature of an educational practice, one needs to contrast the activity of teaching with the 'logic of action' which is characteristic of the 'management of behaviour' just described. By 'logic of action', I mean the logical features of the language by which we describe, understand and explain what someone is doing. Thus, in what has just been described, there is the assumption that an action has an end or goal which can be made precisely, observed and measured – in that sense a 'target'. To reach that target, one adopts certain means via which one is most likely to hit that target. It becomes an empirical matter as to what particular means will enable one to hit the target. There is no logical connection between the means and the end or target. Therefore, in the case of teaching, there can indeed be a 'science'. Hence, the language of 'delivery' – what interventions can be shown to 'deliver' the performance required.

This logical separation of the 'means' from the 'ends' for which they are the 'means' might be clarified through the following example. A target may be to get to the station for the 8.30 a.m. train. The most efficient means could be shown from previous experience that the 8.00 a.m. bus is the most likely means of getting there on time. However, there is no logical connection between getting that bus and arriving 'at the station by 8.30 a.m. Indeed, the hypothesis might be negated as a result of constant experience of missing the train. Along similar lines, teachers might be seen to be rather like the bus driver. They need not be concerned about the ends of education. These are fixtures, given to them from on high, specified in some detail through national tests, examination boards or a detailed National Curriculum. Rather are teachers, like the bus driver, experts in delivery, that is, in the pedagogical skills or the means by which these targets might be reached most efficiently and effectively in the classroom. Teaching is a technical service of 'delivery'.

On the other hand, the actions we engage in, do not necessarily fit this 'logic of action'. In deliberating about what I am to do, there is no clear distinction between the ends and the means. My aim, for example, might be to help someone in distress; the action is to engage in those activities which embody the kindness and caring which are what it means to relieve that distress. I need, as I am acting, to be making judgments about the person, what constitutes relief for him, and how my actions are changing the very understanding of the aims themselves. The nature of the distress becomes apparent and the relevance of what I do is constantly being transformed through the shifting conception of the aims. My actions are shaped by the values through which I see the situation and the virtues which direct my intervention.

The 'logic of action' — the way in which we understand and explain the act of teaching — is, therefore, very different. Michael Oakeshott likens education to a

> conversation — an endless unrehearsed intellectual adventure in which, in imagination, we enter into a variety of modes of understanding the world and ourselves. (Oakeshott, 1975, p. 39)

Teachers, therefore, are much more than managers of the conversation. They are participants in it — both as persons who understand and can participate in that conversation between the generations and as ones who, in the light of that understanding, are able to engage in a conversation with the young learners. The educational practice is that very engagement with the learner, namely, on the one hand, an understanding of the mode of thinking and the level of understanding of the learners; on the other hand, an acquaintance with the inherited culture ('the best that has been thought and said'); and finally making the connection between the two. The humanities teacher is able to show the relevance of literature, poetry and the arts to the self-understanding of the young person. An 'educational practice' is this transaction between teacher (drawing on the understandings and values embodied in the voice of poetry, the voice of science, the voice of history) and the neophyte needing to enter into that conversation. The action of the teacher therefore is as much a deliberation about the aims of education as these apply to these particular learners as it is about the means of implementing those aims in the very act of teaching. Teachers of literature, left to their own devices, would from their own understanding of literature choose those plays, novels or poetry which 'spoke' to the learners, given their perceived needs, and they would introduce them in such a way that the transaction itself embodied the values to be transmitted.

To understand teaching in this way is to transform our understanding of the role of teachers in society and in particular the way in which they should be seen as leaders rather than managers, though, of course, there must always be a degree of management requiring management skills. In teaching well, they must necessarily be reflective, thinking about the aims of what they are doing, about the values which are embodied in their actions and about the changes in thinking, understanding and valuing which occur in the learners.

As such understanding on the part of the learners develops, so too must the aims of the teachers' lesson. Their teaching should not be determined by precise, fixed and unchanging targets, but by the direction of the 'conversation' through which the learner comes to grasp the key concepts of the subject or to appreciate the significance of a piece of literature or to see the significance of an historical event. And such grasp of key concepts (partial and at different levels of understanding) and such literary appreciation and historical insight will necessarily be a little different in each learner and but a stage in the development of greater understanding. In the same way, the doctorate provides opportunities for candidates to engage with professional learning and 'learning' leadership through research and scholarship that brings together theory and practice (Stenhouse, 1983).

It is for this reason that 'action research' is seen so important in professional development. Teachers are encouraged to research their own teaching, coming to see in the light of evidence how their teaching embodies certain values which may not initially have been clear or how there are unintended consequences which require change in pedagogy. There is a need to reflect and to ponder whether these values are compatible with the original vision of the teaching. Furthermore, as the original goals are pursued, so they too will change in the very pursuit. Increased knowledge of the learners and of the attempt to communicate with them will affect how one understands those goals.

Educational leadership, therefore, lies in showing how teachers might engage in such an educational practice, providing the opportunities for cooperative research and support, ensuring coherence across subject areas and classes and years so that greater progress can be made. The teachers are learning all the time. The educational leader would create a 'community of learners' within which teachers would share problems amongst themselves, support those teachers who are struggling, encourage that critical reflection upon the aims and values which are implicit in the teaching.

In the logical confusion between managing and educating, that community of learners is undermined, that examination of the aims and values of educating these learners made redundant because those have been fixed. Once there were Teachers' Centres where teachers from different schools would come together to share their difficulties and to explore possible solutions. What was suggested by one would be tested out and adjusted by another in a 'conversation' that had no end. Now, in the more managed and competitive world of a fragmented educational system, there are examples of 'successful schools' insisting upon the 'property rights' over lessons which have 'worked' – certainly not a community of learners.

ETHICS

The ethical dimension to this understanding of educational leadership has been hinted at so far, but it needs to be made explicit. There are two aspects in which the ethical is intrinsic.

First, to educate (as opposed to indoctrinate, to condition or merely to train) is like the word 'to reform'. It implies making someone better in some respect. In some way, the learners are developing distinctively human qualities and abilities. They are acquiring the understanding and knowledge which enables them to manage their lives more intelligently. It is to open the eyes of the learner to different ways of appreciating the world in which they live. It is inducting them into what is seen as a valued way of life. Therefore, the educational leader must ensure that those qualities which make us distinctively human (and the development of which are what the teachers, in their different subjects and activities, are striving for) are examined, discussed and communicated. Teachers are engaged in a moral activity and the moral nature of that activity needs constantly to be examined. How might it be described? And how then might it be implemented in the diversity of activities which make up the school?

Second, however, there is another ethical dimension to teaching, and thereby to educational leadership, which rarely gets mentioned and yet which is central, namely, the development and promotion of the virtues which are intrinsic to the teaching profession – and which challenge the dominance of the managerial 'logic of action' which increasingly prevails.

By 'virtue', I mean the *disposition,* deep and enduring, which motivates a person to pursue a course of action, despite difficulties and challenges, which the person conceives to be good and appropriate. Any list of virtues, therefore, embodies the values which prevail in a social tradition. Within a profession (a specific social tradition), there are virtues which are intrinsic to carrying out one's professional duties. The doctor, for example, would be expected to make a decision about the appropriate treatment of a patient in the light of the patient's best interests, not in terms of his own fiduciary benefit. Or again, parents need to be able to trust the teachers to exercise judgment about the best course of action for the children rather than for the school as it seeks to progress up the league table. One is aware of the dilemma experienced by many teachers who, forced by 'management' to concentrate on borderline C/D GCSE students, find it necessary to neglect those who are unlikely to boost the school's ranking.

Few moral situations require a great deal of deliberation. Teachers act out of their 'natural' inclinations. They see a situation as unjust, and, if they are so disposed, seek to remedy the injustice. The courageous teacher will not be disposed to abandon his or her obligations when those are challenged by 'management' who have had targets imposed upon them. To resist 'management' where that goes against the educational judgment of the educator may require a great deal of courage, another virtue much needed in teaching. It is important for the 'community of learners', spoken about above, to recognise this ethical dimension to teaching – the virtues which are intrinsic to acting professionally – and to support them.

It is quite possible for a teacher to accept the reasons for behaving in a particular way but not be disposed so to act – not having the relevant virtue. That is why educational leadership should ensure that the virtues of fairness, justice, honesty and care, for example, characterise the running of the school. Adults, as much as children, develop the relevant virtues through the prevailing social ethos, example and encouragement.

For example, one can have a whole school policy on developing the virtue of 'caring'. Noddings (1992) spells out the conditions for such social development: the *modelling* of caring by teachers and the school as a whole; the place of *dialogue* (the open-ended conversations in which each contribution, however disagreeable, is taken seriously); the *practice* of caring (such as taking care of a pupil who feels isolated or engaging in a project aimed at helping the less fortunate); and *confirmation* (that is, showing recognition of the person's contribution, often given with difficulty). All this, of course, requires pedagogical skills (e.g., gaining insights into possible areas of conflict within the group or into the matters which are of deep personal concern). But it requires much more than that. It requires not only the disposition to take such caring for all the learners seriously but also a whole school policy through which such a disposition is made possible to exercise. It becomes, as it were, part of the air one breathes.

For example, a primary school placed the nurturing of caring at the centre of its school's programme. The whole school embodies the values implied in caring for each other – pupil for pupil, teachers for the pupils and each other, and the school for the parents of the pupils. It is crucial to create a caring community. In that school:

> a class of 10 year olds were gathered together for their weekly sharing of their problems and their reactions to them. The school was in one of the most disadvantaged districts of England. Of the class of 30, 11 were on the social services' 'at risk' register. The father of one boy had just been murdered on the nearby estate. Over the last couple of years they had learnt the rules for engaging in discussion (dialogue): only one person at a time (he or she who holds the ball); nothing hurtful of another in the group to be allowed; everyone to listen to what each says; no forced to speak, though everyone has the opportunity to do so. It was crucial to have developed a safe environment in which each could speak honestly about what he or she thought and felt. They were talking about events in their lives which they had found hurtful. Some were of bullying. One was of the anger of her stepfather who had confined her to her bedroom. Discussion was of how one felt, how to deal with one's feelings, how to manage the situation. The courage in engaging in such personal exposure and the caring reactions of the others were quite remarkable.

However, educational leadership should be concerned not only with the development of such moral virtues, but also with the intellectual virtues essential to the development of knowledge and understanding. Moral virtues are dispositions like courage, perseverance, honesty, caring for others' welfare, concern for justice – indeed, very much the Sermon on the Mount with a few additions due to changes in circumstance. Intellectual virtues, on the other hand, refer to *truthfulness*, that is, concern to find out the truth and not to cook the books – what Sockett (2012, p. 57 sqq.), in his book *Knowledge and Virtue in Teaching and Learning*, referred to as 'the linchpin of trust'. It embraces:

- *openness of mind* to criticism for knowledge grows through criticism;
- *concern for accuracy*;
- *interest in clarity of communication*;
- *impartiality* in face of rival interpretations.

A moment's reflection will reveal how defective we often are, when difficult circumstances arise, in being one hundred percent virtuous in this regard. When one acts or makes practical judgments, generally one acts or judges from the deep-seated dispositions which are part of one's very being. Clever people, knowing the conclusions they want, can, if so disposed, find the data and arguments to justify them. The virtuous professional would be horrified at any attempt to 'cook the books' or to stifle criticism or to act partially.

CONCLUSION

This chapter draws a clear distinction between school management and educational leadership. The two are often confused, and, therefore, too often one sees leaders in schools, colleges and universities chosen for their management skills rather than for their educational wisdom and leadership. They have adopted without reflection or criticism a language embodying a 'logic of action' which undermines the educational purposes of schools. They have the 'management speak' of targets, performance indicators, audits and deliverology. The difficulty, of course, lies in the need to reconcile the educational ideals (the ethical ideal of developing 'educated person' and of enabling the learner to make his *debut dans la vie humaine*) with the economic and political context in which it may often be difficult to pursue those ideals. Testing is universal. One has to take part in it even where one recognises its stultifying effect on education (see Pring, 2013, chapter 12 for a detailed account). This conflict gives rise to moral dilemmas, which call upon the deeper sense of values to steer one through. Educational leadership is required to reconcile these differences, guided by the ethical understanding of educational aims and the deep-seated dispositions or virtues to respect those aims even in difficult circumstances.

REFERENCES

Berliner, D., & Nichols, S. (2007). *Collateral damage: How high status testing corrupts American schools.* Cambridge, MA: Harvard University Press.

DES. (2003). *Invitation to negotiate.* London: DES.

Faulkner, D., Freedland, M., & Fisher, E. (1999). *Public services: Developing approaches to governance and professionalism.* Report of a series of seminars. Oxford: St. John's College.

Hay/McBer. (2000). *Raising achievement in our schools: Model of effective teaching.* Report to DFEE. London: Hay Group.

Mansell, W. (2007). *Education by numbers: The tyranny of testing.* London: Politico.

Noddings, N. (1992). *The challenge to care in schools.* New York, NY: Teachers College Press.

Oakeshott, M. (1975). A place of learning. In T. Fuller (Ed.), *Michael Oakeshott and education.* New Haven, CT: Yale University Press (Reprinted in 1989).

Odden, A., & Kelly, C. (1997). *Paying teachers for what they know and can do.* Thousand Oaks, CA: Corwin Press.

Pring, R. (2013). *The life and death of secondary education for all.* London: Routledge.

Smith Report. (2004). *Making mathematics count.* London: The Stationery Office.

Sockett, H. (2012). *Knowledge and virtue in teaching and learning.* London: Routledge.

Stenhouse, L. (1983). The relevance of practice to theory in curriculum change. *Promise and Practice, 22*(3), 211–215.

Wittgenstein, L. (1958, 1.464). *Philosophical investigations.* Oxford: Basil Blackwell.

NEW DIRECTIONS FOR THE DOCTORAL THESIS

Richard Andrews

ABSTRACT

Purpose — *This chapter focuses on the impact of digitization on the conception, development and examination of the doctoral thesis in the contemporary university.*

Methodology — *The approach taken is that of reflective inquiry. The author has taken a lead role in the editing of two handbooks for Sage: one on e-learning research and the other on the digital dissertation/thesis, and this chapter reflects on the changes taking place in higher education as a result of digitization. A number of examples are used to illustrate the possibilities afforded by digitization not only at doctoral levels but also in all dissertations.*

Findings — *It is proposed that digitization affects not only the conception and direction of doctoral research for the student but it has implications also for supervisors, those who 'upgrade' work from MPhil to PhD levels and also for examiners and librarians. Changes in the format of the presentation of the digital thesis allow moving image and sound, as well as still images, to be incorporated into the main body of the text rather than be relegated to an appendix (e.g. in a CD-Rom).*

Investing in our Education: Leading, Learning, Researching and the Doctorate
International Perspectives on Higher Education Research, Volume 13, 75–92
Copyright © 2014 by Emerald Group Publishing Limited
ISSN: 1479-3628/doi:10.1108/S1479-362820140000013004

The storage of the completed thesis in digital form, via a number of different repositories, allows for greater access and use.

Research implications — *One of the major implications of the digital thesis is that all universities must regularly re-visit their regulations to ensure that the parameters for doctoral research are clear, and that they are appropriate for the kind of research that is undertaken by students. Many universities are now making a digital copy of the thesis for principal submission, with print copies as optional.*

Originality and significance — *Consideration of the implications of the digital thesis for students and universities is essential not only in terms of knowledge creation but also in terms of validation of such knowledge and its dissemination and use.*

Keywords: Digital dissertation; digital thesis; higher education; supervision; examination; dissemination

INTRODUCTION

In the *Handbook of Digital Dissertations and Theses* (Andrews, Borg, Boyd Davis, Domingo, & England, 2012), my fellow editors and authors mapped out what impact, we thought, digitization has on the nature and format of the dissertation and thesis. Our approach, though initially focussed on doctorates, was applied in the end to any kind of dissertation — at undergraduate, Masters and doctoral levels. In this chapter, however, I focus more sharply again on the doctoral thesis: its function, its possibilities and what these say about the nature of knowledge creation at doctoral level within a wider context of the present volume, with its focus on leadership and policy implications. I include consideration of the possible direction that digitization can afford to the doctoral student but also look at the kinds of knowledge that are being generated by the contemporary doctorate in the arts, social sciences and humanities. My approach — typical of someone with a background in the communication arts (see Andrews, 2014) — begins with the nature and format of the contemporary doctorate but moves backwards and forwards between the genre itself and the social and political contexts of the genre. It looks at current practice in an education and social science research institution with a large cohort of doctoral researchers where digitization and multi-modality have impacted on the creation, development and examination of the doctoral thesis.

Digitization is changing the nature of doctoral submission, though the possibilities of this shift are yet to be fully realized in practice. For some years, many universities in the United Kingdom have required, like many universities worldwide, that the final written (printed) thesis submission – two copies, softbound until approved by the examiners and then hardbound for the library shelves and public access – should be *accompanied* by a digital version in Word or in a pdf format. It makes sense for candidates to submit the initial version in Word as well as printed form so that amendments and corrections can be incorporated after the viva. The finally approved thesis can be submitted in pdf and then stored digitally by the university in its repository of theses, as well as submitted to EthOS at the British Library. But from the period since 2010, the guidance for submission has been changing. In a pivotal and indicative shift of practice (and possibility) in 2013 at my own university, the digital submission became an option as the *principal* text, with the printed softbound copies an *accessory* to the digital version.

Such practices have been evident since at least 2010 when the University of Illinois at Urbana-Champaign, more radically, indicated to its doctoral students that it would no longer accept printed, softbound or hardbound copies but would receive only the digital version of the thesis. Readership of the submitted digital theses increased 10-fold in the first year. Such a change in submission requirements has a potentially profound impact on the whole doctoral research process. Knowing that digital submission is required will encourage some students to conceive of their research projects, ab initio, differently. A major consideration will be the degree to which multi-modal approaches to the presentation of the thesis are included.[1] Multi-modality suggests the inclusion of word, still image, moving image, sound, gesture etc., and it is possible to conceive of a study that embraces some or all of these modes of communication. Such a broad use of and combination of modes have been possible in arts-based research for decades – art installations, exhibitions and sculptures are presented, usually as *part* of the doctoral submission (accompanied by a 'critical' dimension, conventionally supplied in word form). But the practice is relatively new in the humanities and social sciences, bound as they have been more conventionally in the 'classic' verbal (spoken and written) tradition. However, photographs or other forms of digital still image have already become part of the conventional printed thesis. Now, as digitization influences practice more deeply, an arts, humanities or social sciences research student could incorporate, for example, documentary film as part of their submission.

The reciprocal relationship between new technologies on the one hand and new practices and forms of knowledge creation on the other has implications beyond that of format and presentation. Among these implications are increased researcher agency, a changing relationship between research/ doctoral study and the student researcher and the process of research. In the following sections, I try to chart some of these changes.

CONCEPTION

The *conception* of the research topic, and its subsequent treatment by the research student, needs to be dwelled on further before we move to other implications of the digital thesis. These may continue to be *about* a topic in a post hoc approach. Such post hoc abstraction is partly a result of the nature of the verbal mode: it consists of critical, reflective words about phenomena. However, the inclusion of other modes of communication and representation means that the researcher and the reader can get closer to the primary experience that is being investigated. Instead of (or as well as) writing about film, the researcher can show the film or film extracts; instead of (or as well as) writing about music through the prisms of, first, notation, and second, critical verbal commentary on such notation, the researcher can actually present the music itself as part of the thesis. One could see the proximity of the primary material as a threat to research if we conceive of research only as an abstracted, reflective activity mediated by words. If research means, to paraphrase an eighteenth century definition of research in music, 'the seeking of patterns of harmony which once found, are used in the piece to played afterwards' (think of pattern-seeking in data through analysis, which once found can be applied to real-world problems and solutions), then those patterns need to be identified and shown in primary data, even though they might be analysed in another mode.

Such presentational possibilities raise the question of how studies are framed (see Andrews, 2010), and these need to be made clear in the introduction to a thesis so that all who read it are clear about the paradigm within which the research project is undertaken, and more pragmatically, what to expect – and how to read it – as they embark on the 'reading' of the thesis.

What does this more direct form of communication in the doctoral thesis say about knowledge and the creation of new knowledge? First, that academic framing of knowledge need not be bound by the verbal code, and that other forms of 'knowing' – visual, aural, synaesthetic, tactile, kinetic – can be validated. Second, that the layering of critical commentary can be arranged and weighted by the research student to indicate precisely where his or her focus of attention is, and how that modal focus of attention is related to other modes. Third, that 'an original contribution to knowledge' (never well-defined) can take even more various forms, from the offering of new perspectives, to the re-configuration of existing ideas and assumptions, to the presentation of new material and so on.

Fourth, what kinds of argument are presented by a digital thesis that uses a wide set of possibilities as set out above? Argument (the product) and argumentation (the process) are likely to continue to be central to the criteria for success at doctoral level as they are at both Masters and under-graduate levels. Does the move away from a necessarily linear argumentational sequence in the conventional written/printed thesis – say, in the presentation of a thesis in a website form, where the points of entry are multiple and where the material need not necessarily be read in a prescribed order – compromise the argument of a thesis or could the argument be (partially) constructed by the reader? Can a set of images argue? Can a musical composition be said to make an argument, irrespective of whether it is accompanied by 40,000 words of written critical commentary or not? We are faced here with issues of implied argument and explicit arguments. Doctoral work tends to the explicit because it is set within an academic context. But such explicitness is not always the choice of those presenting theses for examination and is not a worldwide universality: a doctoral study on the historical emergence of manga as an educational tool, for example (Ellis, 2007), eschewed explicit articulation of its thesis within a Japanese tradition of suggestion and implicitness rather than the somewhat less refined practice of explicit exposition.

Issues around the *conception* of the digital thesis are considered here because these are central to the kinds of knowledge that are anticipated in a doctoral course of study and to the student who is embarking on that course. The next matter to consider is the *supervision* of that course of study and its implications for the process of research as the basis of a thesis or dissertation.

SUPERVISION

Supervisors are key not only to the development of a research student's research project, particularly in the structural design of the thesis (the principal aspect that supervisors can be held to account for if the student is not successful), but also for the depth of scholarship, the elegance of the design overall, the degree of theory that is introduced and the methodological rigour. Above all, the supervisor's role is to guide (navigate) the student successfully through the demands and rituals of the doctoral journey. It is thus all the more important, when there is a new direction to navigate, that the supervisor – even if he or she has not travelled the specific territory – is able to map-read and work with the student to ensure a successful passage. Again, this responsibility for navigation comes back to the regulations of the university and the guidance offered to the student in terms of criteria for success.

The regulations at one UK higher education institution include the following (I have included only those that are relevant to the argument of this chapter; details about length of registration, eligibility etc. are left out):

The MPhil/PhD thesis must

6.3.1 consist of the candidate's own account of his/her investigations;
6.3.2 be an integrated whole and present a coherent argument;
6.3.3 include a full bibliography and references;
6.3.4 be written in English and of a satisfactory standard of literary presentation. (2012 regulations, p. 6)

and perhaps more pointedly for the purposes of this chapter:

6.10 If appropriate to the field of study, and subject to approval by the Academic Registrar, a candidate may undertake research leading to the submission of a portfolio of original artistic or technological work undertaken during his/her period of registration. The work may take the form of, for example, objects, images, films, performances, musical compositions, webpages or software, but must be documented or recorded in the portfolio by means appropriate for the purposes of examination and eventual deposit in the Institute library. The portfolio must include written commentary on each item of artistic or technological work and either an extended analysis of one item or a dissertation on a related theme. The written commentaries and extended analysis or dissertation must together be no more than 40,000 words. (*ibid.*, p. 7)

I will take up four main areas in these regulations that a supervisor and student must address if the student decides to go down the route of less conventional thesis. These are the nature of the *argument*, the *bibliography and references,* the *portfolio* and the *written* element. Collectively, these provide the framework for the thesis and, as such, require the guidance of the supervisor.

Discussion of how *argument* manifests itself in a multi-modal, digital thesis was begun above. It also needs to be said that the argument can take various forms. It need not proceed via some of the conventional models, like the proving or disproving of a hypothesis or the sequential and logical or quasi-logical setting out of a position. What it must contain is a series (not necessarily chronological or logical) of propositions supported by evidence and a critically informed position taken by the researcher. This series of propositions can be spatially arranged, like paintings in a gallery or pages on a website where it is up to the reader to determine the sequence in which the elements are experienced, thereby creating their own narrative – and by implication, argument – of the experience. The critically informed position is a matter of development through the material, weighted up by the researcher with a view to find his or her own position in relation to it (to the 'existing body of knowledge').

The *scholarship* in a digital multi-modal thesis need be no different from that in a conventional thesis. There will be references and/or a bibliography. These can be presented separately as they are in a conventional social sciences thesis, or as footnotes, as is the convention in a humanities thesis. Scholarship will also include a critical and careful examination of the problem or the topic analysed.

The *portfolio* is the position taken by the university in question for the specific purposes 'of examination and eventual deposit in the Institute library'. That is to say, the submitted work cannot be a website or a film or an installation per se, but the artefact must be contained with a portfolio (this could be an electronic folder) along with a 'written commentary'. This regulation is central to the argument of this chapter because it defines what is allowed by the university and the format in which the doctoral submission must be contained.

The relatively conservative positioning of this university is reflected in its insistence that there should be 'written commentary on each item of artistic or technological work and either an extended analysis of one item or a dissertation on a related theme' of not more than 40,000 words. The written commentary on one item could be on the only item contained in the portfolio, if there is not more than one. If there is a collection or series of items – as in a critical catalogue of an exhibition – there needs to be a commentary on each item. In addition – not as an alternative – there needs to be an extended (critical) analysis of one item or a dissertation. There is thus some degree of choice for the researcher as to what they put in the portfolio. The written element is deemed to take up about half of the full submission. Sometimes, the artefact is termed the 'creative' element and the written commentary the 'critical' element, but the distinction is a blurred one. There is no reason why the artefact cannot be critical in its response to an existing context. A fuller discussion of the spectrum of possibilities for the submission and form of a doctoral thesis is contained in Andrews and England (2012). We can imagine at one end of the spectrum, the conventional written thesis and at the other end, a thesis that contains no words at all.

UPGRADE AND EXAMINATION

Most doctoral degrees – and certainly the MPhil/PhD route – require the consideration of an 'upgrade' from MPhil to PhD registration during the course of study. In effect, this often takes the form of an interim 'viva' in which the student's work is subjected to close perusal by academics other than the supervisor. Some universities also make provision for an internal reader to undertake a critical look at the draft thesis before it is submitted. Along with the formal examination at the end of the process, these occasions have in common the *critical and formative assessment* of the student's work.

The experience and imagination which the internal readers and internal and external examiners bring to the process of review is crucial to the success and future direction of the student. An examiner or internal reader of work who has digitally submitted (and in which the student brings an iPad or other tablet to the meeting rather than a printed document) must be sensitive not only to the format in which the work is presented but also to the paradigm in which the student is working. Assuming this to be within the framework of regulations, the research paradigm – how the research is approached, what values underpin it, what counts as evidence, what place sequentiality plays in the work etc. – is crucial to its appropriate consideration. It follows that either experience, imagination or training is required for internal readers and examiners who are invited to take part in the doctoral degree process. There are thus implications for institutions to make sure such academic staff are properly prepared.

It is in the management of upgrade and examination, and the wider responsibilities that are bound up with them, that institutions can take a leading role in re-thinking the parameters for the doctoral dissertation or thesis. Heads of doctoral or graduate schools have a complex job, often concerned with applying and interpreting the detailed rules of submission, upgrading and examination. The exciting challenge for institutions, however, and those with leadership responsibilities in these regards, is how to adapt and update the regulations and guidance to reflect the changing nature of knowledge generation and representation.

SOME TECHNICAL AND DESIGN ISSUES

There are some technical issues in the transition from paper-based to digital submission of theses that require brief discussion. Over 100 years of the printed doctoral thesis (see Borg & Boyd Davis, 2012) has established detailed conventions for submission from institution to institution. Some of these look outdated, for example, 'Theses must be presented in a permanent and legible form in typescript or print except that mathematical or similar formulae may be inserted neatly by hand. Photographic and other illustrations should be permanently mounted on A4 size paper and bound within the thesis. In no circumstances should "Sellotape" or similar materials be used for any purpose' and 'Any material which cannot be bound in with the text must be placed in a pocket inside or attached to the back cover or in a rigid container similar in format to the bound thesis.' Furthermore, illustrative material may be submitted in the following forms: 'a) audio recording [on] compact cassette tape C60 or C90, b) photographic slides [should be] 35 mm in 2 inch by 2 inch frame.'

No such detailed instructions exist for digital formatting and presentation but they could include something like the following: 'digital submissions must be in a format that allows weblinks, and links to other modes like sound and (moving) image. Three-dimensional phenomena, like sculpture, installations and performance, must be rendered in two-dimensional form. The submission must give access to the examiners and all subsequent readers the full experience of the proposed thesis. It should be accompanied by a printed version which indicates where, and how material that cannot be included in print form, can be accessed'.

In terms of the actual submission of the thesis, candidates must often wait upon the decision of the examiners who will be asked by the Research Degrees Examination Officer whether they would prefer to read a hard copy or an electronic copy. 'If the examiners request hard copies, you can choose to submit your thesis for examination in one of two ways, *either* softbound in medium blue cloth *or* spiral bound with clear plastic covers'. Again, there is no detailed specification for the electronic submission, other than 'in pdf format'. This requirement appears to assume that the material submitted will be static and renderable in the pdf format − as if the digital version were simply an electronic version of the written, printed submission.

STORAGE AND DISSEMINATION

The regulations, quoted above, stipulate that the portfolio of submitted work must be 'documented or recorded ... by means appropriate for the purposes of ... eventual deposit in the library.' In many cases, in a reverse of the conventional procedure for the submission of a doctoral thesis for examination, the digital copy is usually accompanied by a hard copy for backup purposes. Universities which subscribe to the EthOS national thesis service of the British Library (and students of those universities) can access these digital copies of the thesis – via the full text where possible. Currently there are about 300,000 records of theses from over 120 institutions, with about a third available in full text. Of the remaining 200,000, three-quarters are available to be scanned. Each month about 3,000 new records are added and about two-thirds of these now provide the full texts of the theses. Access is determined by the host institution and may depend on mandatory electronic deposit of new theses, availability of the theses in the institution's own repository and to what extent digitization of print theses is prioritized locally. Doctoral students and others are over 100 times more likely to access doctoral theses via this portal than via conventional means.

Such digital storage and accessibility means that dissemination is partly on demand. Titles and abstracts are available, as well as full texts – though the abstract is often embedded in the thesis – but so far there is no systematic and extensive provision of, say, 10–20-page summaries of theses written for lay or academic audiences that will give a substantial insight into the research that has been undertaken. The closest we have come to such a service is via agencies and research units which provide summaries for different audiences or the Research Impact summaries that universities have provided for the Research Excellence Framework – which do not tend to cover doctoral theses. What this gap suggests is that doctoral students themselves might wish, in future, to provide 10–20 page summaries for their respondents and for interested stakeholders. The public engagement agenda is important here, and projects like Catalyst operate at the interface of research scholarship and public interest.

Most university libraries now house e-repositories for digitized data, e-journals, e-books, digitized course readings and doctoral (and sometimes

Masters) theses and dissertations (e.g. http://eprints.ioe.ac.uk). Furthermore, making a digital version of the thesis available enables the metadata to be 'harvested' by search engines worldwide, for example, via DART-Europe, the European research libraries e-thesis portal (see www.dart-europe.eu). The online catalogue at my own university library, for example, has ambitions for a 'discovery layer' to give access to all of this material. Such a 'layer' would map thematic routes through the material to enable easier access for research students, keying in more to their needs. The key is that digital materials not only enable worldwide access but also enable better access by users with disabilities and/or learning differences.

HOW DO THESE CHANGES AFFECT KNOWLEDGE PRODUCTION AND USE?

There are at least three aspects of knowledge production and use that are raised by the move to digital/multi-modal theses. One concern is what kinds of knowledge are generated in doctoral work, another is whether research knowledge is upstream or downstream of application and third is the extent to which the users of knowledge influence (or should influence) the creation and design of the knowledge that is generated.

It could be said that if research operates without an accessible abstract or summary, it often remains unread – as was the case with pre-EthOS and pre-digitization. If the researcher, on embarking on a doctoral course of study, knows that his or her work will be read and that the available resources include all the modes of communication, the project and the knowledge generated will be different.

Each of the modes of communication has its own affordances. Verbal language, whether spoken or written, has the possibilities of abstraction, generalization (nouns themselves are thought to be generalizations), logical sequencing, hierarchical categorization. The still image has the affordances of direct, potentially visceral communication, whether in photographic or painted (digital) form. Words are still the mode via which search engines operate, whereas images (including signs and icons) are increasingly used to represent ideas. Each of these modes may sit in a dominant position to the other: we can imagine an illustrated book on the one hand, where the written word is primary and the illustrations secondary or, on the other hand, a series of photographs where the written word is secondary, as in captions.

Both of these major modes of communication are *framed* differently.[2] Verbal, written and printed language abides by the medium which carries it: the page and the page on the screen. Currently I am working, in the United Kingdom, on an A4 page on computer screen. Because this is (academic) prose, the words wrap around at the end of the line unless I press 'Enter' for a new line or paragraph. The size of the page changes if the text is moved into a book (very few books are A4 in size) where the framing – as manifested in the words and in the design of the pages in the book as a whole – generates expectations as to the content.

The still image is always more consciously and more evidently framed, even if (or especially if) it is a cropped photograph. The inclusion and placing of a photograph in a thesis says something different from the adjacent written text. It represents a kind of knowledge that is direct, non-sequential, more sensory, observational, of a particular moment. Knowledge that comes in written form, especially academic writing, is almost by definition abstract, generalized, logical or quasi-logical propositional.

The combination of these two modes brings together these two sets of affordances: mostly in complementary fashion, sometimes in tension.

It is the nature of written academic prose in the doctoral thesis that it tends to operate downstream of innovation; in other words, it is post hoc. Its abstract nature allows it to *reflect back* on practice or phenomena, seeking to understand them by the identification of pattern. Once the pattern is identified and transformed into a theory and/or model, it can be applied for future practice and phenomena. But because of the downstream nature of the academic doctoral thesis, many of them remain unread and unused. How can advanced research of this kind be brought more upstream of practice and policy? Part of the answer lies in research teams, some of whom are engaged in post hoc analysis, and others who are applying that knowledge to the design of new products and new ways of doing things – and thus creating new communities of knowledge.

One further specific implication or unforeseen consequence of the move to the digital is obviating of the need for transcription of oral data into writing.

THE END OF TRANSCRIPTION?

While, on the one hand, there has been interesting and valuable discussion in multi-modal circles of the nature of transcription (seeing as one example of transduction from one mode to another), the practice of transcribing from oral recorded data into written transcript must become an increasingly rare activity for researchers. First, the oral data are almost always recorded digitally. They can be stored in sound files. They can be incorporated into the main body of a thesis and/or into its appendices; even in the now outmoded practice of collecting ancillary data on a CD-Rom which is appended to the thesis, sound files can be recorded, stored digitally and presented as part of the thesis as a whole. Transcription is labour-intensive and probably takes up time that could be better spent by the researchers in designing research and collecting or analysing data.

Transcribing one or two interviews, for example, is always useful. The very act of transcription − the transduction from one mode to another − makes one look at the data carefully, seeking patterns that may or may not be replicated in subsequent interviews. The inclusion of a full transcript in an appendix − particularly if translation from one language to another is involved − provides evidence of the nature of the interview and of transcription conventions that have been used. But if the research involves moderate or large numbers of interviews or if the data takes the form of sound (e.g. recordings of naturally occurring sound phenomena) then it makes sense not to transcribe all the data but to let it 'speak for itself'.

The suggestion that transcription may not be necessary is a simple, radical idea that may generate opposition. But it is worth asking: why is transcription necessary? Is the expense in time and/or money worth it? Could the research be presented more engagingly by providing direct access to the sound files themselves? The abstraction − literally − the pulling away from the core, original data that are involved in transcription create a distance between the reader and the data: one which may be conventional and enjoyed in academia but which may be a practice that is increasingly vestigial. *As long as the analytical function is carried out,* which involves standing back from the data so that patterns can be identified, the data itself can be presented more directly. The data can be re-represented in different modes if such an action makes them clearer to the author, and to the reader, where the patterns exist and what form they take.

It is understandable that some researchers may object to the idea that transcription of every digital sound recording may not be necessary. They will argue that analysis must be based on the written transcript, but the argument in the present chapter is that there is more to be gained in presentation of the original data, in the mode in which it was generated (and accessible if needed) accompanied by succinct analysis of its significance, than in the laboursome practice of transcription.

NEW COMMUNITIES OF KNOWLEDGE

Crowdsourcing is one form of collection and generation of knowledge that may well have further impact on the doctoral thesis. By making the thesis publicly available in digested, summary and full forms, it can be reviewed, commented upon, answered and be generally open to discussion in a way that was not possible 10 years ago. Although initially used by companies and other organizations to garner collective wisdom, crowdsourcing can be used as a research tool to generate and refine knowledge on a particular topic. Wikipedia is one result of such crowdsourcing, but it can be used more interactively to continue a dialogue about newly created knowledge.

The principle behind such interactive approaches to the generation of knowledge is dialogism, indicating a move away from one authoritative voice to a more collective creation of new knowledge. Such a move has implications for the doctoral thesis. As a genre and a rite of passage, the doctoral thesis tends to be an individualistic project in arts, humanities and social sciences. It will remain so as the qualification must be awarded to an individual. More team-based research – for example, involvement in a systematic review of research and/or a research project that involves a range of different types of engagement and outcome – will give scope for an individual dimension of the group activity to be separated for research degree purposes, as is often the case in the sciences. As expressed elsewhere in this chapter, such doctoral degrees can be factored into the design of research projects at the bidding stage and have to be managed carefully by both student and supervisor(s) to make sure that the outcomes are successful for all concerned.

One further aspect of new communities of knowledge is the facility for summaries of doctoral theses to be accessed by mobile technologies in a variety of media. It is not beyond imagination to conceive of digests of research findings that can be used by practitioners at the point of need: such is already the case in medical and health care; it could be the same in social care, education and other fields where practice needs to be informed by research. Research thus becomes *upstream* of practice.

PUBLIC ENGAGEMENT

The impact and public engagement agenda is largely concerned with grant-holding higher education institutions, and more specifically through an initiative via Research Councils UK. A number of universities across the

United Kingdom – Aberdeen, Bath, Exeter, the Institute of Education, Nottingham, Queen Mary, Sheffield – have been awarded catalyst funding to strengthen the commitment to public engagement, integrate public engagement into core research activity, support researchers at all levels within their institutions to engage and create networks within institutions to support and develop good practice in public engagement. See http://www.rcuk.ac.uk/per/Pages/catalysts.

To what extent is this movement towards impact and engagement relevant to and feasible for doctoral researchers?

Public engagement generally can take different forms. The approach at my own institution is set out at http://www.ioe.ac.uk/research/86369.html where sharing ideas, forming research partnerships, following good practice and learning about engagement are four dimensions of the work that is being undertaken to forge a better relationship between research and its use.

Research briefings of two pages in length (longer than an abstract and more user-focused) are another way in which engagement and impact can be fostered. As part of a whole series at http://www.ioe.ac.uk/research/87680.html, two examples are (a) a briefing on a study of the evidence available for teaching English as an additional language (EAL) in classrooms, and particularly at training for teachers in the field, which draws mostly on research published in the United States, Australia and the United Kingdom (http://www.ioe.ac.uk/Research_Expertise/RB18_Strategy_EAL_Andrews.pdf) and (b) on the experience of the United States in developing and implementing a National Writing Project for teachers to inform the establishment of a similar project in the United Kingdom (http://www.ioe.ac.uk/Research_Expertise/RB25_National_Writing_Project__Andrews.pdf).

Doctoral research, in arts, humanities and social sciences at least, has been largely individualistic and driven by curiosity of the researcher rather than by any larger social agenda. As noted above, team-based approaches to research which involve doctoral students are rare. As research project proposers include studentships within their work, however, the likelihood for a doctoral study to be aligned with a larger research project is becoming more common, and thus the possibility for stakeholder input at an early stage in the research design process – for example, setting the research question – is growing. The research impact agenda – seen most clearly in the requirement for the 2014 Research Excellence Framework to provide case studies of research that have had an impact on individuals, institutions or in other ways – is part of this wider picture of public engagement. Research impact tends to be seen as one-way; public engagement in research is more reciprocal and cyclical in that such engagement can be included at the start of research projects, throughout their development, and again at the end of the project when dissemination and impact are considered.

IMPLICATIONS FOR POLICY, EDUCATIONAL LEADERSHIP, MANAGEMENT

Finally, what are the implications for policy, educational leadership and management of the move towards the digital/multi-modal thesis? These are broad terms, so it is perhaps best to focus on the implications for doctoral schools and for innovative leadership in the field of research theses.

I would suggest the following:

There will be an increasing integration of research studentships into funded research projects so that early career researchers can respond to issues of public engagement and impact at the start of their research degrees. Early career researchers will learn how their own doctoral research fits into a larger picture of team-based research as well as into different communities of practice (including e-communities).

Highly desirable would be a move of research upstream so that it feeds into the practices and policies that flow from it rather than always addressing the matter 'downstream' or *post facto*/'after the case'. Such a move would make research more productive in that its results would feed into learning design rather than attempt to study learning after the event.

All of the above suggests that guidance for students, supervisors and examiners as to the possibilities afforded by the digital/multi-modal thesis will need to be reviewed and revised. While not being presented as templates for future research, a collection of exemplars of theses that have exploited the possibilities that the digital/multi-modal dimensions would be very useful for research students. These could be stored on the university intranets and/or in libraries. The libraries themselves may need to develop more secure (backup) institutional repositories for digital doctoral theses, as well as national and international collections like EthOS and DART, so that hard copies are no longer necessary.

CONCLUSION

I have argued in this chapter for a shift of practice in the way doctoral theses are conceived, supervised, developed and examined, in response to digitization and multi-modality and also in response to new practices in storage and dissemination. Such changes do not happen quickly in the university sector, but they can indicate changes in the way knowledge is generated.

In particular, the place of the doctoral thesis in the generation of new knowledge is put into question. If the doctoral thesis continues in its individualistic way in social sciences, arts and humanities, it is likely to be seen more as a *rite de passage* for the candidate rather than at the cutting edge of new knowledge. For a start, unless a doctoral candidate has undertaken a full systematic research review of the field in which he or she is working, there can be no guarantee that there is a genuine gap in knowledge being addressed or filled. By definition, individual researchers cannot undertake full systematic reviews because these require a team effort. It is thus the case – not often acknowledged – that the originality of the doctoral thesis is based more upon it not having been done in exactly this form before (its novelty) rather than on an original conception, design, dataset or conclusion.

Perhaps the degree of originality is a problematic concept in itself? Even if an individual researcher, working as part of a research team, identifies his or her contribution as clearly separate from the work of the team as a whole, there are questions about the dividing line between the individual's contribution and that of his/her part in the team.

My argument has been based on changes in the possibilities of new formats of submission and as such is limited to that perspective. Wider issues, like whether and if so, how the doctorate is used as a career stepping stone, about knowledge as generated outside the doctoral thesis and outside the academy and intellectual copyright issues that arise from the open and public availability of doctoral theses – are not addressed in this chapter. On the last issue, the more readily available nature of the doctoral thesis in its digital form is generally seen by students who are studying, by the candidates themselves and by the wider academic community as a positive change in public dissemination and engagement. This degree of accessibility is important not only to fellow research students but also to users in wider communities in distilled forms like the one-page, two-page and 20-page summary (and other variations).

From the point of conception of a doctoral research project to the final points of dissemination, the affordances of new technologies, combined with an understanding of the multi-modal nature of composition, provide a challenge and opportunity to further research practice.

NOTES

1. Digitization and multi-modality are not synonymous, but the advent and wide use of digitization in the early 1990s coincided with the rise of interest in multi-modality, probably as a result of the birth of the Internet and the more widespread use of the computer screen.
2. See   http://multimodalblog.wordpress.com/2013/10/15/framing-as-a-methodo logical-strategy/ (Andrews & Davison, 2013).

REFERENCES

Andrews, R. (2010). *Re-framing literacy: Teaching and learning in english and the language arts* (p. 240). New York, NY: Routledge.

Andrews, R. & Davison, J. (2013). *Framing as a methodological strategy.* Retrieved from   http://multimodalblog.wordpress.com/2013/10/15/framing-as-a-methodological-strategy/

Andrews, R. (2014). *A theory of contemporary rhetoric.* New York, NY: Routledge.

Andrews, R. & England, J. (2012). New forms of dissertation and thesis: A discussion of the seminar series and proposed guidance for universities. In Andrews, R., Borg, E., Boyd Davis, S., Domingo, M., & England, J. (Eds.). (2012). *The SAGE handbook of digital dissertations and theses* (530 pp.). London: Sage.

Andrews, R., Borg, E., Boyd Davis, S., Domingo, M., & England, J. (Eds.). (2012). *The SAGE handbook of digital dissertations and theses* (530 pp.). London: Sage.

Borg, E. & Boyd Davis, S. (2012). The thesis: Texts and machines. In Andrews, R., Borg, E., Boyd Davis, S., Domingo, M., & England, J. (Eds.). (2012). *The SAGE handbook of digital dissertations and theses* (pp. 13−30). London: Sage.

Ellis, K. B. (2007).*The emergence of study manga in Japan: A historical and semiotic approach.* PhD thesis, University of York, UK.

WESTERN DOCTORAL PROGRAMMES AS PUBLIC SERVICE, CULTURAL DIPLOMACY OR INTELLECTUAL IMPERIALISM? EXPATRIATE EDUCATIONAL LEADERSHIP TEACHING IN THE UNITED ARAB EMIRATES

Eugenie A. Samier

ABSTRACT

Purpose – *This chapter approaches the topic of teaching the Western scholarly tradition in non-Western countries like the United Arab Emirates (UAE) from three perspectives employing the following metaphors: as a Public Servant motivated by public service to the goals and aims of the country's development articulated by UAE rulers and its citizens; as Cultural Diplomat, representing the Western tradition and its scholarly achievements while respecting other traditions; and as Intellectual Imperialist, aiming at a colonising incorporation of the UAE into the Western academic world.*

Investing in our Education: Leading, Learning, Researching and the Doctorate
International Perspectives on Higher Education Research, Volume 13, 93–123
Copyright © 2014 by Emerald Group Publishing Limited
All rights of reproduction in any form reserved
ISSN: 1479-3628/doi:10.1108/S1479-362820140000013005

Methodology/approach – *The main methodology adopted is the Weberian ideal type, located within a comparative and historical context that produces the metaphors as analytically possible perspectives as a western expatriate faculty member. Additional critique is drawn from Bourdieu, Said, Freire, Giroux, Foucault, Goffman and cross-cultural organisation studies.*

Findings – *The findings consist of an analytic framework consisting of public servant, cultural diplomat and intellectual imperialist as a set of conceptions for analysing possible orientations of Western expatriate academics in developing countries.*

Social implications – *The implications are threefold: on a personal level, what experientially does each of the metaphors mean for one's sense of identity, profession, values and relationships; on a pedagogical level, what principles and values distinguish the curriculum and teaching styles as well as orientation to Arab and Islamic scholarship; and politically, what is the potential impact and unintended consequences for the indigenous culture, sovereignty and societal survival of a country under the heavy influence of globalisation. The contention of this chapter is that one cannot avoid adopting one or more of these roles and may even perform in contradictory ways.*

Originality/value – *The originality is in establishing a new set of analytic categories drawing on post-colonial, diplomacy and critical studies.*

Keywords: Middle East; globalisation; Islamic scholarship; Weberian critique; critical theory

INTRODUCTION

This chapter was originally developed as a presentation at Oxford Brookes University two years after I arrived in the United Arab Emirates to teach in a new doctoral programme – the first in the country and my first visit to the Middle East. It isn't uncommon for one to change one's perspective, even radically, after initial impressions wear off and a broader and deeper knowledge is gained. This chapter contains early thoughts and later reflections acquired after a further two years working almost exclusively with students and colleagues who are Emirati and from surrounding countries. During this time, we have also experienced the Arab Spring, albeit mostly indirectly, although some of my students and colleagues are from countries that have undergone turmoil and violence, some from the devastated countries of Iraq and Syria and some whose family still lives in Gaza that was bombed throughout part of the last year.

In my experience with doctoral programmes in Dubai, I work closely through supervision and conference and guest lecture travel with mostly mid-career and senior-career professionals whose commitment and perseverance through a difficult and long programme are rarely diminished by extraordinary stresses and strains that many Westerners cannot fathom. Even Emirati students, who enjoy a highly stable and prosperous life, have gone through an almost unique level and depth of change in the last 30 years with a consistent pride in country, in their leaders and in their culture and religion that is a testament to what vision and perseverance can accomplish and the resilience of their traditional culture and Islam. Instead of leadership consultants and gurus coming to the UAE from the West (many of whom have not seen the best of leadership practices), a practice common internationally in education (Walker & Dimmock, 2000), to impart leadership skills and knowledge, I often think that the knowledge transfer should flow the other way.

This account is a personal journey not necessarily generalisable to others who immigrated to the UAE to teach since I spend almost all my time outside the company of Westerners. It is one that is experiential, reflexive, borne of social interaction and cultural engagement and one that contains a shifted perspective on Western and Arab scholarship from many hours in the classroom and in tutorial in a university with a highly diverse faculty. This chapter is a record of this journey.

The chapter will first discuss a number of underlying historical and contextual factors that must be taken into consideration when examining the UAE, a country still establishing its social institutions, with an extremely high level of multiculturalism and as an inheritor of Islamic and Arabic culture and scholarship with distinctive traditions while 'modernising,' in part through the importation of western style degrees and universities. There are both dissimilarities and similarities in comparison with Western traditions, such as a shared intellectual heritage from the Renaissance and, in particular, educational ideals like *Bildung* and humanism that have corresponding theories in Islamic education.

The topic of teaching Western educational administration and leadership is approached from three perspectives employing the following metaphors: as a Public Servant motivated by public service to the goals and aims of the country's development articulated by UAE rulers and its citizens; as

Cultural Diplomat, representing the Western tradition and its scholarly achievements while respecting and in dialogue with other traditions; and as Intellectual Imperialist, aiming at a colonising incorporation of the UAE into the Western academic world. The contention of this chapter is that one cannot avoid adopting one or more of these roles and may even perform in contradictory ways. There are two premises that underlie this discussion: teaching in a doctoral programme is necessarily an existential experience and the construction and use of knowledge is not value-free.

Each of these metaphors implicate a number of issues, many of which are dealt with within the comparative education field (e.g. Dimmock & Walker, 2000); however, here the discussion is extended across three levels as they apply to doctoral programmes creating a different profile for each of the metaphors. First, on a personal level, what experientially does each of these means for one's sense of individual and professional identity, values and relationships, drawing on existential, phenomenological and social interaction theories? Secondly, on a pedagogical level, what principles and values distinguish knowledge construction, the curriculum and teaching style as well as orientation to Arab and Islamic scholarship? And, finally, on a political level, what are the potential impact and unintended consequences for the indigenous culture, sovereignty and societal survival of a country like the UAE under the heavy influence of Western programmes, faculty and other staff?

Drawing on personal experience and observations as well as theory and research in teaching in management and leadership studies, these three levels are examined individually and in how they relate to each other. At all three levels, there also exist problems of adjustment to a different culture, obstacles that exist generally in international comparison and must be overcome not only in studying unlike systems but also, argued here, in teaching as a foreigner. Some of these conceptual obstacles include the 'travelling problem' of concepts that mean different things in societal contexts that are structured differently, theoretical frameworks that differ, jurisdictional variance across political and economic frameworks, differing preferences in research methods that to some extent reflect values and customs and researcher bias often informed by negative stereotypes or sometimes a breath-taking lack of knowledge and interest (see Samier, 2009).

CONTEXTUALISING THE DISCUSSION IN THE UAE

In order to discuss doctoral programmes and the teaching of doctoral students, it is necessary to understand contextual factors. Educational systems vary considerably, in spite of globalisation and internationalisation. In the Middle East, conditions are significantly different from those in Western countries, and vary considerably across the Islamic world, that necessarily affect how one researches, designs curriculum and teaches. The cumulative influences of economic, political, cultural and social forces affect the nature of the educational system and the university as an organisation, the combination of faculty and students, the availability of materials, student preparation and social relations in and out of the classroom. A short sketch of these is necessary in order to explain how doctoral programmes are structured in the UAE, and how this shapes one's intentions, decisions and actions, as well as interpretation and critique.

Politically, the UAE is a very young nation state, formed in 1971 initially by six Emirates, joined a year later by one more. Its federated distribution of powers is similar to Canada and Germany; it is overseen by a Federal Supreme Council consisting of seven ruling sheikhs, a president and vice president who are elected every five years by the Supreme Council, a Federal Council of Ministers composed of government ministers and a Federal National Council that serves in part as a monitoring agency of the government (Kazim, 2000, pp. 329–330), and which is now partially elected. While very young as a nation, it is old in its cultural identity as mountain, coastal and Bedouin communities that first settled at least 4,000 years ago (Heard-Bey, 2004) and was subject to European military and commercial 'penetration' of the area from 1500 to 1820 by the Portuguese, Dutch, English, French and others, followed by English colonisation from 1820 to 1971. Under British colonisation, the shaikhly system of tribal governance through competence-based leaders was transformed into a monarchy, and the treaties signed created the 'Trucial States', giving considerable powers to Britain over external and many internal affairs (Kazim, 2000). It was a form of colonial power that invested very little in the area's development, and for part of this time had a negative impact reducing the local populations to subsistence level (Al-Fahim, 1995).

There are still many political dimensions of traditional leadership that play a strong role in the political life of the country. One of these is the selection of the Crown Prince not determined by primogeniture but chosen through a consultative process from the ruling families on the basis of competence and who may be changed if warranted, carrying on the traditional 'bond of mutual obligation the tribal population and its leaders' (Heard-Bey, 2004, p. xxxi). Another is the majlis, a regular open session that affords anyone an opportunity to gain a hearing (Heard-Bey, 2004; Rugh, 2007). To a large extent, the shaikhly monarchy is a consultative competency-based political system that Western political terms are not constructed to capture, although to some extent Weber's (1949, 1968) ideal types of patrimonial and legal rational are able to accommodate. Another aspect of Weber's system of types that is evident is the charismatic character of Shaikh Zayed, the founder of the country and the president until his death in 2004, and which formed to a large extent what Weber calls 'office charisma' imbuing the formal ruling positions with charisma of their own. While the merits of some traditional practices, like *wasta* (connections or network) debatably carry positive and negative forms, there are still strong functional values, attitudes, practices and relationships that are traditional, and embedded in the social and cultural fabric. Some of these are what Ansari (1998) refers to as 'bedoucracy'(or Al-Rumaihi calls 'bedouinocracy', 1977), although his apposition of modern bureaucratic as positive and bedoucracy as inherently problematic is, in itself, problematic since it reflects a bias towards the bureaucratic as superior (despite the vast bureaupathology literature) and does not allow for a new form of governance and administration that may very well form in the UAE through its own developmental path to becoming a highly modern Arab Islamic state.

The political system in the UAE is a far cry from some Western sources that refer to it as a dictatorship or an absolute monarchy, neither of which is accurate and more likely a product of what Said (2003) describes as 'Orientalism', a projection of characteristics onto an imagined Middle East ontologically and epistemologically that involves 'making statements about it, authorizing views of it, describing it, by teaching it, settling it, ruling over it: in short, Orientalism as a Western style for dominating, restructuring, and having authority over the Orient' (pp. 2–3). He also argues that it is a reflection of a network of interests, and given the UAE's strategic location globally in economic, military and security terms (Mazawi, 2008), the attraction of 'orientalism' is probably stronger now than it was before.

Economically, the UAE has taken an enormous, perhaps historically unprecedented, leap from a subsistence traditional society into a highly modernised (or hyper-modernised), world. Most of this development has taken place in the last 20 years. Where I live, which is one of the more established residential areas, there were sand dunes 12 years ago. My university is in a collection of universities (souk-like) that was at the edge of the desert two years ago but which is rapidly, and sadly, losing dune horizons. One other economic feature that affects higher education is the distinction between public and private prevailing in the UAE. Unlike many countries, 'private' sector does not necessarily mean that there is neither heavy public investment nor that because an individual, perhaps a member of a royal family, 'owns' a university, that they do not operate for the public good and are not governed and administered in many ways as if they are public. 'Quasi-public' or 'quango' would be a more accurate term. The British University in Dubai is a public university created under Royal Decree as a not-for-profit organisation functioning to a large extent on tuition-revenue generation.

The core values in the Arabian Gulf are starkly different from American values (and other Western countries) that affect social interaction and organisational life, including higher education curriculum development and teaching (Fox, Mourtada-Sabbah, & al-Mutawa, 2006). In order of frequency Arabian Gulf core values consist of: the priority of family and its dignity and honour, including respect for elders; religion providing ultimate meaning and morality based on face-to-face interaction; transactions focused on the influence of kin and friends; hospitality, generosity and sharing; loyalty to family and friends, as well as patience and mercy; a pride of and respect for heritage and tradition; sociability; the social group more important than personal achievements; family councils to discuss issues; justice, honesty and compassion for the downtrodden and honest transactions to avoid disgracing one's family name; show of strength and courage and defence of one's family, land and rights at a moment's notice; respect for authority, patriarchy, gender segregation and deference to family/clan/tribal patriarch demands; marriage within the extended family; modesty in dress; religious education, as specified within Islam to take people from the darkness; material wealth; and in-group inclusiveness (Fox et al., 2006, p. 9). However, Simadi and Kamali (2004) have found that values of individualism are gaining ground relative to religious values for UAE university students. In contrast, American core values are secular, materialist and individualist: equal opportunity, achievement and success, material comfort, activity and work, practicality and efficiency, progress, science, democracy and free enterprise, freedom and group superiority (Fox et al., 2006, p. 10). These differences, well demonstrated in cross-cultural literature, affect decision-making, ways of interacting and working, often causing tension and conflict (Ali, Azim, & Krishnan, 1995; Branine, 2011; Mead, 1998; Trompenaars & Hampden-Turner, 2004).

Values are also an issue for the expatriate professional. Ali, Krishnan, and Azim (1997) found that the Western expatriate exhibits a lower level of organisational loyalty in the UAE, not surprising when many of them expect to work in the country only for a relatively short period of time so are less likely to make a high personal investment in changing their practices and entering a steep and demanding learning curve in acquiring knowledge of Islamic and Arab scholarship. Evidence can be seen in the lack of effort made to understand and adjust to local culture (Atiyyah, 1996) that extends into a problem of 'cultural translation' of concepts that are difficult to convey since Arabic and English are embedded in socio-cultural and political constructions (Asad, 1986).

On a socio-cultural level, the UAE consists mostly of expatriates: 85% of the population is non-national (Cevik, 2011) from over 200 countries, which in many organisations creates a highly diverse multi-cultural staff which can create its own stresses and strains. This is evident in higher education and relevant government organisations where a majority of teaching staff in the higher education organisations have been Westerners primarily from the United Kingdom, the United States, Australia and to a lesser extent Canada, with a smaller number from the region, each from systems that have striking differences. This is also the face of globalisation – the effect of import–export in the cultural sector, a problem Al-Ali (2008) describes as an isolation of Emiratis from their own economy and with strong social capital implications, although the political and cultural implications may even be stronger (see Walker & Dimmock, 2000). There are signs of these changes in the UAE as in many countries with large expatriate numbers, with the recently implemented Emiratisation policy aimed at increasing Emirati participation in employment, particularly at more senior levels (Smith, 2008). An increasing number of Emiratis are attaining graduate and professional qualifications, and are consequently moving up organisational hierarchies, a change I see on a regular basis with our doctoral students who are often promoted during the programme, sometimes more than once.

Probably the most important aspect of the socio-cultural realm that is most often misunderstood, and sometimes grievously so, is the role of women in the UAE. Emirati women have all of their rights under Islam: the right to drive, to work, to travel, to get a higher education. Over 70% of Emiratis pursuing graduate degrees are women (UAE Ministry of State; Fox, 2008). I discovered immediately that they are strong in doctoral seminars: they prepare for class, they are articulate and they debate the men, unrelentingly at times. Those I meet are dedicated, intelligent, committed to their studies and professional development and persevere often with a number of small children and a demanding job. They regularly attend international conferences and give guest lectures on academic trips and perform well. They aim their sights high. They envision for themselves performing at a high international level, the standard UAE rulers have set as a goal for the country. This is one topic that I most often have to address abroad: disposing of myths about Emirati women (itself a function of orientalism and negative stereotyping). The cloak (*abaya*), headscarf (*shayla*) and for some the veil (*niqab*), are not associated with repression in the UAE and have little to do with the diminishment of aspirations, capability and achievement. Rather, it is a source of identity, pride and an embodiment of the high goals the country has set for itself, values that are clearly coming through in research results of my female doctoral students. The practice of women having 'chaperones' when travelling does not necessarily have the connotations of power and oppression that the Western negative stereotype assumes – one has to travel with them to understand how supportive it is and how it may have nothing to do with constraining their world. These traditions have not stopped Emirati women from becoming lawyers, judges, pilots, physicians, research scientists, senior government officials, ambassadors, military officers, police officers and professors.

The UAE is a transition country, but, like many in the Arabian (not Persian) Gulf, it is unlike many countries that transition and development models are applied to that modernise with few resources or emerged from a Soviet-style past, the sources for much leadership, policy and management scholarship. The degree of change is hard to describe and very difficult to represent. It is a country unlike any other, even within the Gulf region, following its own developmental path.

Educational history in the UAE does not begin, as some assume, quite recently with the importation of modern formal systems, initially from Kuwait, Qatar and Egypt (Kazim, 2000) and later from mostly English-speaking countries. There were for millennia guild-type professions like pearl diving, boat building, raising herds, agriculture, religious instruction and defensive forces, with trading an occupation of long standing in port cities (Alsharekh & Springborg, 2008). Currently, there are 78 licensed institutions of higher education, most of which are universities, approximately 40 of which are international branch campuses (Wilkins, 2011), many foreign or formed through partnership with foreign universities (MOHESR), predominantly from the United States, the United Kingdom and Australia (Wilkins, 2010). Higher education has become a high priority in the UAE's developmental policies, the increase of investment growing to 22.5% of the 2010 budget (Ibrahim, 2011, p. 149).

One of the major problems of higher education in the UAE, as well as in the Gulf and Middle East generally, is the reliance on imported faculty and curricula predominantly in English from the United Kingdom, the United States and Australia (Donn & Al Manthri, 2010; Mazawi, 2008; Smith, 2008), often viewed as a market activity, or what Al-Sulayti (1999) has noted as an 'investment enterprise'. Shah and Baporikar (2011) reported on

the results of a survey in Oman that demonstrates a high level of dissatis-
faction among faculty and students with curricula that do not meet regional needs and reflect religion and culture as well as socio-political and
economic conditions. Two additional problems are too much emphasis on
quantitative research and on professional degrees instead of primary disciplines to sustain a university system in the country. I find it strange, quite
frankly, that when one goes to Germany, Estonia, Russia, Finland or
Norway to teach, one expects to find a curriculum amply representing their
scholarship. But in the Gulf region, it is customary for many to teach only
English-speaking material as if the Gulf is a black hole of thinking and
sources – devoid of intellectual capital. To a very large extent, higher
education here displays the cultural hegemony Said describes in discussing
assumptions of 'European superiority over Oriental backwardness'(2003,
p. 7). And here I am not inferring a necessary conscious intent – rather it
seems to be carried out in a manner that Giroux and Purpel (1983) call 'hidden curriculum', and Said refers to as 'latent' rather than 'manifest' orientalism (p. 207). The assumption, for example, that knowledge transfer goes
only one way, and that the UAE must build its higher education system on
a 'Western' foundation exhibits the view that involves seeing 'the Orient as
a locale requiring Western attention, reconstruction, even redemption'
(Said, 2003, p. 206). The scale of this problem in the Middle East has
been noted by a number of scholars in the management, leadership and
administration fields (e.g. Abdalla & Al-Homoud, 2001; Ali, 1995).

CONSTRUCTION OF THE THREE METAPHORS
AS IDEAL TYPES

The three metaphors used here, the public servant, the cultural diplomat
and the intellectual imperialist are constructed as Weberian ideal types
(1949, 1968). As such, they are analytic or 'pure' types that one can use to
analyse empirical reality, in this case, Western expatriate faculty and consultants shaping the educational system in terms of their orientations to the
country, to students and teaching and knowledge. As defined by Weber, an

> ideal type is formed by the one-sided accentuation of one or more points of view and
> by the synthesis of a great many diffuse, discrete, more or less present and occasionally
> absent concrete individual phenomena, which are arranged according to those
> one-sidedly emphasized viewpoints into a unified analytical construct (*Gedankenbild*).
> (1949, p. 90)

Such types are analytical, not normative or empirical, although constructed from empirical evidence. For Weber, ideal types are a method for handling the infinite complexity of reality, are constructed within a comparative world historical perspective and demonstrate an appreciation of historical process and its causal nature, as well as underlying value orientations leading to legitimacy and authority structures. In this case, the metaphors also represent an orientation to the public good, but in these cases, the public good is conceived of differently – for the public servant it is the public good as defined by the UAE government and its citizens, for the cultural diplomat, both the UAE and one's home country's good are taken into consideration with the latter taking a dominant role, and for the latter, only the foreign position is taken as a definition of public good. In other words, the three positions determine whose interests are being served.

Using metaphors as analogies is also a common practice in the microinteractionist sociology of Goffman (1990) and the cultural anthropology of Turner (1974) used to specify characteristics that are common to the original object of the metaphor and what it is analogous to for explanatory purpose. Related to these is Said's (2003, p. 7) humanistic critique of 'orientalism', a Western politico-cultural hegemonic construction for intellectual and colonial use that expresses itself through structures and patterns at all three levels presented in this chapter, in other words an ideology that establishes the boundaries and content of conceptual construction (see Hourani, Diallo, & Said, 2011). The metaphors are designed to reflect value orientations and attitudes to both the UAE and to Western and Arab scholarship and learning. In ideal typical form, these take three possible logical forms of value orientation, attitude and social action that, in most individuals, would be some combination of two and in some cases even three. The general characteristics of the public servant, cultural diplomat and intellectual imperialist types are described below.

A public servant is one who is oriented valuationally towards public service of the state, society and community, in this case, the UAE. In Weberian terms, the ideal traits of senior public servants, or mandarins, would fit analytically into a form that combines patrimonial traditionalism with values that are characterised by substantive rationality, that is, higher order political values, an ethos of 'official duty' and the 'public weal' or public interest, whose ethos governs their manner of living and circle of contacts, and who 'lives for the state, rather than from the state'. Their authority and role are imbued with personal qualities of resilience, independence of mind, intellectual prowess, sound judgement and discrimination, loyalty and integrity. They are characterised by 'moral courage' in

'speaking truth to power', and whose responsibilities are tied to the legitimacy of the 'ruling elite', who oversee national interests for political
authority and are protected by anonymity. They are generally a professional class whose education is generalist literary, humanities or liberal arts
rather than technocratic. Their organisational role is quasi-political and
quasi-bureaucratic that forms an informal 'collegial' system, whose rights
and duties are established under Royal Prerogative instead of statute. They
are inducted through patronage and protegéeship, and their practices are
governed by convention (see Samier, 2001). Translated into teaching and
curricular terms, they synthesise international knowledge and custom with
the Islamic intellectual heritage and traditions and Emirati values and
norms.

The cultural diplomat can be described in Weberian terms as a patrimonial traditionalism combined with instrumental legal rationality. Derived in
part from Freeman's (1997) *Arts of Power: Statecraft & Diplomacy*, the
diplomat is valuationally oriented towards the home state's strategic interests, in political, economic, security and cultural terms, and at times, all of
these can serve security interests, for example, during the Cold War when
university activities were used as a means for this purpose (e.g. Cline, 1976;
Lewis, 1996; O'Mara, 2005). At the senior level, diplomats are strategically
and tactically adept in the international arena, abiding by a power ethics
and belonging to formal and informal networks. Their ethos informs their
modus operandi consisting of manoeuverabilities through exaction, accom-
modation, appeasement, coercion, rapprochement etc. In analytical ideal
type terms, like the public servant, they live for the state rather than from
the state. Their authority and role are primarily that of a medium of
communication between states, delegated with authority to speak as a
representative of their home state in pursuing its interests (Lloyd, 2001).
Often scholars act as informal diplomats representing their country and its
intellectual traditions, and the university is often the site of formal and
informal diplomatic activities and can serve as an agent of foreign policy.
Sometimes, this is done unwittingly through the 'hidden curriculum'
(Giroux & Purpel, 1983). In educational terms, academic cultural diplomats
represent their own academic traditions, but in dialogue with, and therefore
to some extent influenced by, a foreign intellectual tradition and values.

Imperialists in Weberian terms are (disenchanted) entrepreneurial
rationalists whose drive is to economic hegemony, emphasising the formal
rationality of processes and techniques, who demonstrate an indifference to
ends (or higher order values) or results since they are taken as pre-
established. Their ideals are the 'leader', 'entrepreneur' and consultant in

Weberian terms exhibiting mercenary competitive self-interest. Their ethos is a set of imperatives that include efficiency, technical effectiveness and objectified performance, human relations and roles ('bottom-line' mentality). They 'live from the state, rather than for the state'. Their ideal personal qualities are to abide by impersonal rules, objective competence and technical business-style management, adhering to goal-oriented accountability (measured by market analysis and performance measurement) aimed at value for money and cost-effectiveness. They exhibit a high mobility between public and private spheres or, in some cases, do not distinguish between them and comprise a technical managerial elite (the 'new nomenklatura', 'technical intelligentsia' or 'consultocracy' (see Samier, 2001), grounded in managerialism. Their authority and role aims at strategies of control, operational monitoring and strategic planning and are 'doers' rather than 'thinkers', creating a conducive environment for the like-minded. In educational terms, they represent their home market, including the values, jurisdictional characteristics and culture within which their 'product' is created for export.

In culturally embodied form, the metaphors can be understood through an everyday experience with something that I call the 'abaya complex' that represents symbolically the problem of researcher bias in international comparative studies pointing to the negative stereotype of a Muslim woman in black abaya, shayla and niqab that connotes for many terrorism and a deprivation of rights and mind. Instead of closing one's world down, I found that wearing an abaya opens a door to another world. In a country where two worlds – the local and expatriate cohabited the country and generally do not socially interact. The social experience, both recognition and interaction one has, is completely different depending on what one wears. The relevance of the abaya as a metaphor for this chapter is a threefold one: a public servant's attitude regards it as clothing, the diplomatic as ceremonial dress and the imperialistic as a garment belonging to the 'other' that is rarely touched, let alone worn.

METAPHORS APPLIED TO LEVELS OF EDUCATIONAL EXPERIENCE

The levels I have chosen to apply the three metaphors to are, first the personal experiential that includes one's values, personal and professional identity, professional ethos and qualities of social interaction, how one perceives and how one constructs meaning. Embedded in this is one's growth as a human being and scholar, viewed as dialectical rather than incremental. The second, the pedagogical, consists of scholarship, curricular principles and teaching styles. It is seen as a dynamic process that evolves from a broad and international range of sources, knowledge as constructed, and is produced through conversation and debate as well as reading – the implication of which, for this chapter, is that one's doctoral students are living curriculum from whom one learns as much as teaches. The political level is viewed here as a complex construction of economic, social, cultural and political factors that collectively, but not uniformly, affect values and belief systems as well as social relations and the nature and structure of social institutions. One of the most important of these is the impact of globalisation, essentially an economic process that consists of mostly Western export of goods that encompasses culture and education as commodities to developing countries. As Maringe and Foskett (2012, p. 1) point out, it demands a 'greater homogenization of fundamental political, ideological, cultural and social aspects of life across different countries of the world', potentially compromising sovereignty, identity, religion, etc. A complementary process is that of Bourdieu and Passeron's (2000) reproduction thesis, that Westerner expatriate employees and consultants will most often reproduce the values, social action and structures that they are familiar with in a new country, including the educational institution, which is necessary to social, cultural and political continuity in a society.

The Personal Level: Existential, Phenomenological and Hermeneutic

The personal level is one that consists predominantly of existential, phenomenological and hermeneutic activity –part psychology, part social action and part ideological as a system of values and beliefs. In higher education, all of these inform one's sense of identity as personality and in social interaction and social relations, as well as professional as scholar and teacher, and, on an organisational level, as one who is managed and in turn manages others. Depending, of course, on which tradition of psychology and sociology one thinks within, these are viewed in different ways. The perspective here is a humanistic one that assumes a dynamic, shared social reality and one in which social action is informed by values (Weber, 1968) as well as personality, and in which the scholarly and teaching processes are complex, multi-faceted and influenced by culture and social structures. They also inhere in the way that social interaction shapes our organisational worlds, in the manner that Goffman (1990) contends consists of a dramaturgical presentation of self with others that is partly shaped by contextual factors in which self and identify are continuously shaped, and similar to Weber's social action theory, form the basis upon which groups and larger structures are formed.

From this perspective, teaching is personal: it engages personality, character, values, world view, one's biases and prejudices, as well as one's aspirations. Teaching is an interactive implicit and explicit social process involving establishing rapport and finding a common language to work through, in other words Habermasian 'communicative action', which establishes the 'language' of interaction and boundaries of behaviour. In teaching cross-culturally, one can meet students halfway over the gap between many Western and Arab and Islamic interaction practices, a mode of teaching that is derived from finding commonality on a deeper subjective and human level from which one as a foreigner can reconstruct an interaction style that incorporates cultural constructions of respect, manner, humour, dress, etc. – in other words allow oneself to become acculturated. It lies within the framework of creating a professional ethos and demeanour, or repertoire in Schön's (1993) terms, as a reflective practitioner. This necessarily affects one's conceptions of professional identity, teacher and student roles, and issues of power and authority, which in the UAE is, from the students' perspectives, heavily derived from Islam and culture. I would argue that this does not mean abandoning one's values and standards but in acculturating to find the expressive modes for these in the Gulf. The abaya and shayla provide one means of demonstrating respect, recognising the boundaries between male and female – which in my experience, produces a more constructive relationship with male students – and carries a political message on an individual level of acceptance rather than rejection of their deeply held values and cultural practices. In other words, it is a hermeneutic adventure.

In no way does it require the reduction of standards, expectations for quality of work, lowered dedication to studies or diminished aspirations to a high international level of scholarship. From a valuational perspective, the teacher–student relationship described above can be seen as a convenantal one.

There are a number of important features distinguishing many Western perspectives from Arab and Islamic that I meet in the UAE, two of which I would like to emphasise here. On the experiential level, Islam, unlike Christianity, does not recognise a secular and sacred separation (see Halstead, 2007). Their world view, and the legal system of shariah, is integrated and synthesised into daily life, similar in some respects to the European ontological and epistemological character of the medieval period, described by Berman (1981) in *The Reenchantment of the World*. This principle permeates all aspects of teaching and curriculum. The other is that of using English language, a colonising problem Freire (1985) analysed. However, it depends upon what English one is using and how one uses it – a reflexive and critical English provides them with the ability to analyse the impact of values embedded in English language curriculum and draws on Idealist philosophy and critical theory as well as intellectual traditions that are related to Islamic intellectualism, such as humanism and hermeneutics that can mitigate the colonising influence of foreign programmes.

To conclude this section, I would like to cast this discussion into the three metaphoric types, drawn from Said's (2003, p. 201) work in portraying typical structures representing ideological tendencies as well as Weberian ideal types.

1. The public servant's values are dominated by local culture and serve the state's strategic goals and whose identity, as a participant–observer, may consist to some extent of living liminally even though highly engaged and immersed in local social interaction. Professional qualities could be seen as international but oriented towards an ethno-hermeneutic reconstruction on a deep valuational and personality level to meet local needs and terms of engagement.
2. The cultural diplomat's values are representative of his/her own culture but mediated through a two-state understanding of strategic goals that may not coincide, and whose identity remains national but engaged with the local on a more surface level than the public servant, and using a mediated style of social interaction and presentation of self. Professional qualities will represent the 'home' ethos with respect for the 'other' but more distanced than the public servant's.
3. The Intellectual Imperialist's values are exclusively 'home' referenced, and identity is unchanged and in tension with or contradictory to local conditions and culture with a social interaction style that is aimed at socialising (colonising) locals into foreign patterns of value, role and practice.

The last is most problematic from an international perspective consisting, as Said contends of stereotyped individual characteristics of 'orientals': sensuality, despotism, aberrant mentality, inaccuracy, backwardness (2003, p. 205). The orient is also portrayed in 'Orientalism' as a 'locale requiring Western attention, reconstruction, even redemption' and as a problem to be solved (2003, pp. 206–207), including through scholarship by 'pioneers' to the Orient (p. 221).

The Pedagogical Level: Hermeneutic, Interactional, Legitimating, Reproductive

The pedagogical level is taken here to be the teaching, curricular and learning part of education, understood as growing out of the foundation presented previously so that it is in part an interactional process, particularly so at the doctoral level, and is hermeneutic in that one is constructing knowledge and meaning rather than simply conveying what one learned previously (important in expatriate adjustment to a foreign context). There are also other dimensions within a society that involve establishing what is legitimate knowledge and values and how the educational system provides continuity or what Bourdieu describes as the 'reproduction' function.

The tendency for Western expatriate policy advisers and faculties is to define the purpose of education in western terms, drawing on US, UK and Australian public policy views that have been using a predominantly neoliberal framework and on their own educational philosophy at the exclusion of a rich and long tradition of Islamic educational theory. The regional tradition, for example, encompasses Ibn Khaldun who argued for its importance in social development (Halstead, 2004; Hilgendorf, 2003; Ibrahim, 2011), as well as foundations for history that incorporate a strong sociological, anthropological and political theory (not unlike Weber's work), and Ibn Sina and al-Ghazali who contributed to educational ideas as well as work in primary disciplines (Lootah, 2011).

There is a misunderstanding that seems to be widespread that the Islamic educational heritage has only been the maligned 'madrasa' image of rote memory schools. However, this is not Islamic intellectualism or scholarship; for various historical and political reasons, the rich and varied schools of scholarship that thrived during the early Islamic period went into eclipse in many territories but in essence Islamic educational philosophy is close to many interpretive traditions in the West. The Qur'an and Sunnah both recognise and promote the full range of thinking and critical abilities, with knowledge emphasised in its many forms more than 750 times in the Qur'an alone, including the moral implications and uses of knowledge (Halstead, 2004, 2007; Lootah, 2011, p. 210). What does differentiate most 'Western' educational theory from Islamic is the secular ideology of the first and the religious nature of the latter that places the

Qur'an and Sunna at the centre (see Lootah, 2011). An important feature of Islamic education, and exhibited by almost all the Emirati EdD applicants I have interviewed, is the notion of life-long learning (Halstead, 2004) they interpret to include the responsibility to continue their education to the highest degree level.

Drawing on Goffman (1990), teaching can be viewed as a presentation of self that can be represented through three metaphoric modes. One can, as a public servant, acculturate and as a cultural diplomat one can retain most of one's cultural presentation but be respectful of the religious and cultural patterns in the UAE. As an intellectual imperialist, one can maintain a sense of self 'undisturbed' − as one person I heard describe it, 'I was born X and that is what I am, and they simply have to accept it'. One aspect of the teaching role that many from Western countries do not consider is that a teacher should be a role model − not just of learning but of values and manners. In a society predicated upon social relations and strong Islamic values, the role model is someone who should exhibit these virtues or be 'righteous' as one of my doctoral students describes it. At the doctoral level, even though students are more mature are more independent and already well socialised into their cultures; teaching initiates a transformation from students into junior colleagues. This means that one should model and assist them to shape a culturally appropriate professionalism as a teacher and scholar in their own culture enabling them to serve as role models in turn.

Teaching in a culturally sensitive manner involves much more than excluding language, behaviour and content. I discovered quite early that my students think in Islamic terms and are frequently comparing Western material taught to Islamic principles. This first came up explicitly in a manner that changed how and what I taught when I was presenting a series of slides on Kantian principles of ethics for leadership. Halfway through I asked what they were conferring with each other about in Arabic and found that they were comparing the values, principles and steps in Kantian moral reasoning with principles in the Qur'an and Hadith. I returned to the first slide and we went through, comparatively, slide by slide. Given the idealist nature of Kantian ethics, as higher order values that require a reasoning process that has strong hermeneutic character, the comparison was close, an argument for which I later discovered in Tampio (2012) that a close correspondence exists, in part due to the intellectual history of the Renaissance. This notion is found in Said who argued for a broad and all-inclusive notion of humanism that provides a means of bridging this gap, through its nature as 'a means of questioning, upsetting, and reformulating so much of what is presented to us as commodified, pack-aged, uncontroversial, and uncritically codified certainties' (2003, p. 28). It was after that class that I decided to more systematically integrate Islamic sources in my modules and use the work of Arab scholars on leadership and management. A related false assumption I ran into made by many foreign faculties in the UAE is that one should not discuss religion and politics in the classroom. I found that to be entirely untrue, and in teaching leadership and administration it is simply not possible; however, it requires not only a respectful attitude but also a commitment to learning again (see Nydell, 2006).

Integrating Islamic ethics and writings about the political system and leadership in the UAE is necessary if one takes an interactional approach to doctoral studies and has to prepare local and regional students to participate in their own societies. One can apply these principles to an understanding of curriculum as a shared exploration and construction of knowledge. As Shah and Baporikar (2011, p. 280) argue, a curriculum is not just materials it consists also of 'skills, the manner of teaching and assessment, the philosophical outlook of the teacher and who the learners are. Curriculum is the planned process, the actual implementation of the teaching, and the students' "experiences" of the learning process'. One implication of this is that knowledge will become a complex and dynamic construction of 'Western' traditions with Islamic principles, concepts and traditions of knowledge. Another is that sensitive issues like not wanting to be photographed or reduced access across genders and to homes have to be accepted in research (Thomas, 2008) and learning to draw on 'insider' culture that is not one's own.

One of the most problematic pedagogical issues in the UAE under globalisation is the lack of knowledge by many Westerners about the Islamic intellectual tradition and its relationship to 'Western', at least European scholarship. This is a topic that has received considerable atten-tion in the academic and trade press in the last few years (e.g. Al-Khalili, 2010; Freely, 2009; Lyons, 2009; Mahdi, 2006; Masood, 2009; Morgan, 2007). Through its transmission to the West during the Renaissance and subsequently, Islamic scholarship provides a strong foundation based on a common classical Greek heritage, and influence over many humanities and social science traditions, for creating a synthesised and inclusive curricu-lum. While scholarship and knowledge management one would assume, through an academic ethos, to be disinterested in the origins of knowledge, the politics of curriculum do not function this way under the globalised importation of much education into the Gulf region.

One question that needs to be explored in examining the globalisation and internationalisation of education is, how well does Western (or any) teaching and scholarship travel? Among those in comparative educational leadership who have examined these topics are Walker and Dimmock (2000) who raise questions about the relevance of some material that is imported as well as assumptions that are made in English-speaking countries about the nature of knowledge and curriculum, the teacher—student relationship and the learning process in terms of socio-political and cultural contexts in other parts of the world. They also point to one area of deficit in the field — 'an alarming ethnocentricity' in 'the most recent journals in educational administration, management and leadership' (p. 227). Another point of consideration is that policies and practices transferred from the West across national boundaries and cultures do not take into account sufficiently local culture.

Critiques that are relevant to these pedagogical issues, but for which there is no room here for detailed discussion are the colonisation critique of Freire (e.g. 1985), Galtung (1981) and Donn and Al Manthri (2010) through language that carries ontological, epistemological and valuational content that produces a linguistic power that can be translated into resource and structural power, means by which colonisation is effected. These complement critiques of the 'hidden curriculum' and ways in which communicative action are disrupted and excluded. It is similar underlying ontological, political and epistemological concepts that are fundamentally hegemonic in nature, according to Said (2003, p. 202) that have defined 'oriental' and then are embedded in the historical development of disciplines carried down to the present day. On this point, Said (2003, p. 203) quoted Nietzsche (1954) on the depth of embeddedness of the doctrine of the Orient:

> A mobile army of metaphors, metonyms and anthropomorphisms — in short, a sum of human relations, which have been enhanced, transposed and embellished poetically and rhetorically, and which after long use seem firm, canonical and obligatory to a people: truths are illusions about which one has forgotten that this is what they are. (pp. 46—47)

This section concludes with a characterisation in pedagogical terms of the three metaphors that derive from the above:

1. The public service approach includes an inclusive synthesised scholarship formed dialectically through mutually informing intellectual history from the Islamic and many Western traditions, assuming that

knowledge transfer moves in both directions. Their teaching style is a recombinant one that incorporates local interaction styles, values, forms of sociability and structured around calls for prayer, observation of Ramadan and Islamic and national holidays and aimed at contributions to nation building and national goals.

2. The cultural diplomat, as a representative of home interests, including foreign policy, engages in an unequal dialogue that may still aim at a 'westernisation' of curriculum and students that promotes knowledge transfer predominantly from the home country. This may be practised through a toleration of local ethos but serves globalised and international goals that most often privilege the West.

3. The intellectual imperialist exclusively uses Western scholarship and regards knowledge transfer as uni-directional. In an educational setting, this means that a foreign curriculum is not only used exclusively but also is expected of others, if not imposed on others, to create a dependency that serves the market model of globalisation.

One potential consequence of intellectual imperialism is a 'golemisation' of UAE history that erases the detrimental effects of previous colonisation and recasts it into economic and development terms that both legitimise and promote a world view that is highly secular, material and individualist to the benefit of those 'doing business' in the Gulf.

The Political Level: Entente, Rapprochement or Global Monopolism?

And, finally, what is the potential impact and unintended consequences for the indigenous culture, sovereignty and societal survival of a country like the UAE allowing for such a heavy influence through imported programmes and staff? And, is there a way that a foreigner teaching leadership and administration doctoral programmes cannot contribute to a colonising process and may even mitigate the effects? At its essence, this level is that of power – involving countries have installed themselves strategically in the UAE, whose knowledge will be used and thereby what values are promoted, who determines what is taught and how and whose language and conceptual framework will be used. The basic issue is cultural or intellectual imperialism and colonisation that can have a detrimental effect on a nation going through such a rapid and fundamental nation-building process. Al Farra (2011, p. 219) asks a pertinent question: 'what kind of educational model should be adopted to ensure the continuation of being

"United" and "Arab" while aiming to develop the well-rounded person who will help create a better, more peaceful and just world through inter-cultural understanding and empathy?'

The greatest external impact on the country, one could argue, is the neoliberally driven globalisation that rarely considers indigenous factors of 'markets', including an educational one. As Kazem (1992, p. 117) has pointed out, where Western education for Westerners can 'deepen loyalty and a sense of belongingness', for the non-Westerner this form can be 'dysfunctional' – creating 'cultural pockets of individuals alienated from their people and cut off from their roots'. This is a part of the world where the role of universities and their professors are more commonly called up on as leaders for ministerial and other posts, often playing a major role in the development process. Since this requires, as Kazem notes, stimulating and guiding social movement, the sense of social responsibility has to be strong. I would more explicitly argue that expatriate universities and professors should consider whose interests they are serving in the process – are they consciously or unconsciously trying to transform Arab students into Westerners and aid the globalisation agenda or are they there to serve the indigenous population and its culture and government? Put in blunter terms – where do their loyalties lie?

These are concerns that are shared among many nationals in Gulf countries, including the UAE, where 'unwanted influences on their political systems, societies and cultures' is a concern and seen by some to be a 'destabilizing force' (Atiyyah, 1996, p. 38), although recent nationalisation, labour policies and educational support are intended to reduce the depen-dence on foreign labour. As H. H. Sheikh Mohammad bin Zayed Al Nahyan, Crown Prince of Abu Dhabi and Deputy Supreme Commander of the UAE Armed Forces, and one must add, carrying a heavy portfolio of broader public sector responsibilities, 'the UAE ... pins great hope on citizens who are armed with knowledge and science in building the nation ... [requiring] an excellent, comprehensive and integrated educa-tional environment that will contribute to the preparation of Emirati students who are the real wealth of the nation' (in Al Farra, 2011, p. 223). At stake, I would argue that the development of a very young country that is still in sensitive phases of institution building in a highly politicised part of the world due not only to the 'Arab spring'-related politics surrounding it but also because it is seen as a strategically important country to many Western powers. All of these factors make the development of education a highly political issue on many levels, many of which are identified by Al Farra (2011), some of which are important here: a high drop-out rate of

Emirati boys, a very low participation rate of Emirati men in higher education, relative to Emirati women and an emphasis on education as an end
product that tends to exclude intrinsic values of higher education.

There are a number of questions here that involve the use of more than
one theoretical framework. First is Weber's work that is relevant in terms
of his 'Central Question', that is the fate of liberalism in the modern world,
that works on four levels: the individual's valuational orientation, freedom
of the individual within a framework of responsibility (Weber's ethical
position), basic human rights and self-determination for nations (see
Hennis, 1983). Second is Habermas's – does the educational institution
and those it is connected to provide for communicative action, for the
meaningful dialogue that respects different traditions, values, communicative styles and knowledge and recognises a colonisation of the life-world of
Emirati society? And third, from a Saidian perspective, how strong is the
relationship between 'colonial knowledge' and the 'exercise of imperial
power' combined with the role of the intellectual in 'speaking truth to
power' (see Rizvi & Lingard, 2006). I would like to add a corollary to this
theoretical position: the Enlightenment project does not have to be dead –
there are 'grand narratives' that have been, in Said's terms, in 'abeyance,
deferred or circumscribed' (2003, p. 351) that could provide a critical foundation from which to examine globalised education as a market commodity
serving foreign political economy interests. And some of these radical
humanistic positions are not necessarily greatly at odds with the Islamic
humanist tradition.

A country that has such a large proportion of its workforce composed
of expatriates runs the risk of cultural security in many respects. First, there
is the problem of English as a foreign language playing such a large role in
all societal sectors outside of the family and religion, and to some extent
politics. Findlow (2006) examines a number of issues associated with
English as the major medium of higher education. Drawing principally on
Bourdieu, English as a foreign language can affect symbolic interaction, the
construction of 'communicable meaning', the adoption of a language that
'embod[ies] alien mindsets and mentalities', given its role as a carrier of
values and the colonial language becoming one of higher status (p. 20),
constituting what Bourdieu (1992) regards as a form of symbolic violence.
Since the impact on conceptualisation, communication and culture can be
so radically altered through the colonial and post-colonial-globalisation-
colonial language of English, identity itself is at risk, implicating also conceptions of authority and leadership. While Arabic may not succumb to
'language death' (Brenzinger, 1992), given the large population of Arabic

speakers in the region, in certain sectors, English replaces not only the language but also central concepts of education and authority, as well as personal development. For example, the reasons one could give for pursuing higher education in English and Arabic, where the former could be 'reaching the top' has connotations of economic and entrepreneurial terms, where in the latter the same type of answer connotes service to family and country, and acquiring knowledge, skills and a suitable position are understood within these contexts (Findlow, 2006, pp. 27–28).

Some of these ideas, as Rizvi and Lingard (2006, p. 297) point out, are also found in Foucault's (1980) view of knowledge as power, particularly in Said's use of this view to regard the West's representation of the Orient as a Western 'will to power' expressed through a linking of 'material realities of political and economic domination'. They also find support in Bourdieu's (1969) discussion of the 'intellectual field' in terms of intellectualism as symbolic power, a network of ideas that includes the concepts of cultural capital, intellectuals as creators of symbolic power and contributing to the reproduction of self-perpetuating hierarchies of domination, the shaping of politics through symbolic power and the web of symbolic interests, power and capital in political economy terms that lead to power structures (habitus), occurring on micro to macro levels producing fields of production, circulation and consumption. In Rizvi and Lingard's (2006, p. 296) reading of Said's orientalism, one finds the nub of the problem for a globalised higher education, that is, 'imperial expansion'. Firstly, it carries assumptions (even unconscious ones) of orientals, in this case Arabs, as 'separate, eccentric, backward, silently different, sensual and passive'. Secondly, they are seen as 'a fixed and unchanging Other, lacking subjectivity and variation'. Thirdly, their 'capabilities and values are judged in terms of, and in comparison to, the West', rather than in terms of their own society (collectively as political and economic system, social and cultural traditions and religious concepts and values). And finally, 'they are the conquerable, the inferior or those in need of Western guidance and patronage'.

There are distinctive values and practices characterising leadership that a doctoral programme in this region must incorporate that are described by a number of authors, including Branine (2011, pp. 453–460), many of which are religious and cultural, although in significant transition due to modernisation and the impact of globalisation. These include a number of norms and values, such as direct, face-to-face communication, respect for age and seniority, drawing on personal connections and kinship relationships to get things done. Included also are wasta (connections), saving face (avoiding direct conflict and confrontation), a number of Islamic values involving vice-regency (to be a trustee of Allah on earth) by upholding principles of courtesy, fairness and work that benefits the individual and community. This Islamic 'work ethic' is understood to be an act of worship — in Islam one does not recognise a distinction between the sacred and profane or the sacred and the secular. These are supported by many other values like truthfulness, kindness and care, justice, trust, patience and keeping one's promises. One of the most important practices in this tradition, and a strong element of rulership, is consultation.

Translating this into the three metaphoric terms, modulated through diplomatic positions, produces distinctive goals and purposes to doctoral education for the UAE:

1. Public servant/entente in which coalitions and alliances are formed between equals that are mutually enriching, and which celebrate traditions. It is able to form a distinctive Emirati scholarship and education to service the intellectual, cultural, religious, social, political and economic traditions of the nation, and which reproduce Emirati classes and status groups authentically but in modern form, and located within the international community of scholarly traditions.
2. The cultural diplomat/rapprochement in which education takes a beneficial mutual evolution, however, society remains a multi-cultural one that retains many of its 'solitudes' and to some extent will, on a conceptual and cultural level, be segregated into 'western' versus Islamic. This approach is aimed at serving globalised and foreign interests, however modulated to accommodate the local.
3. The intellectual imperialist/global monopolist that exacts an educational market by commodifying education, and producing cultural and intellectual colonies that in the case of developing countries, can exert a strong influence in reproducing foreign structures, governance, responsibilities, roles, practices and values, producing possibly, what Banerjee (2008) calls 'necrocapitalism' — a dispossession modified to accommodate 'social' or 'cultural' death.

CONCLUSION

The processes we now see as globalisation, and the colonisation that occurs from it, were already well established by the 1980s. Ramirez and Boli (1987), for example, saw the development of an educational ideology premised on a progressive capitalist basis that harnesses nation states to a 'global social system' in their development that necessarily transports values, constructs of the individual and the institutions of implementation, what Yang (2003) calls the 'new coloniser' in the case of globalised education. The problem here, of course, is that these are not culturally neutral structures, but transform and even colonise the developing world. In other words, it was well established by the time the UAE's greatest growth and institutional development was underway. Lawn and Lingard (2002) described this 'working space' for global educational elites as 'magistracy' – a 'bureaucratic interpenetration' of a habitus. Donn and Manthri describe it in the Gulf states as 'magistry' – that are key players who are 'magistry of influence'. Can their globalised and market-based approach to education (as commodity) really serve the strategic goals of the UAE on levels other than employment and the economic sector? Is it a picture of higher education, as Donn and Manthri regard it, as 'a baroque arsenal, a valuable economic and political cargo for the sellers/exporters but of little educational value to purchasers/importers' (2010, p. 15).

The UAE's success is a convergence of political will, resources, consensus and trust. It is also the convergence of socio-cultural and religious values and maintaining strong traditional social structures while modernising. However, there are two most probable paths that this dynamic can take: either modernisation and its global pressures will overwhelm and undermine the society that has brought it this far or the nation has an historic opportunity to show that there is not just one, Western, form of modernisation – that an Arab and Islamic form is possible. It saddens me to hear, occasionally, remarks from Western expatriates that 'They are learning ... and they will change' to indicate that somehow they will become more like 'us' and give up their quaint customs and values. I find this an interesting inversion, as a Weberian scholar, of Weber's famous (if not infamous) 'iron cage of modernity' – that modernised societies become bled of all values but the legal rational, creating the 'dead soul' of bureaucracy, with no passion, no tradition and no higher order values.

The UAE needs a sustainable higher education system in terms of cultural security for the continuation of the culture and state but not sustainability in terms that Western countries and many of their human resource exports understand. Doctoral programmes are a critical factor in creating a sustainable educational institution – it is through such programmes that credentialing is done, that legitimacy is created, and that full participation in international scholarship is achieved, as well as providing continuity. But they have to also be authentically Emirati from a valuational perspective. The route to creating a doctoral programme is one that bridges religious and cultural differences while challenging notions of 'otherness' and 'clashes of civilisations' (à la Huntington, 1997). The title of Fox et al.'s (2006) chapter is instructive: 'The Arab Gulf region: Traditionalism globalized or globalization traditionalized?' Given the richness of Emirati culture and of many of the Arab cultures in the region, of its many virtues, its toleration, hospitality and warmth, I would hope that it is the latter that emerges in the tensions between imported globalised knowledge and culture rather than the former.

ACKNOWLEDGEMENTS

Writing about and understanding a foreign culture can only be done with sufficient acculturation, experience and interaction that allow one to enter its world. I was most fortunate in the Emirati doctoral students I first worked with after my arrival in the UAE – their acceptance, warmth, support and generosity, values deeply embedded in Emirati culture, enabled me to make that journey smoothly and with good humour. My deepest indebtedness to those who shepherded my transition and welcomed me into their lives: Faisal Albakeri, Kaltham Kenaid, Rabaa Alsumaiti, Tarifa Al Zaabi, Hamad Al Rashdi and also Nadera Alborno. There are no words sufficient to thank them for their gift to me. Any errors and misunderstandings in the chapter are wholly mine.

REFERENCES

Abdalla, L., & Al-Homoud, M. (2001). Exploring the implicit leadership theory in the Arabian Gulf states. *Applied Psychology, 50*, 506–531.

Al-Ali, J. (2008). Emiratisation: Drawing UAE nationals into their surging economy. *International Journal of Sociology and Social Policy, 28*(9/10), 365–379.

Al-Fahim, M. (1995). *From rags to riches: A story of Abu Dhabi.* New York, NY: I. B. Tauris.

Al Farra, S. (2011). Education in the UAE: A vision for the future. In Emirates Center for Strategic Studies and Research (Ed.), *Education in the UAE: Current status and future developments* (pp. 219–237). Abu Dhabi: ECSSR.

Al-Khalili, J. (2010). *Pathfinders: The golden age of Arabic science.* London: Penguin.

Al-Rumaihi, M. (1977). *Obstacles to social and economic development in contemporary Gulf societies.* Kuwait: University of Kuwait.

Al-Sulayti, H. (1999). Education and training in GCC countries: Some issues of concern. In Emirates Center for Strategic Studies and Research (Ed.), *Education and the Arab world: Challenges of the next millennium* (pp. 271–278). Abu Dhabi: ECSSR.

Ali, A. (1995). Cultural discontinuity and Arab management thought. *International Studies of Management and Organization, 25*(3), 7–30.

Ali, A., Azim, A., & Krishnan, K.(1995). Expatriates and host country nationals: Managerial values and decision styles. *Leadership & Organization Development Journal, 16*(6), 27–34.

Ali, A., Krishnan, K., & Azim, A. (1997). Expatriate and indigenous managers' work loyalty and attitude toward risk. *Journal of Psychology, 13*(3), 260–270.

Alsharekh, A., & Springborg, R. (2008). *Popular culture and political identity in the Arab Gulf states.* London: Saqi Press.

Ansari, S. J. (1998). *Political modernization in the Gulf.* New Delhi: Northern Book Centre.

Asad, T. (1986). The concept of cultural translation in British social anthropology. In J. Clifford & G. Marcus (Eds.), *Writing culture: The poetics and politics of ethnography* (pp. 141–164). Berkeley, CA: University of California Press.

Atiyyah, H. (1996). Expatriate acculturation in Arab Gulf countries. *Journal of Management Development, 15*(5), 37–47.

Banerjee, S. (2008). Necrocapitalism. *Organization Studies, 29*(12), 1541–1563.

Berman, M. (1981). *The reenchantment of the world.* Ithaca, NY: Cornell University Press.

Bourdieu, P. (1969). Intellectual field and creative project. *Social Science Information, 8*(2), 89–119.

Bourdieu, P. (1992). *Language and symbolic power.* Cambridge: Polity Press.

Bourdieu, P., & Passeron, J.-C. (2000). *Reproduction in education, society and culture.* London: Sage.

Branine, M. (2011). *Managing across cultures: Concepts, policies and practices.* Los Angeles, CA: Sage.

Brenzinger, M. (Ed.). (1992). *Language death: Factual and theoretical explorations with special reference to East Africa.* Berlin: Mouton de Gruyter.

Cevik. (2011). *Policy coordination in fiscal federalism.* International Monetary Fund Working Paper. Retrieved from http://ideas.repec.org/s/imf/imfwpa.html

Cline, R. (1976). *Secrets, spies, and scholars.* Washington, DC: Acropolis Books.

Dimmock, C., & Walker, A. (2000). Developing comparative and international educational leadership and management: A cross-cultural model. *School Leadership & Management, 20*(2), 143–160.

Donn, G., & Al Manthri, Y. (2010). *Globalisation and higher education in the Arab Gulf states.* Oxford: Symposium Books.

Findlow, S. (2006). Higher education and linguistic dualism in the Arab Gulf. *British Journal of Sociology of Education, 27*(1), 19–36.

Foucault, M. (1980). *Power/knowledge: Selected interviews and other writings.* New York, NY: Pantheon.

Fox, J., Mourtada-Sabbah, N., & al-Mutawa, M. (2006). The Arab Gulf region: Traditionalism globalized or globalization traditionalized? In J. Fox, N. Mourtada-Sabbah & M. al-Mutawa (Eds.), *Globalization and the Gulf* (pp. 3–59). Abingdon: Routledge.

Fox, W. (2008). The United Arab Emirates and policy priorities for higher education. In C. Davidson & P. M. Smith (Eds.), *Higher education in the Gulf States: Shaping economies, politics and culture* (pp. 110–125). London: SAQI Press.

Freely, J. (2009). *Aladdin's lamp: How Greek science came to Europe through the Islamic world.* New York, NY: Vintage.

Freeman, C. (1997). *Arts of power and diplomacy: Statecraft and diplomacy.* Washington, DC: United States Institute of Peace.

Freire, P. (1985). *The politics of education: Culture, power and liberation.* Westport, CN: Berin & Garvey.

Galtung, J. (1981). Structure, culture and intellectual style: A essay comparing saxonic, teutonic, gallic, and nipponic approaches. *Social Science Information, 20*(6), 817–856.

Giroux, H., & Purpel, D. (1983). *The hidden curriculum and moral education.* Berkeley, CA: McCutchan.

Goffman, E. (1990). *The presentation of self in everyday life.* London: Penguin.

Halstead, M. (2004). An Islamic concept of education. *Comparative Education, 40*(4), 517–529.

Halstead, M. (2007). Islamic values: A distinctive framework for moral education? *Journal of Moral Education, 36*(3), 283–296.

Heard-Bey, F. (2004). *From trucial states to United Arab Emirates.* Dubai, UAE: Motivate Publishing.

Hennis, W. (1983). Max Weber's 'central question'. *Economy and Society, 12*(2), 135–180.

Hilgendorf, E. (2003). Islamic education: History and tendency. *Peabody Journal of Education, 78*(2), 63–75.

Hourani, R., Diallo, I., & Said, A. (2011). Teaching in the Arabian Gulf: Arguments for the deconstruction of the current educational model. In C. Gitsaki (Ed.), *Teaching and learning in the Arab world* (pp. 335–355). Bern: Peter Lang.

Huntington, S. (1997). *The clash of civilizations and the remaking of world order.* New York, NY: Touchstone.

Ibrahim, N. (2011). The UAE and higher education in the 21st century. In *Education in the UAE: Current status and future developments* (pp. 147–158). Abu Dhabi: ECSSR.

Kazem, M. (1992). Higher education and development in the Arab states. *International Journal of Educational Development, 12*(2), 113–122.

Kazim, A. (2000). *The United Arab Emirates A. D. 600 to the present: A socio-discursive transformation in the Arabian Gulf.* Dubai: Gulf Book Centre.

Lawn, M., & Lingard, B. (2002). Constructing a European policy space in educational governance: The role of transnational policy actors. *European Educational Research Journal, 1*(2), 290–307.

Lewis, L. (1996). *Cold war on campus.* New Brunswick, NJ: Transaction.

Lloyd, L. (2001). 'Us and Them': The changing nature of commonwealth diplomacy, 1880–1973. *Commonwealth & Comparative Politics, 39*(3), 9–30.

Lootah, H. A. (2011). Transdisciplinarity or integralism in the sciences. In Emirates Center for Strategic Studies and Research (Ed.), *Education in the UAE: Current status and future developments* (pp. 209–217). Abu Dhabi: ECSSR.

Lyons, J. (2009). *The house of wisdom: How the Arabs transformed western civilization.* London: Bloomsbury.

Mahdi, M. (2006). *Ibn Khaldûn's philosophy of history: A study in the philosophic foundation of the science of culture.* Kuala Lumpur: The Other Press.

Maringe, F., & Foskett, N. (2012). Introduction: Globalization and universities. In F. Maringe & N. Foskett (Eds.), *Globalization and internationalization in higher education: Theoretical, strategic and management perspectives* (pp. 1–13). London: Continuum.

Masood, E. (2009). *Science & Islam: A history.* London: Icon Books.

Mazawi, A. (2008). Policy politics of higher education in the Gulf cooperation council member states: Intersections of globality, regionalism and locality. In C. Davidson & P. M. Smith (Eds.), Higher education in the Gulf states: Shaping economies, politics and culture (pp. 59–72). London: SAQI Press.

Mead, R. (1998). International management: Cross-cultural dimensions. Oxford: Blackwell.

Ministry of Higher Education and Scientific Research (MOHESR) Commission for Academic Accreditation. Retrieved from http://www.caa.ae/caa/DesktopModules/Institutions.aspx

Morgan, M. H. (2007). Lost history: The enduring legacy of Muslim scientists, thinkers, and artists. Washington, DC: National Geographic Society.

Nietzsche, F. (1954). On truth and lie in an extra-moral sense. In W. Kaufman (Ed. & Trans.), The Portable Nietzsche. New York, NY: Viking Press.

Nydell, M. (2006). Understanding Arabs: A guide for modern times. Boston, MA: Intercultural Press.

O'Mara, M. (2005). Cities of knowledge: Cold war science and the search for the next silicon valley. Princeton, NJ: Princeton University Press.

Ramirez, F., & Boli, J. (1987). Global patterns of educational institutionalization. In G. M. Thomas, J. Meyer, F. Ramirez, & J. Boli (Eds.), Institutional structure constituting state, society, and the individual (pp. 150–172). Newbury Park, CA: Sage.

Rizvi, F., & Lingard, B. (2006). Edward Said and the cultural politics of education. Discourse, 27(3), 293–308.

Rugh, A. (2007). The political culture of leadership in the United Arab Emirates. New York, NY: Palgrave Macmillan.

Said, E. (2003). Orientalism. London: Penguin.

Samier, E. A. (2001). Demandarinisation in the new public management: Examining changing administrative authority from a Weberian perspective. In E. Hanke & W. J. Mommsen (Eds.), Max Webers herrschaftssoziologie: Studien zu entstehung und wirkung (pp. 235–263). Tübingen: Mohr Siebeck.

Samier, E. A. (2009). Towards a model for international comparative educational administration: A critical, contextualised, and interpretive approach. Journal of Humanities and Social Sciences, 3(3), 35–64.

Schön, D. (1993). The reflective practitioner: How professionals think in action. New York, NY: Basic Books.

Shah, I. A., & Baporikar, N. (2011). The suitability of imported curricula for learning in the Gulf states: An Oman perspective. In C. Gitsaki (Ed.), Teaching and learning in the Arab world (pp. 275–292). Bern: Peter Lang.

Simadi, F., & Kamali, M. (2004). Assessing the values structure among United Arab Emirates university students. Social Behavior and Personality, 32(1), 19–30.

Smith, P. M. (2008). Introduction. In C. Davidson & P. M. Smith (Eds.), Higher education in the Gulf states: Shaping economies, politics and culture (pp. 9–22). London: SAQI Press.

Tampio, N. (2012). Kantian courage: Advancing the enlightenment in contemporary political theory. Bronx, NY: Fordham University Press.

Thomas, A. (2008). Focus groups in qualitative research: Culturally sensitive methodology for the Arabian Gulf? International Journal of Research and Method in Education, 31(1), 77–88.

Trompenaars, F., & Hampden-Turner, C. (2004). *Managing people across cultures.* Chichester: Capstone Publishing.

Turner, V. (1974). *Dramas, fields and metaphors: Symbolic action in human society.* Ithaca, NY: Cornell University Press.

Walker, A. & Dimmock, C. (2000). Mapping the way ahead: Leading educational leadership into the globalised world. *School Leadership & Management, 20*(2), 227–233.

Weber, M. (1949). *The methodology of the social sciences.* Glencoe, IL: The Free Press.

Weber, M. (1968). In G. Roth & C. Wittich (Eds.), *Economy and society: An outline of interpretive sociology.* Berkeley, CA: University of California Press.

Wilkins, S. (2010). Higher education in the United Arab Emirates: An analysis of the outcomes of significant increases in supply and competition. *Journal of Higher Education Policy and Management, 32*(4), 389–400.

Wilkins, S. (2011). Who benefits from foreign universities in the Arab Gulf states? *Australian Universities Review, 53*(1), 73–83.

Yang, R. (2003). Globalisation and higher education development: A critical analysis. *International Review of Education, 49*(3/4), 269–291.

CAN WE IMPACT LEADERSHIP PRACTICE THROUGH TEACHING DEMOCRACY AND SOCIAL JUSTICE? ☆

Carolyn M. Shields

ABSTRACT

Purpose — *The purpose of this chapter is to determine whether graduate classes in deep democracy and social justice can actually effect change in educators' leadership practice.*

Methodology/approach — *This chapter draws on a survey of all doctoral students in educational leadership from a major research university who were concurrently school principals. From those willing to engage in follow-up, surveys were conducted of their teachers, and follow-up interviews and observations were conducted with the principals themselves.*

☆ An earlier version of this chapter, comprising only the data from the 13 cohort members was published as Shields, C. M. (2012). Can we teach deep democracy: And can it make a difference? In P. R. Carr, D. Zyngier, & M. Pruyn (Eds.), *Can education make a difference? Experimenting with, and experiencing democracy in, education.* Charlotte, NC: Information Age Publishing.

Investing in our Education: Leading, Learning, Researching and the Doctorate
International Perspectives on Higher Education Research, Volume 13, 125–147
Copyright © 2014 by Emerald Group Publishing Limited
ISSN: 1479-3628/doi:10.1108/S1479-362820140000013006

Findings — *We identified six main themes; courses related to deep democracy and social justice brought about deeper understanding of the topics, helped leaders acquire language and "new paradigms," sometimes caused confusion and a sense of being overwhelmed by the challenges, assisted leaders to engage staff in dialogue, and prompted action related to social justice. Leaders also sometimes experienced a sense of being alone as they engaged in a difficult struggle.*

Practical implications — *The findings highlighted the need for instructors to walk "alongside" their students as they tried to change their practices, to become critical friends and to offer on-site support.*

Research implications — *Findings also highlight the importance of teaching both theory and practical applications together. Further research about the pedagogies that make this possible is needed.*

Social implications — *If graduate coursework can impact leaders' practice, it can effect changes in schools so they become more welcoming and inclusive of all students so that those who come from minoritized or disadvantaged backgrounds may experience greater school success.*

Originality/value of chapter — *Demonstrating a link between graduate coursework and the ability of school leaders to emphasize social justice, equity and deep democracy in their practice is not only original but extremely important.*

Keywords: Leadership preparation; social justice; praxis; changing practice

There is a general lament that education and educational leadership in particular are in crisis. In the United States, acerbic critiques from scholars such as Levine (2005) have been influential in persuading policymakers and the general public alike that higher education has not, and more particularly cannot, play a major role in transforming schools. Scholars like Giroux (1995) have agreed with the notion of crisis, while Macedo (1995) went further, arguing almost two decades ago, that the crisis "is not an isolated crisis ... [but] a crisis that is implicated in and produced by a transformation in the very nature of democracy itself" (p. 295). Later, he described it as a "crisis of citizenship and ethics" (p. 297). Macedo (1995) argued that the crisis is exacerbated by a "myth that schools are very much kept independent of society and dislodged from the political reality that shapes them historically." At the same time, Berliner and Biddle (1995) were positing that the crisis was manufactured and indeed, isolated, with many schools continuing to perform well, while others continued to be abysmal. For Berliner and Biddle, and many others, the crisis was one of equity and not a generalized failure to perform.

A decade later, in his 2005 study, *Educating School Leaders*, Levine argued that school leaders "are being called on to lead in the redesign of their schools and school systems" (p. 12) but that few "are prepared to carry out" the agenda he described. His list included "rethinking of goals, priorities, finances, staffing, curriculum, pedagogies, learning resources, assessment methods, technology" and many more items, but interestingly did not address either social justice or equity as being the province of school leaders. Moreover, although his nine-point framework for assessing the quality of school-leadership preparation programs included the program's purpose, curricular coherence, and admissions criteria, among others, nowhere were these issues of equity addressed.

As Ravitch (2010) has recently acknowledged, the press for accountability and the punitive aspects of failing to achieve specified standards (in the United States to make "adequate yearly progress") have narrowed the focus of education and made its implicit purpose to prepare all students to pass whatever tests have been mandated as the standard. Additionally, the increasing competition from private and charter schools and home schooling seems to have diluted the public purpose of education and emphasized individual choice to the detriment of the collective good. These mandates have taken on such significance that many educational leaders have lost sight of the wider purposes of democratic education – including preparing students to participate fully and critically in civil society (Shields, 2008). They have also supplanted Starratt's (1991) notion of an ethical school as one that incorporates the ethics of care, critique, and justice with what might be called (somewhat tongue-in-cheek) an "ethic of accountability."

In attempts to address increased demands for accountability and improvement, the current policy climate is replete with a reform agenda intended to promote individual student learning by focusing on remedial instruction, by teaching test-taking skills, by attending to issues of school safety and bullying, or by restructuring the governance of "failing schools." Alternative education providers have multiplied, but the achievement gap between middle and upper-class majority children and their less advantaged peers continues with little signs of narrowing.

Oakes and Rogers (2006) contend that the continued lack of equity in the outcomes of schooling should not come as a surprise. In fact, they argue that, "Merely documenting inequality will not, in and of itself, lead to more adequate and equitable schooling" (2006, p. 13). They further suggest that it is important to attend to the type of reform being instituted, because "technical changes by themselves, even in the hands of committed and skilled professional 'change agents' or backed by court orders, are too weak to interrupt the intergenerational transmission of racial inequality" (pp. 21–22). In short, their argument is that if one is seeking equity, then one must choose a reform specifically designed to accomplish that end.

> Quite simply, educational equity is entangled with cultural and political dynamics that extend beyond the school; therefore, equity reforms must engage issues of power by extending beyond the school. (p. 31)

The underlying assumption of this chapter is that the aforementioned "crisis" of democracy has not abated, but indeed has been exacerbated by recent policy emphases, and that it is critically important to understand whether graduate programs in educational leadership have the potential to prepare school leaders to address these important 21st century issues. Moreover, the foregoing suggests that despite growing social disparities in almost every country, unless these graduate programs explicitly address issues of deep democracy, social justice, transformative leadership, and power, equity reforms are likely to remain far from the educational agenda.

PURPOSE

Thus, the purpose of this chapter is to describe a study in which I explored the potential of graduate work to transform the understandings and practices of school leaders. Specifically, I wanted to explore whether doctoral work could actually promote more democratic and ethical approaches to educational leadership and ultimately help leaders to achieve equity reform and a social justice education. The goals of this investigation were to consider whether (and if so how) the democratic purposes of public education may be advanced through graduate preparation of school leaders, and to consider the implications of these data for leadership preparation programs.

METHODOLOGY AND PARTICIPANTS

The data for this chapter come from two major sources. The first was a cohort of 13 doctoral students enrolled in a course named "Democracy and

Politics." The second was a larger group consisting of all school principals ($N = 25$) who were enrolled in a doctoral program in educational leadership studies in a given year at a major American research university. Prior to beginning the course, the first group was asked to voluntarily complete a survey about their understanding and practice of democratic principles. Then, as they progressed through the course, the students were asked to write weekly, reflective journals to demonstrate their understanding and critique of course content, as well as to describe any application of the ideas to their settings and the challenges the application might have presented.

The larger group was also asked to complete an anonymous survey consisting of questions about their leadership priorities and practices and the impact of their doctoral studies on their work. Subsequently, eight principals were chosen for a follow-up phase in which they were interviewed, a total of 210 teachers from their eight schools were surveyed, and a site visit was conducted at their school. Each of these data-collection strategies was intended to verify the self-responses to the surveys and to confirm the presence (or absence) of certain practices.

All the students in these EdD programs were practicing professionals (most were school principals, but three in the first cohort were district human resource directors or curriculum directors); each was already working in a position of leadership and responsibility. All forms of data reported in this chapter were collected after receiving Institutional Review Board approval; all surveys were anonymous; however, once permission for the interview was given, the identity of the participants and sites was known to the researcher, although held confidential in this chapter.

As a result of this analysis of student responses, I will argue here that graduate programs have the potential to change school leaders' perceptions of their goals and roles, and ultimately to affect their practice as they reflect on the implications of their insights and integrate them into their daily work lives. Prior to examining the methodology and data, it is important to provide a brief overview of the program undertaken by these students.

THE EDUCATIONAL CONTEXT

Students were enrolled in a doctoral program that presented traditional topics such as law, finance, and the role of the superintendent as well as two courses entitled "leadership and social justice" and "democracy and politics." Overall, the program goals were to ensure students were prepared to assume leadership roles in schools, school districts, and higher education and to do so cognizant of issues of equity, inclusion, and social justice.

It is important to note that this was not designed as a "social justice" program, although certainly two of the required courses took that as a central mission. Because of the dual emphasis that combined a traditional educational administration focus with courses related to democracy and social justice, I wondered whether students had acquired enough information to develop a commitment to socially just and deeply democratic practices and if so, what had influenced them in that way. Moreover, I wanted to explore whether the specific courses in democracy and social justice had influenced their practice.

Here, I provide a brief overview of the two "social justice" courses included in students' programs before proceeding to an analysis of whether they might have impacted student practice. Both courses were conceived as dialogues that permitted these doctoral student-educators to explore, not only multifaceted meanings and interpretations, but also how more robust conceptions of democracy and social justice might affect their practice. The anticipated outcomes of these courses were that graduates would a) develop better understandings of a number of different conceptions of democracy, leadership, and social justice, b) reflect on the relationship between various concepts and the ways in which they might practice educational leadership and governance, and c) develop skills in examining, critiquing, and perhaps changing, the ethics and outcomes of their own practices. The democracy course introduced students to concepts of "deep democracy" (Green, 1999) and to "critical democratic perspectives" (Carr, 2008; Portelli, Solomon, Barrett, & Mujawamariya, 2005); while the course related to leadership and social justice introduced students to various leadership theories and approaches, but emphasized the role of transformative leadership (Quantz, Rogers, & Dantley, 1991; Shields, 2011, 2012; Starratt, 1991). Thus the theories that were studied were selected to ensure that students were confronted by the unequal lived realities of students, the social injustices that perpetuate an uneven playing field in educational institutions, and leadership approaches that attempt to mitigate and overcome these inequities.

Both courses required a relatively large amount and wide range of scholarly reading, including historical, conceptual, and empirical work. The text, Goodlad's (2001) edited *The Last Best Hope*, provided a basis for thinking deeply about the topic of democracy. It was supplemented and extended by numerous additional readings from such seminal authors as Buber (1937/2000) and Freire (2000); as well as more critical and current perspectives by authors such as Delpit (1993), Giroux (2005), Lipman

(2002), Shields (2008, 2009), Starratt (1991), and Torres (1998). Similarly, Shields' (2008) work provided an introduction to transformative leadership, again supplemented by numerous texts related to leadership, organizational theory, and social justice.

Numerous activities were employed – in-depth discussion of the articles and of their relationship to current education policies or newsworthy current events; role playing how Delpit's (1993) rules of power might play out in various educational settings; examinations of disparities in academic achievement (and income levels) of various groups in America and elsewhere; simulation games relating to the inequitable distribution of resources; critical discussion of videos, and the creation of imaginative vignettes of others' lives based on photographs and other images. Often a student comment or question prompted a particular exercise. For example, when one high-school principal stated, "I have absolutely no interest in travelling outside the United States," several activities were introduced to demonstrate how understanding another culture through travel or at minimum, through global curiosity, could extend one's knowledge and appreciation of other cultures and hence, lead to greater sensitivity in dealing with the increasing diversity of school populations in one's own school. Another time, in response to a reading from Bigelow (1998) discussing the role of child labor in the construction of many commonly used items, a student asked whether, if we teach our students about global disparities and child labor, they will still be able to enjoy shopping. This led to a further examination of the interconnectedness of our world and of the need for the practice of democratic leadership to look beyond one's own shores to understand both equitable leadership and deep democracy (Green, 1999). These, and other student comments, suggested the need for students to better understand the interrelatedness of our world and the cultures from which their students may come, if they are to be successful and sensitive leaders.

STUDENT OUTCOMES

For the purposes of this analysis, I examined and analyzed survey responses and weekly critical reflective journal entries from one class of 13 EdD students (6 men and 7 women), the 25 surveys from the wider cohort of school leaders, and the interview and observational data from the in-depth studies of students in the whole EdD program. As I approached the data, I was conscious of the positional power I held over some of students who had been in my classes and the fact that students often write what they believe a professor wants to read. Given that most of them held formal positions of educational leadership yet had never found it necessary to interrogate their location and positional power, this tendency would not have been surprising. To mitigate the impact of any perceived power relations, and to better understand the impact of the program as a whole, a department secretary administered the surveys to the whole EdD cohort without any attribution to a specific professor. Had the study focused only on an analysis of assignments written by students for one course, one might argue that students were simply "playing the academic game" and responding as they assumed the professor desired. Here, however, the intent was broader and no one professor's ideologies were associated with the survey. Teacher surveys were conducted in the eight schools selected for follow-up to attempt to verify whether changes in practice reported by the school leaders had, in fact, been noticed at the school level. This form of data triangulation helped to confirm the veracity of the self-report data.

The data analysis first examined the students' responses on the survey taken prior to the beginning of the "democracy" class and then moved to analyze responses on the wider survey given to all doctoral students. I then re-read each reflective journal entry and interview transcript, chunked and coded the content, and identified the persistent and recurrent themes, which I present here. I attempted to triangulate the data and verify the themes by further analysis of the teacher surveys and observational data from the eight schools selected for follow-up in-depth study. Finally, I reflected on the potential implications of each insight for helping to prepare ethical, socially just, critically democratic and transformative school leaders.

EXAMINING THE SURVEY DATA

From the pre-democracy course survey, consistent with Carr's (2008) findings, I noted a "predisposition among university students to understand democracy and politics in a thin way" (p. 147). Students defined democracy in terms of "one person, one vote" and in terms of governmental processes, without demonstrating much further thought about its meaning. Typical responses were the following: "Democracy is a form of government that should be carried out by the people through publicly elected officials," "representation of individuals by themselves or elected officials," "democracy is when people are governed by the people where the people vote and the majority will usually rule." One group of responses included the concept of participation and voice, such as "everyone having a voice" or "the ability to participate in the governance of a society." Only one response out of 13 (8%) showed a somewhat more complete and critical understanding of democracy: "To me, democracy represents a social order that is built on fundamental principles of freedom, liberty, and justice. It is characterized as government by the people." Overall, it is fair to say that at the outset of this course, which came near the middle of their doctoral programs, most of these students' concepts of democracy focused almost entirely on governance processes to the exclusion of either the content or the outcomes of democratic society.

Despite these "thin" understandings (Carr, 2008; Strike, 1999), the responding graduate students showed an awareness that neither their own schooling experiences nor those of their students were particularly "democratic." Although some indicated that they had "not really thought about democracy in teaching or leading," others − perhaps because of the failings of their own education − believed schools should do more to promote democracy. Typical comments included: "The public schools in the United States are inequitable. Most educational leaders in the United States should feel guilty knowing that the system is essentially designed to inculcate and strip low SES and students of color of their backgrounds," "there were plenty of examples of inequity and decisions made that were not democratic." One stated that "Society should be educating students on how to be better citizens for our country," although another was clear that teachers "should not spew their own political views as gospel!"

Overall, these graduate students were "concerned about the direction education reform was taking, especially in the areas of curriculum development," and believed that "we need to have conversations in schools about this important topic." Acknowledging that they were, for the most part, "untrained to teach" democracy, they did show some eagerness to learn, making comments like "what will happen to our society as people continue to think it is someone else's problem?" Yet, students were somewhat skeptical that anything could change: "Improvement assumes there is a definitive structure or practice in place. Democracy is more of an ideal and set of beliefs than a machine that can be adjusted." It is clear teachers need guidance in how to begin these conversations, for as one stated, "We really need to understand what democracy means!"

From the second set of surveys, it quickly became apparent that students' insights and understandings had changed during the course of their doctoral programs. They claimed that their doctoral programs had, indeed, both shaped and changed their understanding of leadership and helped them to understand ways in which traditional practices continue to marginalize and exclude some students. They emphasized notions like "deficit thinking and removing blame," the concept of social justice itself, differentiating between equality and equity, transformative leadership, and the necessity of knowing your own grounding and values. Comments included:

> The biggest "ah ha" I have had yet is the idea of social justice and the need for open dialogue with staff around these topics ... There are many ways we aren't equitable to our students that I had never considered before. I've also deeply been changed by the discussion thus far around transformative versus transformational leadership.

> I believe that my entire approach to leadership was formed at [...] where I learned that I must be secure in my beliefs and values.

> I had never thought about social justice issues prior to this education. It has evolved my way of thinking and expanded how I handle situations at my building. Prior to this work, I do not think I would have addressed deficit thinking with the staff or even advocated for those in the minority.

> My entire thinking about school leadership has changed as a result of the [...] program. When I first started, I never considered issues of equity, access, social justice, democracy, inclusivity, dialogue, etc. Now, I believe that without these core foundations, schools will continue to perpetuate past systems which marginalize students.

Thus, in general, it became apparent from these comments that graduate studies could actually influence, and even dramatically change, the leadership practice of practitioners. To better understand how these changes occurred, we turn to comments made by the cohort in their course journals as well as to elaborations and explanations that occurred during the interview process.

Delving Deeper

It had long been my prior experience that many students, even practicing school leaders, had never taken an opportunity to encounter or think deeply about the concepts of democracy, social justice, or equity as it related to the overall operations of their school and/or student achievement. Nevertheless, I had also realized that many students were open to these concepts and in fact, often amazed and somewhat ashamed at their prior lack of exposure and awareness. Many immediately wanted to learn how to change their practice and became firmly dedicated to changing their roles.

As I examined student comments from the journals and the interviews, this perception was again borne out. As described in my earlier chapter,[1] student responses fell primarily into five areas: achieving deeper understanding, acquiring language and new paradigms, feeling confused and overwhelmed, preparing for action, and taking action. Below I give a few samples of student comments that reflect each of these general areas. In the follow-up discussion, I reflect on the implications of these responses for graduate preparation in general.

Achieving Deeper Understanding
Included in this category are student comments that suggest they are encountering particular topics and concepts for the first time or that they have been prompted to think in new ways as a result of course readings and/or discussions.

- Actually, until this class and this article, I never really had any real discussion about democracy and the affects of 9/11. That's pretty sad since I'm in education.
- One of the ideas that has become more clear to me is the difference between thin democracy and deep or thick democracy,
- I never thought about education being in a crisis based on democracy.
- It has taken coursework toward the pursuit of a Doctoral Degree to finally consider the relationship and connectedness between all of these [ideas]...

That these educational leaders had simply accepted the idea that schools were democratic and had never considered the connections among conceptions of democratic education, social justice, patriotism, or citizenship was of tremendous concern to me. I began to believe that continuing to teach the more traditional topics related to the role of the superintendent or school law or finance disconnected from concepts related to deep democracy and social justice failed to provide school leaders with the language and concepts needed to make significant changes in their buildings and districts. As students shared their puzzlement and sometimes their anger at not having encountered some of these concepts in prior courses, the urgency to reconsider graduate preparation programs became evident. Moreover, during the second survey in which students were asked about the impact of their programs, they frequently made comments identifying the two social justice-oriented courses, and "not necessarily all my coursework" as courses that had made them feel their role was "very crucial in not only improving the lives of my students, but also bringing a social awareness to my entire school community."

Acquiring Language and New Paradigms
More than simply providing a foundation for deeper understanding of their educational contexts and roles, these school leaders indicated that the readings and class discussions had given them new frameworks and the necessary language to articulate some of their deep convictions and to change the focus of some of their leadership activities.

• From my classes that I have taken for my Doctorate, I am starting to ask questions that make my teachers think about our children in a different light (rather than the parents don't care and don't help the child at home). I had never heard of the term social justice before starting my doctoral program.
• Social justice, equity, dialogue, and discussions regarding students of poverty have influenced me the most. … my coursework has really brought these issues into the forefront.
• I often indicate that these readings have provided me with the language to describe my thoughts and the reality I have come to know as an educational administrator.
• So, how did we get here? How did I miss this? Where was I?…

Where did we fail these already practicing school leaders if they had neither the language nor the understanding of inequity prior to this program? One cannot assume that all school principals will have the time and resources to enroll in doctoral studies, nor should it take this long for them to begin to confront the inequities that underlie schooling practices that result in the "failure" of so many minoritized students. Indeed, the failure is not that of the students, as I have often maintained elsewhere (Shields, 2008, 2011) but that of schools and systems, and certainly of higher education preparation programs. Given Lewin's (1951) often cited dictum that "there is nothing so practical as a good theory," it seems almost self-evident that helping educational leaders develop additional frames for analyzing and addressing the challenges they face on a daily basis would enhance their praxis. One African American woman, who had been relatively quiet in discussions over most of her program, suddenly came to life – in her writing and her verbal contributions. She wrote:

> Remember when I talked about the anger that I see moving as an undercurrent in too
> many African Americans who have made it?… I now have a better explanation as to

why it exists. Dantley (2005) also states, "Their sense of a greater purpose cultivated their resilience to allow them to consistently bounce back and resurrect from the acts of silencing and marginalization of the dominant culture." Can you understand why I am excited about having these concepts in my repertoire? Being able to say it in that way says more about me and gives my argument more credibility. I feel like I am being armed and properly equipped to fight the battle on behalf of those who cannot.

When an African American school leader emphasizes that a doctoral program is equipping her to help "her people," there is little doubt that the program is making a difference. It speaks to the power of ensuring that course readings reflect a variety of perspectives – not only in terms of scholarly or ontological perspectives, but that they are expressed in different voices and by authors from different cultures and scholarly traditions; in short, it speaks to the power of dialogue in a Bakhtinian sense (1973) of promoting understanding of divergent perspectives.

Feeling Confused and Overwhelmed
At the same time, giving students language and new frames for thinking about their roles can, and often did, seem overwhelming. Students frequently wrote or stated, "I have no idea how to do this!" and indicated that they really had no idea where to start or how to go about achieving, what for many, were new goals. Some were "overwhelmed by the need for change" but indicated, "I really don't know how to go about it ...." Obviously it is critical in doctoral preparation not only to provide students with new ideas, language, or frames for thinking about changes in practice, but to ensure they have time to explore in detail some substantive ways of actually implementing the new concepts.

This concept was brought home to me clearly when one of my students invited me to address her staff at an early morning meeting and then to spend the day meeting with small groups of teachers. We talked about many of the issues raised in class including creating alternatives so that children from disadvantaged families would not feel embarrassed and would not be put in the position of having to say they had no money to pay for materials or no ability to complete an assignment. When I returned home, the principal (my student) wrote to me saying, "Don't be surprised if a teacher writes asking you to explain a comment. I have used your name to 'call some of them out.'" For example, she has said to one man, "Dr. Shields wondered why you seemed so disengaged today." Now, I had not noticed this person specifically, but if my student felt the need to appeal to my perception in order to make her point, I was willing to have this occur. Sometimes educators need support as they change their approaches and work to change the understandings of their teachers. If we hope our doctoral programs will result in change, I have learned we must be willing to take a stand alongside our students when they ask.

Preparing for Action

Perhaps the most frequent theme I noted from students, as they began to internalize the new ideas, was their intent to do something differently. Hence, they made comments such as the following:

- I'll have to take this [...] article to the staff to prompt some further dialogue.
- In order to address the impact of poverty on our families and students, I think we need to increase the level of dialogue we have with our families and students.
- I'm thinking that we can use some of the readings from this course to spark dialogue and debate among teachers.
- I have a faculty meeting next week and am planning on opening the conversation with the faculty about [citizenship]. I am planning on challenging my staff ...

Once again, student responses indicate that scholarship may have a transformative impact. The desire of these practitioner scholars to share their new insights was laudable, but left me wondering what response they might have and how push-back on the part of their colleagues might influence their ability to continue.

As I conducted observations and follow-up visits to some schools, the need to help my students implement dialogic approaches became evident. Generally, after I had spent a day conducting interviews as part of this research project, I was asked to meet informally with any staff members who wished to interact with me. This resulted in some surprising exchanges, and permitted me to model for my students, the use of dialogue. On one occasion, I asked teachers how they dealt with students who expressed negativity towards other children or groups of children. One spoke up immediately, saying "We do not need to address prejudice; all we need to do is model acceptance and respect." As the conversation continued, with some agreeing and others disagreeing, a woman spoke up.

> I came to this school just last fall as assistant principal. On the first or second day of school, one young boy asked me who I was. When I told him I was the new assistant principal, he looked surprised, and then responded, "No, You can't be. You are Latina and a woman."

This type of stereotypical perception cannot be addressed simply by modeling respect and good behavior. Sometimes, it is necessary to probe the deeper concepts underlying student perceptions if we are to address negative and incorrect assumptions.

Hence, I once again learned, that class discussions provide a starting point and may prompt a desire to change behaviors, but it is important to help students take their learning back to their workplace and to implement it there.

Taking Action

A final group of student comments related to how they actually attempted to implement course ideas. These leaders shared how they had initiated conversations and begun to press for change.

- I am beginning to have conversations with my staff about our curriculum. I am bringing up the issues about whether our curriculum addresses the needs of all the children who attend our school. Are we promoting equality for all?
- [Following the election of Obama], I asked my teachers in a middle school serving grades six through eight to describe the **conversations** they had with their students. I also asked them to describe the **interactions** between the students. I received answers like, "The *kids are too young to recognize this historical moment*" and *"I'm a math teacher, I teach math"* and *"We didn't have time."* Wow! I fault myself for not making it an issue at the staff meeting prior to the inauguration. I should have created a list of sample questions ...

These selections highlight, not only the fact that these school leaders began to take action based on their new insights and understanding, but also that they began to feel a sense of guilt for not having done so previously. Once again, this points to a specific need for dialogue. The goal of graduate instruction is not to impart guilt but to raise awareness that leads to action. It is important for preparation programs to reassure educators that they could not have been expected to know all theories in advance.

DISCUSSION: INCREASING THE POTENTIAL IMPACT OF GRADUATE PROGRAMS

We have previously noted that some school leaders indicated that prior to embarking on their doctoral programs, they had not had the language to address inequities, with several, remarkably stating they had never even heard the term "social justice" prior to their classes. These school leaders made comments about their overall doctoral programs like: "When I started it was all about test scores. It was about data and numbers and test scores and curriculum, and now ... through the social justice lens, it's let's look at the bigger picture of access and opportunity." Another indicated, the program has "forced me to think about myself, my upbringing, the lens that I see life through" and indicated that this was healthy for him both as a person and as a principal. Others made comments like, "My personal goals have shifted ... to more of that citizenship piece or that global aware- ness piece," or "I couldn't have verbalized it ... I feel like I have a vision now, and I recognize how important vision is and how important that con- ceptual understanding is and how important democratic engagement is ...." Still another reported that while he had always "believed that school leaders should be catalysts for social change, [he] did not have an adequate understanding of what that might look like in the daily context of public schooling." These comments are particularly important because, through coursework, we can energize students to want to act; nonetheless, we must also find ways, both in our coursework and in following up with students in their contexts, to ensure that they do gain an understanding of what social justice might look like in the "daily context of public school."

We cannot stop at imparting knowledge of theory; but must help students develop working models of inclusive and socially just education. This is particularly true given that there is often push-back about issues of social justice. Some feel that it is a waste of time; others insist that it is not the educator's task. Yet, I wonder how we can ever narrow the achievement gap if educators do not recognize how material inequities in the daily lives of children play out in schools. The point was brought home to me in one interview, when the principal reported that "without a doubt social justice is now the primary lens through which I view every situation." He laughed and continued:

> I can be candid enough about this now. I remember thinking, 'Oh my gosh. This class on social justice, it's all going to be this touchy-feely stuff,' and it just absolutely opened my eyes.... It really did,... and then obviously that tied into my finance background.

Social justice must not be taught in a touchy-feely way, but with data, statistics, and stories that demonstrate clearly the impact of social, cultural, and economic inequities and disparities on student achievement.

Although these inequities can negatively affect student performance, and sometimes also make the role of educators more challenging, it does not follow that they cannot be overcome. In fact, the data here suggest the importance of educators knowing how to take disparities into account and to incorporate the lived experiences of all students into the classroom discussions and activities. Additionally, educators must ensure all students have an equitable opportunity to perform to similar high levels and to successfully meet expectations that must be equally high for all students.

Going Beyond

It becomes apparent from the foregoing, and many other similar comments that a doctoral program can play a significant role in changing the perceptions and intentions of school leaders. Yet, as previously indicated, these students also often expressed the need for additional guidance and support. Frequently they indicated that, in their roles as school leaders, when they introduced new ideas they often encountered resistance (either covert or overt) and considerable "push-back" from teachers and other school leaders. One reported, "The first time I brought this discussion up with the staff, they looked at me like I had two heads ... they have finally figured out, I am going to keep asking the questions." Another recognized that push-back might be inevitable but stated that "we as educators need to be willing to take some heat for championing this cause." Others indicated that faculty had branded them as "the liberal" taking university courses; or that teachers insisted they did not have time for social justice because they have to teach standards. One summed the difficulties up by saying, "We preach democracy and equity, but we practice marginalization." These scholar-practitioners indicated that such responses from their colleagues left them "disheartened and frustrated," but also that they were committed to continuing the dialogue and the struggle.

Here, once again, we can see that encouraging educational leaders to change their practice may result in both an amplified sense of isolation and increased frustration and disappointment. Thus, it is important for faculty members attempting to teach about social justice and about deeply democratic, transformative leadership not only to teach about advocacy and activism, but also to reflect carefully on the ethical implications of doing so.

It seems to me that if we encourage our students to take action, we also need to ensure that we, and they, are cognizant of the risks and that we provide adequate support. Thus, if we argue for advocacy and activism on the part of educational leaders, we must be willing to become involved with them and to support their daily efforts to promote deep democracy.

The data from this study demonstrate clearly that a graduate program can promote new understandings of deep democracy, social justice, and transformative leadership – understandings that lead to a new commitment to action. This commitment is exactly what Oakes and Rogers (2006) posited is needed – a commitment to equity reform that will have the potential to truly create more inclusive and socially just learning environments. But the path is difficult; the challenges and push-back are both enormous and often dangerous. As educators, we must acknowledge, as Weiner (2003) did, that school leaders are often appointed because they conform to the expectations of the status quo and have demonstrated their support for the current practices related to accountability, effectiveness, and efficiency. He argues that leaders are "actors, inside dominant structures" but that "transformative leadership must always make problematic the institutional power it wields" (p. 93). He claims that just as

> Transformative leadership, [...] must have one foot in the dominant structures of power and authority, and as such become 'willing' subjects of dominant ideological and historical conditions. (p. 91)

so it must also

> Confront more than just what is, and work toward creating an alternative political and social imagination that does not rest solely on the rule of capital or the hollow moralism of neoconservatives, but is rooted in radical democratic struggle. (p. 97)

It is therefore incumbent on faculty from institutions of higher education who want to refute Levin's assertions of the inefficacy of graduate programs, to align themselves with their students as they strive to create alternative visions and versions of the social and political institutions called schools.

In other words, if we remain within the theoretical confines of our classroom, students may well be left wondering how to apply the concepts discussed in class. One student explained during the interview process:

> It's taken me a while to sort of figure out how to make that relevant to what I'm doing here in the school. 'Cause I think I saw it, read it, understood it. It was still abstract to me, and as I'm going through this process right now (i.e., the interview), it's really helped to solidify my understanding.

I was surprised. After all of the dialogue and discussion from his peers, he was still having difficulty applying the concepts. It wasn't until I was actually in his school interviewing him, discussing the concepts with his specific context and challenges in mind that he began to see more clearly how to proceed. Once again, the lesson for me (and hopefully others) was that we must be willing to move out of our "ivory towers" and into the workplaces of our students, standing alongside them and offering support.

I was not aware that this approach was rare until one evening, during class, several of my students were whispering to each other. The whispering grew louder and soon involved more students. As I stopped talking and stared quizzically they asserted, "We were just saying that you are the only professor who knows what we are talking about when we mention specific policies or reforms we are dealing with." The class proceeded, and at one point, when I mentioned a common policy initiative of the local government, the students burst out laughing, "See," they shouted. "You not only know the name of the reform, but you understand what we are being asked to do." I was both amazed and saddened that they found this knowledge rare and even surprising. Because I was often in schools conducting research, visiting teachers and classrooms, and talking to staff, it seemed natural for me to know something about their challenges; however, the message is clear that faculty must be aware of the learning environments and political contexts that students strive to transform. This awareness must become the norm for those wanting to help school leaders change their practices.

I am firmly convinced that if we are to make a difference in the praxis of educational leaders who are also our students, we must help them reflect on ways to become more ethical as leaders, more socially just, and more deeply democratic. In our classrooms, this requires us to use pedagogical methods that are themselves, dialogic, ethical, and democratic; that we do not stop with the discussion of theory, but that we teach praxis – attending first to our own, then theirs and that of their fellow educators and students as well. It requires that we, as educators, eschew typical higher education lecture and power point presentations – pedagogies described by Freire (1970) as "banking methods" which deposit information into the heads of students, with little interest and less benefit for democratic schools or citizenship. In contrast, we must design our content and our pedagogy to promote the conscientization (critical consciousness) that Freire so powerfully advocated. We must find ways to make our instruction both rigorous and relevant, always helping students to make the connections between the theory and their practice, and at the same time, rejecting prescriptions and easy answers (Shields, 2008; Starratt, 1991).

Yet, despite the urgency that I and other faculty sometimes feel about encouraging educational professionals to become activists focused on developing socially just and deeply democratic schools, it is important to acknowledge that not every student will adopt our normative concepts of critically democratic educational leadership or our vision for their organizations. At the same time, as my data have clearly shown, as students engage in critical discussion and reflection, their own critical consciousness may be awakened and ultimately, we can anticipate that change will occur. In 1991, Quantz, Rogers, and Dantley wrote: "Those who know only the discourse of the status quo can hardly be expected to challenge the undemocratic aspects of the status quo" (p. 109). Our role, as educators, therefore, must be to ensure that students not only know a different discourse but also that they become comfortable with its challenges and implications. If we want to restore robust democratic societies where we live, we will need to enhance the democratic principles taught in our classes and our students' understanding of these principles.

This is not easy − either for faculty or students; in fact, it is messy and time consuming. Moreover, because transformative change includes both moral purpose and ethical, deeply democratic approaches to schooling and leadership, we must teach by example, engaging in caring and supportive ways with our students; in other words, it requires a level of engagement with our students and their contexts that may go beyond the norm in educational leadership to a more collaborative relationship of learning and service.

The value of persisting, sometimes in the face of ridicule from academic colleagues, sometimes in the face of push-back from students, and always cognizant of the risks and dangers of doing so, was emphasized for me when I received an unsolicited email from a student who had proclaimed social justice and deep democracy "nonsense" during our first class. She wrote, in part:

> Your class has probably had the greatest influence upon my thoughts about education since I was in undergrad. However, this class has reshaped my paradigm about education for a deep democracy and my responsibility to assume, formally or informally, that role.

A few years ago, Seddon (cited in Carr, Zyngier, & Pruyn, 2010, p. 27) asked:

> How can education be remade to serve the purposes of a just and democratic society? How can education, in the context of a social order torn between neo-liberal free markets and neo-conservative family values and 'them'−'us' differentiations, develop an ethical citizenry and capable and creative contributors to the common good who will enable and protect civic society in a sustainable way?

My student's testimony suggests that one way to respond to Seddon's call is through offering rigorous academic programs in our higher education institutions. Moreover, the data provided here indicate that most prescriptions for improving the quality and outcomes of higher education programs are inadequate in that they continue to ignore issues of equity and social justice.

As Palmer wrote in 2011:

> Our democratic institutions are not automated. They must be inhabited by citizens and citizen leaders who know how to hold conflict inwardly in a manner that converts it into creativity, allowing it to pull them open to new ideas, new courses of action, and each other. (p. 15)

The data presented here provide evidence that university faculty can play a role in preparing the kind of citizen leaders that Palmer advocates — leaders who understand the concept of deep democracy, who are able to resist the pressures and push-back, and to convert the inherent tensions and conflicts into creativity. I believe, as I have argued here that we must step up to the plate, stand alongside our students, and help them to prepare the new generations of democratic citizens and citizen leaders.

NOTE

1. This section draws heavily on data already published in my 2010 chapter; however, the analysis of interview and observational data and the subsequent discussion is new.

REFERENCES

Bakhtin, M. M. (1973). *Problems of Dostoevsky's poetics*. Ann Arbor, MI: Ardis.

Berliner, D. C., & Biddle, B. J. (1995). *The manufactured crisis: Myths, fraud, and the attack on America's public schools*. New York, NY: Basic Books.

Bigelow, B. (1998). The human lives behind the labels — The global sweatshop, Nike, and the race to the bottom. In W. Ayers, J. A. Hunt, & T. Quinn (Eds.), *Teaching for social justice* (pp. 21–38). New York, NY: Teachers College Press.

Buber, M. (1937/2000). In R. G. Smith (Trans), *I and Thou*. New York, NY: Simon & Schuster.

Carr, P. (2008). Educators and education for democracy: Moving beyond "thin" democracy. *Interamerican Journal of Education for Democracy, 1*(2), 146–165.

Carr, P. R., Zyngier, D., & Pruyn, M. M. (Eds.). (2012). *Can education make a difference? Experimenting with, and experiencing democracy in, education.* Charlotte, NC: Information Age Publishing.

Dantley, M. E. (2005). African American spirituality and Cornel West's notions of prophetic pragmatism: Restructuring educational leadership in American urban schools. *Educational Administration Quarterly, 41,* 651–674.

Delpit, L. D. (1993). The silenced dialogue: Power and pedagogy in educating other people's children. In N. M. Hidalgo, C. L. McDowell, & E. V. Siddle (Eds.), *Facing racism in education* (pp. 84–102). (reprint series No. 21). Cambridge, MA: Harvard Educational Review.

Freire, P. (1970). *Pedagogy of the oppressed.* New York, NY: Continuum.

Freire, P. (2000). Education for critical consciousness. In A. M. A. Freire & D. Macedo (Eds.), *The Paulo Freire reader* (pp. 80–110). New York, NY: Continuum.

Giroux, H. A. (1995). Educational visions: What are schools for and what should we be doing in the name of education? In J. L. Kincheloe & S. R. Steinberg (Eds.), *Thirteen questions* (pp. 295–302). New York, NY: Peter Lang.

Giroux, H. A. (2005). The terror of neoliberalism: Rethinking the significance of cultural politics. *College Literature, 32*(1), 10–19.

Goodlad, S. J. (2001). *The last best hope: A democracy reader.* San Francisco, CA: Jossey-Bass.

Green, J. M. (1999). *Deep democracy: Diversity, community, and transformation.* Lanham, MD: Rowman & Littlefield.

Levine, A. (2005). *Educating school leaders.* Washington, DC: The Education Schools Project.

Lewin, K. (1951). *Field theory in social science: Selected theoretical papers.* New York, NY: Harper & Row.

Lipman, P. (2002). Making the global city, making inequality: The political economy and cultural politics of Chicago school policy. *American Educational Research Journal, 39*(2), 379–419.

Macedo, D. (1995). Power and education: Who decides the forms schools have taken, and who should decide? In J. L. Kincheloe & S. R. Steinberg (Eds.), *Thirteen questions* (pp. 43–57). New York, NY: Peter Lang.

Oakes, & Rogers. (2006). *Learning power: Organizing for education and justice.* New York, NY: Teachers College Press.

Palmer, P. (2011). *Healing the heart of democracy.* San Francisco, CA: Jossey-Bass.

Portelli, J. P., Solomon, R. P., Barrett, S., & Mujawamariya, D. (2005). Standardized teacher testing fails excellence and validity tests. *Teaching Education, 16*(4), 281–295.

Quantz, R. A., Rogers, J., & Dantley, M. (1991). Rethinking transformative leadership: Toward democratic reform of schools. *Journal of Education, 173*(3), 96–118.

Ravitch, D. (2010). *The death and life of the great American school system: How testing and choice are undermining education.* New York, NY: Basic Books.

Shields, C. M. (2008). *Courageous leadership for transforming schools: Democratizing practice.* Norwood, MA: Christopher-Gordon.

Shields, C. M. (2009). Leadership: Transformative. In E. Baker, B. McGaw, & P. Peterson (Eds.), *International encyclopedia of education* (3rd ed., Vol. 5, pp. 26–33). Oxford: Elsevier.

Shields, C. M. (2011). Introduction. In C. M. Shields (Ed.), *Transformative leadership: A reader* (pp. 1–20). New York, NY: Peter Lang.

Shields, C. M. (2012). *Transformative leadership: Equitable change in an uncertain and complex world.* New York, NY: Routledge.

Starratt, R. J. (1991). Building an ethical school: A theory for practice in educational leadership. *Educational Administration Quarterly, 27*(2), 185–202.

Strike, K. A. (1999). Can schools be communities? The tension between shared values and inclusion. *Educational Administration Quarterly, 35*(1), 46–70.

Torres, C. A. (1998). Democracy. In *Democracy, education, multiculturalism* (pp. 145–173). Lanham, MD: Rowman & Littlefield.

Weiner, E. J. (2003). Secretary Paulo Freire and the democratization of power: Toward a theory of transformative leadership. *Educational Philosophy and Theory, 35*(1), 89–106.

THE EDUCATION DOCTORATE (Ed.D.) AND EDUCATIONAL LEADER DISPOSITIONS AND VALUES IN ENGLAND AND THE UNITED STATES

Alison Taysum and Charles L. Slater

ABSTRACT

Purpose — *This chapter focuses on the dispositions and values of The Education Doctorate (Ed.D.) students in England and the United States as they conducted research, graduated, and entered their work communities.*

Methods — *We will present a brief review of the history of the Ed.D. and an explanation of signature pedagogy, which leads to a consideration of values, particularly as they relate to the connection between the researcher and the community. A synthesis of Banks (1991, 1998) description of the researcher's position and stages of ethnic development provide a framework to analyze the experience of a doctoral student in England and a doctoral student in the United States.*

Investing in our Education: Leading, Learning, Researching and the Doctorate
International Perspectives on Higher Education Research, Volume 13, 149–170
Copyright © 2014 by Emerald Group Publishing Limited
All rights of reproduction in any form reserved
ISSN: 1479-3628/doi:10.1108/S1479-362820140000013007

Findings — *The leaders developed multicultural dispositions through doctoral pedagogies that included the supervised creation of a doctoral thesis in a Higher Education Institution with access to resources. The resources included pedagogical relationships with program providers, a library and access to intellectual networks that built leadership capacity within the doctoral education system. Leaders designing and implementing their research and drafting and redrafting their doctoral thesis, engaged with pedagogies that developed a deep understanding of "what counts as evidence," and critical and reflective thinking tools that enhanced their multicultural dispositions and habits of hearts, minds and hands.*

Practical and social implications — *The findings may contribute to informing decisions to invest in the doctoral dividend, policy and a research agenda into doctoral pedagogies.*

Original value — *New insights into the benefits of educational leaders investing in the doctoral dividend are revealed.*

Keywords: Critical thinking; reflective research; doctoral pedagogy; multicultural identity; deep democracy

INTRODUCTION

Teachers College Columbia University established the first practitioner focused Ph.D. in 1898. In 1920, the Graduate School of Education at Harvard University established the Educational Doctorate (Ed.D.) for those with teaching experience who sought additional knowledge and skills to assume positions of leadership in educational administration. The intent was to have a rigorous research program like the Ph.D. and to provide a focus on practice. By 1940, many schools had begun to offer the Ed.D. including Berkeley, Stanford and Michigan.

The Ed.D. was first offered in England at the University of Bristol in 1991, and it was later established at several other universities including Durham University, the Institute of Education in London, the University of Birmingham, Kings College, the University of Leeds, the University of Leicester, Kingston University, Warwick University, the University of Lincoln, and the University of Bath. The Ed.D. is equivalent to the Ph.D. in terms of rigor although the dissertation may be shorter and more focused on practice. The Ed.D. also includes coursework whereas traditionally the Ph.D. has not, though this is now beginning to change with the introduction of modular-based PhDs and practice-based PhDs.

Over the years, considerable confusion has spawned over the difference between the two degrees. Perry (2012) summarized research that has attempted to offer clarification. Levine (2005) argued that there were too many degrees and certificates in educational administration and varying purposes for the degrees from one institution to another. He suggested elimination of the Ed.D. in favor of a stronger Master's degree program.

SIGNATURE PEDAGOGIES

Shulman, Golde, Bueschel, and Garabedian (2006) argued for change as well, but suggested continuing with a program at the doctoral level that would better connect theory and practice and prepare highly qualified educational leaders. In 2007, the Carnegie Project on the Education Doctorate (CPED) joined with universities to strengthen the education doctorate through the adoption of new pedagogies.

CPED has proposed new ways for doctoral programs in education to be delivered. A key to understand doctoral education is what Schulman (2005) referred to as *signature pedagogies* that "form habits of the mind, habits of the heart, and habits of the hand ... they prefigure the cultures of professional work and provide the early socialization into the practices and values of a field" (p. 59).

He defined signature pedagogies as the characteristic form of teaching and learning, "that organizes the fundamental ways in which future practitioners are educated for their new professions" (p. 52). Many fields already have signature pedagogies. The case dialogue method in law and clinical rounds in medicine are examples. These practices that are common across universities affect the way that students think and how they practice their profession.

In addition to signature pedagogies, CPED proposed laboratories of practice, scholarship of teaching, and capstone projects as other key elements of the education doctorate. Laboratories of practice refer to "structured experiences, designed to teach ways of doing and provide an important opportunity for students to view work in situ and to work alongside practicing professionals" (Perry & Imig, 2008).

Hutchins and Schulman (1999) added scholarship of teaching to the CPED framework. It is based on Boyer's (1990) proposal for a

combination of research and teaching that would allow teachers to critically reflect on their work and share it with others publically so that it
could be replicated. Finally, the capstone project has traditionally been a
five chapter thesis, but CPED advocated for many different forms to
demonstrate understanding of the core knowledge of the profession and
application to problems of practice.

The CPED concepts of signature pedagogy, laboratories of practice,
scholarship of teaching, and capstone project provide a way of understanding the impact of doctoral programs on the research perspectives of students. In this study, we examine how educational leaders report that the
Ed.D. impacted their research disposition, values, and those aspects of the
program that were most crucial. In asking about values and research disposition, we are going beyond the skills and knowledge imparted and asking
about the philosophy and the extent to which it was adopted by the
students.

The Impact of Inquiring into Values Systems through Doctoral Signature Pedagogies

Pedagogy informed by philosophy implies a value orientation that varies
from one program to another and is influenced by globalization, and value
systems of communities that cross borders. The influence of the program
on student values may be invisible because they do not articulate changes
they experience. However, the influence becomes visible as educational leaders inquire into the practice(s) of their communities, and the changes of
their values are revealed in their behavior and in their writing up of
research.

Pring (2011) described a way of life understood through values, and
behaviors that shape human reaction to the physical world. These values
and behaviors change over time. Banks (1998) outlined a conceptual framework to map shifts in a researcher's value system in relation to the community being studied. The indigenous insider shares the values of the research
community under study and is seen as a legitimate community member.
The indigenous outsider has been socialized into the research community
values system, but has maintained an oppositional culture and is viewed as
a community outsider. The external insider rejects his or her own values
and adopts the values of the research community. Here the researcher is
viewed as an "adopted" insider. Finally, an external-outsider has been
socialized within a different community from the one being studied, has

limited understanding of the research community, and misunderstands behaviors and underpinning values.

These categories provide a helpful view of how values change but there may be other more nuanced categories as well. For example, a person may develop a "hybrid" that includes 'the best of what has been said and done' of both values systems. Such a position neither wholly rejects a formal value system nor wholly accepts a new one.

Banks' (1991) earlier work outlines additional value positions vis-a-vis the research community and provides stages of development of ethnicity. The stages progress from the primitive to the more complex and from monocultural to multicultural. The first stage is ethnic psychological captivity in which members of a minority ethnic group internalize negative attitudes toward them from the dominant group. The second stage is ethnic encapsulation where people are not exposed to other cultural groups and only understand themselves in relation to the in-group. The third stage is ethnic identity clarification in which there is self-acceptance and thus the beginning of acceptance of others. The fourth stage is biethnicity in which a person is capable of functioning in two cultures in a healthy way. The fifth and highest stage is multiethnicity, in which a person is able to function in a number of cultures with an appreciation for values, symbols, and institutions.

Table 1 is a synthesis of Banks' two models that will provide a framework to understand our data.

The synthesis of cross-cultural researcher positions and multiethnic stages of development suggests multiple areas in which there may be misunderstandings between the researcher and the community. They may come

Table 1. Adaption of Banks (1991) and Banks (1998) Synthesis of Cross-Cultural Researcher Positions and Multiethnic Stages of Development.

Type of Educational Leader	Description
Stage one cultural psychological captivity	A leader of a minority cultural group internalizes negative attitudes toward them from the dominant group.
Stage two cultural encapsulation	A leader is not exposed to other cultural groups and only understands themselves in relation to the in-group.
Stage three cultural identity clarification	A leader has self-acceptance and thus the beginning of acceptance of others.
Stage four bicultural disposition	A leader is capable of functioning in two cultures in a healthy way.
Stage five multicultural disposition	A leader is able to function in a number of cultures with an appreciation for values, symbols, and institutions.

from the insider-outsider position of the researcher or from the researcher's stage of ethnic development. These dispositions, in turn, will indicate the level of care that the researcher has for the community.

Relationships between the researcher and participants need to be based on trust, respect, unconditional positive regard and treatment with an ethic of care (Noddings, 1994). These are virtues that Pring considers in an earlier chapter of this volume where he identifies lists of virtues that are tied to particular cultures or communities of practice. For respondents to have faith in the research process and believe that their reality will be faithfully represented, they must also have faith in the researcher (Blumenfeld-Jones, 1995).

A person higher on the synthesis of research positions and ethnic development likely has a greater degree of self-awareness and a higher level of values. Having such values predisposes researchers to recognize their behavior patterns (Bourdieu, 2000). When students carefully consider their disposition and values in relation to their research community, they may face possibly for the first time, an insight into their own behavior.

Research that inquires into policy may cause students to reconsider the rules that shape acting in one way rather than another, and the values underpinning those reasons (Pring, 2000). Specific rules required by sponsors or the government are often expressed a priori so that when "x" happens then "y" will happen. There is no room for interpretation, rather the rules are positivistic.

Values have the logic of rules but they are a posteriori and are dependent on examples that are more disposed to interpretation. This is important because researchers may call for a list of rules, but these rules may marginalize particular groups because they do not recognize their values' systems. Communities' values systems may be hidden from the dominant group, as a survival strategy within a dominant group, which dehumanizes them. This is demonstrated by Stuart Mill's argument in his essay *On Liberty* (1859) cited in Pring (2000):

> The peculiar evil of silencing expression of an opinion is, that it is robbing the human race; posterity as well as the present generation; those who dissent from opinion, still more than those who hold it. If the opinion is right, they are deprived of the opportunity of exchanging error for truth; if wrong, they lose, what is almost as great a benefit, the clearer perception and livelier impression of truth, produced by its collision with error. (p. 146)

This means that educational leaders engaging with signature pedagogies of doctoral study, will need to engage in moral deliberation and consider the synthesis of their research positions with their ethnic development (see Table 1), and how they might move to the next stage and why this might be important for them and the other cultures they engage with.

We have argued that constructing positivist a priori rules for conducting research is not enough. If there is to be moral deliberation, the research would also require clarification of underpinning interpretivist, a posteriori values (Pring, 2000). This is further problematized when consideration is given to the possible clashes between principles and their underpinning rules. For example, if the overarching principle is to find the truth, there may be a clash if respect for a person's dignity may result in telling untruth (Pring, 2000).

Signature pedagogies of doctoral research provide educational leaders the opportunity to explore what are and what are not appropriate dispositions or attitudes for them. Pring (2000) states: "on the whole we act from character or from our dispositions to see, value, and behave in a certain way" (p. 143). The doctorate offers students the chance to examine their values and moral reasoning.

These values can be mapped throughout a lived life from the formation of character (Taysum, 2012). The researchers' values may have been shaped by the values of an outsider illustrated by Banks (1998) "external-outsider" researcher. The community may have become dominant through the oppression of the other communities' values (Freire, 1972). "Researchers, too, can easily be led to see things as the wider society sees them, particularly where a government, with a specific agenda and thinking in business terms, sets the conditions for research funding" (p. 144).

Doctoral research has great potential to enable educational leaders to think carefully about the values that are underpinning their leadership, learning, and plans for change. This study is an examination of the extent to which two doctoral graduates were able to develop these values and dispositions.

RESEARCH QUESTIONS

The research questions were:

How do educational leaders report that the Ed.D. has had an impact on their research dispositions?

How do educational leaders report that the Ed.D. has had an impact on their values?

What aspects of the Ed.D. program do they cite as having the most impact?

What are the differences between the experiences of a doctoral graduate in England and a doctoral graduate in the United States?

METHODOLOGY

This research draws upon data gathered in a larger research project reported in Taysum (2012, 2013) where detailed accounts of the methodology are provided. The research design took an interpretivist approach with a qualitative research design (Newby, 2010). The original sample was 24 educational leaders doing doctorates located in four Higher Education Institutions in England and four Higher Education Institutions in the United States.

In reporting the research, it was found that fuller case studies would enable the reader to get a sense of one student's learning journey through the doctorate. Therefore, in this chapter, we are providing two in-depth cases of a school leader from the United States and a school leader from England doing an Ed.D. looking at exploring their life narratives (Goodson, 2012). We organized the results according to our research questions beginning with the students' dispositions, and values with a focus on respect and inclusion, and the impact of the Ed.D. program on the students' research dispositions and values.

The very difficult nature of this work makes the respondent validation very important. Therefore, we prioritized sending our final paper and interpretation of the findings to the two case study participants so that they could have the final say as to whether we represented them faithfully. In this way, we believe we are beginning to bridge the divide between the academy and the practicum by developing partnerships between the academy and schools/colleges.

The research cannot claim any kind of generalizations, but we hope that readers, leaders, policy makers, and stake-holders may be able to connect with the findings to inform their thinking and practice. Thus, we begin to address the important issue of beginning to understand what is happening in different countries and why, which will enable those responsible for educating future generations to understand their own systems better. Such understanding provides a platform to develop strategies to improve systems, and enhance community members' cultural capital, and their contribution to systems of production and exchange (Brock & Alexiadou, 2013). Further, the understanding may inform strategies for addressing societal challenges such as removing oppressive practices and enhancing social cohesion. We also hope that the research will help guide the research agenda that focuses on the potential impact of postgraduate research on school and college leadership development (Deem, 2012; Lieberman & Friedrich, 2010).

FINDINGS

The Case of Martina: The Teacher Activist

Martina grew up in a middle class white community, which is very different from her school with an almost 100% Latino population in the western United States (U.S.). Martina speaks Spanish like a native now but grew up speaking English. Her father who was Portuguese, lost his native language when he moved to the U.S. Martina was therefore inspired to ensure that her own students would not lose their native language. She teaches Spanish and dance, and her husband was the president of the teachers' union. She was also active in the union.

She enrolled in an Ed.D. program with a cohort of 10 students that involved three universities. The other students were experienced educators like her, but they were all administrators. She decided to study parent involvement in her school. Early in the program, she changed dissertation advisors to find someone with more experience in her topic.

She was interviewed a year after she completed her program. Her comments are reported in terms of the research questions on research disposition, values, and program impact.

RESEARCH DISPOSITION: CREDIBILITY

How do educational leaders report that the Ed.D. has had an impact on their research disposition?

Martina talked about her research mainly in terms of the credibility it gave her with colleagues, administrators, and the community. She felt that the doctorate gave her voice that added weight in policy discussions so that others would not be able to take advantage of her.

Often times these administrators ..., who are not that well educated, are telling me the
research ... I think that's basically the reason why I did it (pursued the doctorate). I
didn't do it to become an administrator or to become rich or to walk round and say I'm
a doctor (but) to be able to fight the good fight and to have the ammunition I needed.

She enjoyed being able to cite research and defend her position publicly.
She might have known the information already, but the research gave her
added authority. Using research, she wrote a letter to the editor of a newspaper challenging the point of view presented in the newspaper editorial by
a community member who was funding school board candidates. She also
used parts of her dissertation to argue against a proposed tracking system
in her district. She described the meeting this way:

I write on the card Dr, and I stand up and everybody sitting at that school board, even
the administrators don't have doctorates I have more education than any of you sitting
there. It is not that I feel superior but in situations like that when you know they are
doing wrong and you know they have to listen to you, it gives you that little edge.

Martina was glad to learn research vocabulary because along with citing
research, use of research terms helped her to bolster her arguments and
understand better what she was doing. She distinguished between academic
sense, which was the research vocabulary and common sense vocabulary,
which were the ones she had been using that arose out of her own practice.

She cited an example of the importance of critiquing programs with
research. These critiques would support her arguments for changing programs even as the principal may have just wanted her to say it was an
exemplary program.

VALUES: RESPECT AND INCLUSION

How do educational leaders report that the Ed.D. has had an impact on
their values?

Martina's values centered on respect and inclusion of all groups. She
saw herself as an activist who would take risks and challenge the status
quo. She cited:

community frustration that they (parents) didn't have a voice in the decision making
and wanting to create some kind of model locally to where we could show, yes we can
create the forum and the possibilities for especially Spanish speaking parents to have
some kind of opinions and voice in the decision making.

She fought hypocrisy when the administration designed a plan ahead of
offering to involve parents in its development, and she expressed her
respect for community groups when she insisted that she did not come with

answers but rather with empowerment and said, "What I was trying to do was something from the grass roots up rather than coming in and saying, 'Oh I've got an idea, I know how to fix you.'"

She also challenged the principal's language that was offensive to the students and parents.

She was unafraid to take risks when the goal was to establish a greater degree of justice even as she realized that activating parents would be dangerous and upsetting to administrators and could get her into trouble.

> Administrators get very upset, they will tell you oh yes we want parents' input we want to collaborate they will tell you all the right answers if you ask them. But the truth is they are extremely threatened the minute you do.

Her courage came from her own will and from the knowledge that others were fighting with her.

> I am pretty tough. And I have tenure okay, so he couldn't just fire me that kept me safe ... this isn't the first time naming injustices and not remaining neutral ... I have been there before and what I have found is that you have to have a mass behind you, you have to have a community behind you.

Her dedication to acting on behalf of the community resulted in conflict with her role as a student. She felt that her study and writing were taking precious time that could be used to take action and make changes.

> I felt like I'm not able to get out there and hit the pavement like I need to be doing because I have to write another draft of this damned paper and who is going to read it. In a certain way I thought it was futile sitting there writing instead of organising or being out there doing something.

Martina took an activist role to make sure that the community was involved, but she put limits on how much of herself she was willing to dedicate to the task. She believed in a balance of life and work that limited the hours worked and the degree to which teachers should be completely wrapped up in their work.

> You don't have to be a martyr to your job ... If you learn how to teach right, and you learn procedures, and that is the only way I could do a doctorate and teach at the same time. I had to figure out how to make it a nine to three job .... I have to go home and do a data analysis.

Martina's new found credibility from having a doctorate not only allowed her to take part in policy discussions, but she also gained more of a personal sense that she did not have to do what others expected and could follow her own dreams and desires.

I don't have to conform to whatever the expectation for a woman my age is supposed to do, and I feel I am completely out of the box, I don't think I was completely in the box before, but I think now I am completely busted out of the box ... just having the confidence that you are going to be okay no matter what, that you can live your dreams your desires ....

IMPACT OF THE PROGRAM

What aspects of the Ed.D. program do they cite as having the most impact?

Martina praised her doctoral program for the support from her dissertation advisor and committee members, the new networks to which she was now connected, and the extensive library resources. She also learned from dialogue with other students in the cohort who were administrators. She debated with them as to whether the union was having a positive or negative effect on education.

Initially, as Martina stated above, she expressed frustration with having to write many drafts of her dissertation, but then found that she may have learned from the process.

It was helpful to me discovering things through writing ... through the different drafts in getting comments and reflecting and just articulating, putting what I read, articulating that into thoughts, and relating that to what I saw and what I experienced and the data I was collecting.

If Martina's experience was like other students' experiences, then this doctoral program could be inferred to have a signature pedagogy that put students into the field. Her laboratory of practice was her own school where she worked to organize parents. The capstone project was the traditional dissertation which combined collection of data in the field with a multi-draft review by supportive faculty.

LOCATING MARTINA ON A TYPOLOGY OF EDUCATIONAL LEADERS' CULTURAL DEVELOPMENT AS ED.D. SIGNATURE PEDAGOGY

Martina was multicultural because she could operate in her white middle class culture, her school community culture, the university Ed.D. program culture, and the culture of members of the school board. Martina was inspired to enable Latino students she taught to be bilingual and not monolinguistic as her father had become in an education system that did not recognize his own culture and language. She felt that parents in the almost 100% Latino population were left out of the decision-making process, and she championed their cause, which she came to see as her own. She said that she drew on resources:

> the community knowledge and community frustration that they didn't have a voice in the decision making and wanting to create some kind of model locally to where we could show, yes we can create the forum and the possibilities for especially Spanish speaking parents to have some kind of voice in the decision making.

She fought against a tracking system that would limit opportunities for Latino children and reduce them to being monolinguistic, and she challenged an influential community member who was advocating a market system of education that Martina felt would weaken the school. She had originally learned about this approach in her doctoral classes at the university where she was also an indigenous outsider. She adopted the arguments against a market approach to education and tracking of students that she had learned from her professors. While she was initially skeptical of the dissertation process of writing many drafts, she came to accept the academic values of thoroughness and attention to detail, and she saw writing as a way to articulate her thoughts. She also saw the value of collecting and weighing data to make an argument. Her reward for adopting university values was the Ed.D., and having a direct impact on improving the education opportunities for students at her school.

Martina appears to have gone through cultural identity clarification in relation to the university. At first, she felt apart from her cohort because she was the only teacher among administrators. She was impatient with the dissertation process and wanted to be the activist that she felt herself to be. By the end of the program, she had accepted the value of the process and embraced the academic mantel of the doctoral degree. She then became like a missionary spreading the word of the importance of research. She also became more confident in herself.

> I think as a person, I am much more confident ... I didn't expect at all on a personal level to feel like I can do anything I want, I don't have to conform to whatever expectation for a woman my age is supposed to do, and I feel I am completely out of the box, I don't think I was completely in the box before, but I think now I am completely busted out of the box.

Martina seemed to be most at home when she was advocating for people in her school community. She advocated for parents when they wanted to bring issues of discrimination and she challenged the principal when he used language that was offensive to some students.

Martina has been clear about staying in her position as a teacher. She does not want to be an administrator. Yet, she demonstrated she could function effectively in the School Board administration culture as a change agent. The evidence reveals that in learning about the culture of administration, she has been able to function more effectively as a change agent and this represents her growth to the fifth stage of being able to function in a number of cultures with an appreciation for values, symbols, and institutions of "A Typology of Educational Leaders' Cultural Development as Ed.D. Signature Pedagogy."

MAYA, THE TRANSFORMATIVE LEADER

Maya is a headteacher of one of the two secondary schools that she has turned around from failing schools to highly successful schools. Maya left school at 16 and began working because her father was ill and for her, going on to A level and University was not possible. Maya worked full time and took A levels from evening school and got access to University and trained to become a teacher. Maya reports that she has always needed to complete because she has a sense she did not complete school, and now considers her need for completion has driven her to turn around failing schools, and to do a doctorate.

Maya enrolled in the Ed.D. with a cohort of students who were or had been educational leaders. Maya decided to do research on principals. She was interviewed as she had just finished her program. Her comments are reported in terms of the research questions on research disposition, values, and program impact.

RESEARCH DISPOSITION: CREDIBILITY

How do educational leaders report that the Ed.D. has had an impact on their research disposition?

Maya talked about her research in three ways. First, she gained a sense of completion as a successful human being, second, she developed the disposition of a researcher by being able to conduct systematic and rigorous research, and third, she became more reflective. We begin with the sense of completion the Ed.D. gave her.

> I did the Ed.D. because I left school at sixteen and I've been searching for completion ever since. I had to leave school at sixteen because I was a girl and my father was not very well. There was not a lot of money in the family and really I needed to go out ... You know what really interests me now is you bring yourself, my personal history and my background, my outlook, my emotional experiences and I have brought them into a situation which is damaged, a school that has failed is damaged. And I found that with other heads, there were other heads like me that went looking for these damaged places. A lot of those heads I met when I was interviewing them, had failed the 11 +, but had been driven by that ever since. Who obviously have the same desire for completion and recognition. So there is obviously a need in us that was met by that situation. I think I have got this big need for completion and in a school like this, I can complete on a big scale .... You know I have always enjoyed the job, but I do enjoy it now in the sense that I have not got anything else to prove to people in terms of academic qualification.

Second, the Ed.D. enabled her to develop a systematic and rigorous approach to conducting research that informed decision making and strategies in her leadership and management of the school staff.

> I think I was always interested in the power dimension because I am a historian by trade and I have read about the micro politics of school, that Steven Ball book which is just so wonderful isn't it? It's the first time you read a book about education that is actually like it actually is and that inspired me. I thought I want to write a thesis which is about what it is really like and not about theory of what it is like.

The third impact was becoming more reflective.

> Yes I think I am more reflective .... I think I have been keener to bring on other people's leadership skills. I have got two staff doing the Nation Professional Qualification of Headship (NPQH). They both came back the other day and they had their standard NPQH leadership theory. They were saying have you got a contingency view of leadership or, you know, some of those managerial theories? I gave them something out of Ket de Vries ....

Maya identifies that she has used her understanding of her values and disposition as a researcher to invite her colleagues to think about their practice as educational leaders using literature she thought might be useful.

> What I have done with them now is feed them with little bits of reading. I gave them Machiavelli the other week that gave them something to think about power, with a little note: "would you rather be feared or loved"? So I think I am trying to nurture that in them. The thing I have got against the National Professional Qualification for Headship (NPQH) is it does not examine its own stance and the Ed.D. certainly makes you look at lots of different stances ... it (the NPQH) is a sort of mono-culture.

VALUES: RESPECT AND INCLUSION

How do educational leaders report that the Ed.D. has had an impact on their values?

Maya's values centered on respect and inclusion of all groups, and she is keen to transform a damaged school into a healthy one so that the students and teachers can thrive. Although she did not share the same cultural identity of the diverse school community, Maya recognized the diversity within her school, celebrated it, and encouraged all students to realize their dreams. As such Maya was recognized and accepted by the school community as someone who they could trust.

> An Asian girl is under the threat of an arranged marriage if she does not get her qualifications to go onto A level. She is fine except for her maths and she is desperate to pass her maths, but she is a bit weak. So we keep giving her extra maths coaching, obviously because we do not want her to go back to Pakistan and have an arranged marriage if that is not what she wants. And I just thought poor kid, she's only sixteen. She has got huge obstacles ahead of her and I was just trying to boost her up and say of course you can, so when I got her report, I wrote … your education is a life's journey, make it when you can really. And yes, I feel for her, I wonder what the future holds for her then.

IMPACT OF THE PROGRAM

What aspects of the Ed.D. program do they cite as having the most impact?

Maya praised her doctoral program for the support from her dissertation supervisor, the new networks to which she was now connected, and the extensive library resources. Maya states of her supervisor:

> I had an HMI who came to this school, and his technique was to rattle your cage as hard as he damn well could and if you stood up he would then help you. I think there was an element of that with 'Name of Supervisor'. He would really seriously rattle you really unsettle you and then he would help you pick up the pieces, but you could have easily have given up at that point, it was a sort of test of commitment almost. You would come from school if I had to go down for a meeting with him I would walk in with my head full of school things and he would come out with something like; 'oh yes it is the heuristic fallacy you need to be considering here isn't it'? I had not got a clue what he was on about. My vocabulary is only in the basic five hundred words. I have not got these words … and that was one of my worries that I just would not have the facility with the vocabulary to manage it. I think I could do it if I was writing it but I was really worried about the Viva because I thought I will never be able to put this into

sophisticated enough terms and use that vocabulary of academic speak that they use so naturally. By and large you get through things and you learn from them. You know that you can learn from them, so I think I have probably reached a stage where I know that whatever happens I will have a reasonable go at making it work. You know, even though I have not experienced all the things that can happen, I have got that confidence .... Now I am a doctor. My chair of governors was lovely. He wrote a really nice letter and put it in all the local press.

Maya enjoyed the networking with other educational leaders:

and I liked meeting up with the other people in the group and that sort of sense of working on things together.

Maya found the library useful at the University, but did not find the local libraries useful. She knew that she wanted her thesis to become a public document.

I was really keen that I wrote something (my doctoral dissertation) that people would actually read. And I did not want it to be on a shelf somewhere in that part of the library; gender studies.

If Maya's experience was like other students' experiences, then this doctoral program could be inferred to have a signature pedagogy that put students into the field. Her laboratory of practice was her own school where she worked to transform the school culture, and for students to be part of a successful school community and have the chance to realize their dreams. The capstone project was the traditional dissertation which combined collection of data in the field with a multi-draft review by supportive faculty. The evidence reveals that in learning about herself, her own school, the experiences of other headteachers who have turned round failing schools, and the University values and dispositions, she has been able to function more effectively as a change agent. On "A Typology of Educational Leaders' Cultural Development as Ed.D. Signature Pedagogy," her learning and her growth locate her on the fifth stage of being able to function in a number of cultures with an appreciation for values, symbols, and institutions.

LOCATING MAYA ON A TYPOLOGY OF EDUCATIONAL LEADERS' CULTURAL DEVELOPMENT AS ED.D. SIGNATURE PEDAGOGY

Maya was multicultural because she could operate in her school community culture, the university Ed.D. program culture, and the culture of HMI.

Maya came from a working class background and had to leave school at 16 to find employment because her father was ill. Maya worked very hard to catch up on the education she missed because she was unable to continue at school, and considers that she failed and has been looking for completion. Maya turned around two large secondary schools which enabled her to give students the chance to build a life narrative that would enable them to engage in economic and cultural systems of production and exchange in informed ways. She also supported a student who faced leaving education to go to Pakistan if she did not get her maths qualification.

Maya initially did not trust that writing many drafts of chapters would help her. However, she came to accept the academic values of thoroughness and attention to detail, and she saw writing as a way to articulate her thoughts and to learn. She also saw the value of collecting and weighing data to make an argument. Her reward for adopting university values was the Ed.D., and having a direct impact on improving the education opportunities for students at her school. Maya wanted to share this approach with others and mentored her leadership team by facilitating their critical reflection on texts. Maya wanted the community members to apply their thinking to their practice in terms of whether they wanted to be a leader who is loved or hated. Maya considered that her own critical and reflective position that was developed on the Ed.D gave her the confidence to be able to face any situation and to know that she would do her best. Thus Maya found the culture of the school very important and wanted to develop community members' authentic engagement with the school processes and practices for school improvement.

Maya appears to have gone through cultural identity clarification in relation to the university. Initially she thought of herself as a failure because she had left school when she was 16. However, at the end she was more confident:

> you can learn ... so I think I have probably reached a stage where I know that whatever happens I will have a reasonable go at making it work. You know, even though I have not experienced all the things that can happen, I have got that confidence .... Now I am a doctor.

She was impatient with the dissertation process and wanted to engage in dialogues with her supervisor with appropriate language and grammar. By the end of the program, she had accepted the value of the process and embraced the academic mantel of the doctoral degree. The evidence reveals that in learning about the culture of administration, Maya has been able to function more effectively as a change agent and this represents her growth to the fifth stage of being able to function in a number of cultures with an appreciation for values, symbols, and institutions of "A Typology of Educational Leaders' Cultural Development as Ed.D. Signature Pedagogy."

COMPARING THE CASE OF MAYA AND MARTINA

Research Disposition: Credibility

Maya is an established headteacher who has turned around two secondary schools and has credibility with her peers, however, Maya wants to have the Ed.D. so that she does not have anything left to prove to herself or anyone else regarding her qualifications. Martina on the other hand is a teacher, and feels she needs the Ed.D. for credibility with school boards when she is fighting for her school community's rights. Therefore, both are motivated to get the Ed.D. to give them some kind of power to make others take them seriously and listen to them.

Both Maya and Martina identify that their vocabulary and grammar has changed and they can now use that language to communicate with others which is empowering, and gives them confidence. Part of the development of their vocabulary and grammar may be located in them having to write draft after draft which at the time they both found frustrating, but may have enabled them to rehearse their new vocabulary and its application to language to form meaningful and worthwhile sentences that enabled them to develop persuasive arguments. Maya expresses that she has become more reflective which is demonstrated with her recognizing her need to rescue others, which may be rooted in her need to rescue herself from a situation where she could not continue at school at the age of 16. Maya says she takes a reflective approach in mentoring her school leadership team which enables her to build capacity within her school system. Similarly, Martina demonstrates a highly reflective approach to her professional practice, where she states she could: 'hit the pavement' or in other words be pounding the streets, as an activist, rather than doing a doctorate. Here Martina has carefully considered how she could better spend her time to get the best outcomes for the marginalized community. However, her doctoral research enabled her to stop the school board from implementing policy that she showed to be illegal. Martina's careful reflection on how best to focus her energies was right because "hitting the pavement" would have been unlikely to have gained her the same outcome though Martina would have demonstrated the same desire for justice.

The signature pedagogy of the Ed.D. from Maya's and Martina's cases is the formal qualification that empowers people. The researcher's disposition is underpinned by a learned vocabulary and grammar that enables the presentation of persuasive arguments that effectively engage the opposition and are therefore critical. The researcher's disposition is also hallmarked by being reflective. In summary, a signature pedagogy of the Ed.D. is that it enables students to become critical and reflective, which empowers them to present persuasive arguments from which their confidence and self-belief flows (Taysum, 2012).

VALUES: RESPECT AND INCLUSION

Both Martina and Maya respected the members of their community. Maya gave a concrete example of how she respected an Asian member of her school community and included her, and tried to support her in her personal pathway to prosperity. Using a typology of educational leaders' cultural development as Ed.D. signature pedagogy, Maya is an interesting case, because she shares many characteristics of the community, but is not a member of the community. However, she can function in the school community culture, in the School Inspector's culture and the culture of the university Ed.D. program. Maya has led the way in affirming values of respect and inclusion and has focused on mentoring others to think about these values, and whether they would rather be hated or loved for example. We do not believe that Maya rejects her own community values. However, the evidence reveals that she was frustrated with the conditions of her working class position that meant that she did not have the capital to continue at school. Maya works to try to understand the community and provide an environment where colleagues are supported to enable the students to achieve and attain. Both Martina and Maya function in the University community. Therefore we suggest that Martina and Maya have similarities in that they can function effectively in different cultures, particularly their own culture, their school culture, and the university culture. These findings of fact locate Martina and Maya as multicultural on the typology. As such the cultural development of the US leader and the English leader are similar, which confirms the Ed.D. signature pedagogy of developing multicultural dispositions and values that impact on leaders' professional practice.

The signature pedagogy of the Ed.D. is developing researcher multicultural dispositions and values. Both Martina and Maya recognize and respect and/or can function in their own culture, and the culture of others, and work for cultural alignment (Taysum, 2013). The multicultural aspect of the Ed.D. journey enables them to develop as leaders and helps them to critique, reflect upon, and develop understandings of other cultures which enables them to move toward cultural alignment and engage with advocacy work, (Anderson, 2009) social justice, and work for deep democracy (Shields, 2013). Working for deep democracy involves critiquing and reflecting upon inequitable practices and working for cultural alignment that enables greater individual achievement and a better life with shared values, behaviors, symbols, and institutions that are in common with others (Shields, 2013). Shields continues that work for deep democracy will be different in different contexts and therefore cannot be prescribed. Rather it requires transformative leadership or agents of change to embed a few common principles and values of respect and inclusion that connect individual accountability with social responsibility.

IMPACT OF THE PROGRAM

The doctoral journey was challenging for both Maya and Martina. Maya said she had "her cage rattled" and Martina found writing and rewriting drafts frustrating. However, both have demonstrated resilience to keep going, and this has enabled them to gain self-confidence. The program also enabled Maya and Martina to develop networks of supportive colleagues made up of academics and peers. Thus it could be argued that a signature pedagogy of the Ed.D. put students into the field, with confidence. The Ed. D. facilitated engagement with clinical research in a laboratory of practice; their respective schools supported them with networks of academics and peers. The capstone project was the traditional dissertation, which combined collection of data in the field with a multi-draft review by supportive faculty.

A multicultural disposition can be developed with the thinking tools of being critical and reflective, which is a signature pedagogy of the doctorate. The doctorate may provide educational leaders with the opportunity of developing critical and reflective multicultural identities that equip them to negotiate power structures to work for deep democracy (Shields, 2013).

REFERENCES

Anderson, G. (2009). Advocacy leadership: Toward a post-reform agenda in education (Critical Social Thought). London: Routledge.

Banks, J. (1991). *Teaching strategies for ethnic studies* (5th ed.). Boston, MA: Allyn and Bacon.

Banks, J. (1998). The lives and values of researchers: Implications for educating citizens in a multicultural society in. *Educational Researcher, 27*(7), 4–17.

Blumenfeld-Jones, D. (1995). Fidelity as a criterion for practicing and evaluating narrative enquiry. In J. A. Hatch, & R. Wisniewski (Eds.), *Life history and narrative*. London: Falmer Press.

Bourdieu, P. (2000). *Pascalian meditations*. Cambridge: Polity Press.

Boyer, E. (1990). *Scholarship reconsidered: Priorities of the professoriate*. Princeton, NJ: The Carnegie Foundation for the Advancement of Teaching.

Brock, C., & Alexiadou, N. (2013). *Education around the world. A comparative introduction*. London: Bloomsbury.

Deem, R. (2012). The twenty-first-century university: Dilemmas of leadership and organizational futures. In A. Nelson & W. Ian (Eds.), *The global university* (pp. 105–132). New York, NY: Palgrave Macmillan.

Freire, P. (1972). *Pedagogy of the oppressed*. Harmondsworth: Penguin Press.

Goodson, I. (2012). *Developing narrative theory. Life histories and personal representation*. Kindle Edition.

Hutchings, P., & Shulman, L.S. (1999). The scholarship of teaching: New elaborations, new developments. *Change*, (October/November), 10–15.

Levine, A. (2005). *Educating school leaders*. The education schools project. Retrieved from http://files.eric.ed.gov/fulltext/ED504142.pdf. Accessed on February 27, 2014.

Lieberman, A., & Friedrich, L. (2010). *How teachers become leaders learning from practice and research*. New York, NY: Teachers College press.

Mill, J. S. (1859). On liberty. In M. Warnock (Ed.), *Utilitarianism*. London: Collins.

Newby, P. (2010). *Research methods for education*. Essex: Pearson Education Ltd.

Noddings, N. (1994). *A feminine approach to ethics and moral education*. London: University of California Press.

Perry, J. A. (2012). What does history reveal about the education doctorate? In L. Macintyre & S. Wunder (Eds.), *Placing practitioner knowledge at the center of teacher education: Rethinking the policy and practice of the education doctorate*. Charlotte, NC: Information Age Publishing.

Perry, J. A., & Imig, D. (2008). A steward of practice in education. *Change Magazine*, November/December.

Pring, R. (2000). *Philosophy of educational research*. London: Continuum.

Pring, R. (2011). Culture a neglected concept. In J. Elliott, & N. Norris (Eds.), *Curriculum pedagogy and educational research. The work of Lawrence Stenhouse* (pp. 49–60). London: Routledge.

Schulman, L. S. (2005). Signature pedagogies in the professions. *Daedalus, 134*(3), 52–59.

Shields, C. (2013, September). Leading creatively in high poverty schools: A Case for transformative leadership. *European conference for educational research*, Istanbul.

Shulman, L., Golde, M., Bueschel, A., & Garabedian, K. (2006). Reclaiming education's doctorates: A critique and a proposal. *Educational Researcher. American Educational Research Association, 35*(3), 26.

Taysum, A. (2012). *Evidence informed leadership in education*. London: Continuum.

Taysum, A. (2013). *Educational leaders' doctoral research that informed strategies to steer their organizations towards cultural alignment*. Educational Management, Administration and Leadership. Retrieved from http://EMA.sagepub.com/content/early/2013/09/24/1741143213496660.full.pdf+html. Accessed on October 3, 2013.

DEMOCRATIC CITIZENSHIP EDUCATION AND ISLAMIC EDUCATION: ON SCEPTICAL DOCTORAL ENCOUNTERS

Yusef Waghid

ABSTRACT

Purpose — *There is a dearth of literature dealing with Islamic education that embeds the notion of democratic citizenship education for at least two reasons: firstly, democratic citizenship education is not always considered as commensurable with Islamic education and secondly, Islamic education is aimed at producing just persons, whereas democratic citizenship education aims to engender responsible citizens.*

Methodology/approach — *My approach is philosophical/analytical and argumentative.*

Findings — *I argue that the two concepts do not have to be considered as mutually exclusive and that cultivating just persons invariably involves producing responsible persons. Hence, as my first argument I show that through the practices of Islamic education, which is just action (ijtihād), deliberative engagement (shūrā) and recognition of the other (ta`āruf),*

Investing in our Education: Leading, Learning, Researching and the Doctorate
International Perspectives on Higher Education Research, Volume 13, 171–186
Copyright © 2014 by Emerald Group Publishing Limited
ISSN: 1479-3628/doi:10.1108/S1479-362820140000013008

democratic citizenship education has the potential to enhance the pursuit of a doctorate on the basis that the latter connects with multiple forms of enactment. My second argument relates to offering some sceptical encounters with a doctoral candidate, in particular showing how just action (ijtihād), deliberative engagement (shūrā) and recognition of the other (ta`āruf) were manifested in our encounters. Drawing on the seminal thoughts of Stanley Cavell (1997), particularly his ideas on 'living with scepticism', I argue that doctoral supervision in the knowledge fields of democratic citizenship education and Islamic education ought to be an encounter framed by scepticism.

Research limitations − *Although I combine philosophical and narrative inquiry, I do not consistently accentuate various dimensions of the latter − that is, narrative inquiry, as well as drawing on other cases of my supervision.*

Practical implications − *I envisage that the commensurability argued for between democratic citizenship education and Islamic education can impact the supervision of doctoral candidates.*

Originality/value − *I point out that supervising students sceptically might engender moments of acknowledging humanity within the Other (autonomous action or ijtihād), experiencing attachment to the Other's points of view with a readiness for departure (deliberative engagement or shūrā) and showing responsibility to the Other (recognition of the other or ta`āruf). In turn, I show how sceptical encounters along the lines of autonomous action, deliberative engagement and responsibility towards the other connect, firstly, with liberal education and secondly, the possibilities of such encounters for Muslims involved in advocating for just and/ or responsible action.*

Keywords: Democracy; citizenship; encounters; Islam; education

ON THE COMMENSURABILITY BETWEEN ISLAMIC EDUCATION AND DEMOCRATIC CITIZENSHIP EDUCATION: IMPLICATIONS FOR THE DOCTORATE

At first glance, it might seem as if the rationales for both Islamic education and democratic citizenship education are incommensurable. For obvious reasons, this seems to be the case because Islamic education has its roots in primary sources of revelation (i.e. Qurān and Sunnah — the Word of God and practices of Prophet Muhammad, respectively), whereas democratic citizenship education is guided by liberal thought. However, without suggesting that these two different conceptions of education are equal or the same, one finds, on closer examination, that to some extent there might be greater commensurability between the two notions than would be expected, particularly on the grounds of their practical orientations. Although Islamic education is meant to engender just persons — that is, persons of *adab* (just action), democratic citizenship education aims to cultivate persons who can enact iterations (listen and talk back to one another), recognise one another's rights in terms of differences and similarities and recognise that people have the right to live their lives according to what they deem to be fit and not according to how someone envisages it for them. More specifically, a person of *adab* is one who acts with 'the discipline of the body, soul and mind in order to act with justice and to ensure that everything is in its right and proper place' (Al-Attas, 1991). It therefore follows from this that such a person's actions cannot be distanced from enacting justice towards self and others. In this way, *adab* (just action) becomes a way of enacting justice towards society, which is an idea not foreign to the Qurānic injunction (*amāl al-sālihāt*, the doing of righteous deeds) of benefit to the society at large. *Adab* (just action) seems to be a desirable practice that can raise the consciousness of people against forms of human rights violations and atrocious acts perpetrated against humanity. There is no doubt that, in the African continent, the societal ills in certain communities, such as perpetual genocide, rape, mass enslavement, political dictatorships, xenophobic violence and religious intolerance, are calling for some form of just intervention that can deter people from acting violently against societies. Similarly, a responsible person, as envisaged by a democratic citizenship education framing, is one who engages the other freely, openly and critically about solving societal problems, holds open a space for non-instrumental thinking (i.e. thinking that is concerned with the intrinsic worth of just and autonomous actions) and constantly resists or disrupts practices that move towards completion (i.e. practices that recognise that there is always something new to be learnt and that nothing is perfect and completed) (Derrida, 2001, pp. 35–36). Consequently, both a person of *adab* (just action) and a responsible person are intent on achieving fair and autonomous action aimed at resolving particular societal problems. Hence, it follows that a just person (a person of *adab*) can also be a responsible person, which makes the rationales for Islamic education and democratic citizenship education quite commensurable.

Now that I have shown that the rationales for Islamic education and democratic citizenship education connect, I shall examine how instances of Islamic education, such as autonomous action (*ijtihād*), deliberative engagement (*shūrā*) and recognition of the other (*ta`āruf*), have the potential to enhance the pursuit of a doctorate on the basis that the latter connects with multiple forms of enactment. Firstly, autonomous action (*ijtihād*) involves the capacity of people to reach their own justifiable conclusions, for which they are to be held accountable by and to others – referred to by MacIntyre (1999, p. 83) as the ability to evaluate, modify or reject one's own practical judgments. People develop the capacities of evaluation and modification, that is, what others consider to be sufficiently good reasons for acting and for imagining alternative possibilities, so as to be able to rationally re-educate themselves – to become practical reasoners (MacIntyre, 1999, p. 83). By implication, doctoral supervisors act autonomously when they encourage themselves and students to develop the capacities of evaluation and modification, that is, students are taught to become 'reflective and independent members' of the society and are imbued with virtues that allow them to act imaginatively as individuals and members of groups. Thus, autonomous action has the task of initiating students into a 'community of thinking'. In the words of Derrida (2004, pp. 148–150), 'this [community of] thinking must ... prepare students to take new analyses' and 'to transform the modes of writing, the pedagogic scene, the procedures of academic exchange, the relation to languages, to other disciplines, to the institution in general, to its inside and its outside'. Also, a 'community of thinking' would go beyond the 'profound and the radical' (Derrida, 2004, p. 153). The enactment of such thinking is 'always risky; it always risks the worst' (Derrida, 2004, p. 153). A community of thinking that goes 'beyond' with the intention of taking more risks would become more attentive to unimagined possibilities, unexpected encounters and perhaps the lucky find. Nothing is impossible because it opens the university not only 'to the outside and the bottomless, but also ... to any sort of interest' (Derrida, 2004, p. 153). And, if students and supervisors are prepared to take more risks, what seems to be unattainable could well be achieved easily. Certainly in South Africa, where the moral fabric of post-apartheid society is withering away, universities require thoughtful, highly inspired and risky research contributions that can address issues of racism, gender inequality, patriarchy, domestic violence and the HIV and AIDS pandemic – that is, research for non-instrumental purposes. Risky efforts would enhance the possibility of highly contemplative and theoretical contributions that go beyond practical usefulness and provide us with more to know than any other instrumentalist form of action (Derrida, 2004, p. 130). I am thinking particularly of the need for risky intellectual contributions in cosmopolitanism, which might address the sporadic xenophobic outbursts in South Africa.

Secondly, doctoral supervisors embarking on deliberative engagement (*shūrā*) afford students the opportunities to engage in public deliberation. They are taught about their rights to various speech acts, to initiate new topics and to ask for justification for the pre-suppositions of the conversation (Benhabib, 2002, p. 107). Public deliberation takes place when students speak their minds (but only up to the point where injustice to others begins) and no one has the right to silence dissent (Callan, 1997, p. 215). Public deliberation is different from debate and discussion or conversation. Although debate involves offering arguments for or against points of view, it does not necessarily imply that people should reach some consensus or dissensus about the topic under scrutiny in the debate – that is, a debate does not necessarily have a fixed outcome. Similarly, discussion or conversation can go on endlessly without the participants reaching any form of conclusion. In fact, participants in discussion do not have to be attentive to one another's points of view. The point about public deliberation is that there can be a temporary conclusion, whether consensus or dissensus, with the possibility that something new and different can emerge. In a way, a public deliberation is reflexive in the sense that there need not be any fixed, final or conclusive outcome (as some doctorates want to be presented). The possibility should always exist for new meanings to unfold.

Thirdly, recognition of the other (*ta`āruf*) implies that a doctorate also initiates supervisors and students into discourses about rights to the protection of life, liberty and property, the right to freedom of conscience and certain associational rights (Benhabib, 2002, pp. 163–164), of course in relation to education. Through an understanding of recognising others, students are taught that, to enjoy these rights, they should accept appropriate responsibility for the rights of others and not just make a fuss about their own rights (Callan, 1997, p. 73). Thus, to be educated as a just or responsible person involves being initiated into a process of recognising the legitimate rights of others, whether these are social, cultural, political or economic rights. The point about recognising these rights occurs concomitantly with the responsibility to ensure that these rights are attained and not just given lip service. The upshot of such a view of recognising the rights of others is that students are initiated into discourses aimed at contributing to changing undesirable and unjust situations in the society, particularly those related to gender inequality, religious bigotry, mass starvation and hunger, and political dictatorships – after all, a doctorate is not just meant to remain on the shelves of universities but actually to engender meaningful change in the society.

In the following section, I expound on my sceptical encounter with a doctoral candidate with the aim to show how autonomous action, deliberative engagement and recognition of the other possibly manifest.

A SCEPTICAL DOCTORAL ENCOUNTER: ON THE MANIFESTATION OF AUTONOMOUS ACTION (*IJTIHĀD*), DELIBERATIVE ENGAGEMENT (*SHŪRĀ*) AND RECOGNITION OF THE OTHER (*TA`ĀRUF*)

I now offer a narrative account of my sceptical encounter with Nerina – a doctoral candidate I supervised over a three-year period – where scepticism refers to raising doubts about the encounter. Drawing on the seminal thoughts of Harvard philosopher Stanley Cavell (1997), particularly on his ideas on 'living with scepticism', I argue that postgraduate student supervision ought to be an encounter framed by scepticism. I point out that supervising students sceptically might engender moments of acknowledging humanity within the Other (autonomous action), developing attachment to the Other's points of view with a readiness for departure (deliberative engagement) and showing responsibility to the Other (recognition of the other).

Acknowledging Humanity within the Other

It seems quite apposite to use Cavell's depiction of one's relationship with the Other to attend to postgraduate student supervision; in this instance, some of the experiences with doctoral students and my pedagogical encounters with Nerina over three years. Central to one's connection with the Other is the view that one has to acknowledge humanity in the Other, of which the basis for such action lies in oneself: 'I have to acknowledge humanity in the other, and the basis of it seems to lie in me' (Cavell, 1979, p. 433). Nerina became a doctoral student on the basis of having been introduced to me by a colleague. Her eagerness to pursue doctoral studies, coupled with her critical acumen, astuteness and independence of mind, made an indelible impression on me to the extent that I was persuaded to begin a doctoral journey with her.

Hailing from Cape Town, she had completed (i.e. had complied with institutional regulations) her Master's degree at another South African university and subsequently applied to Stellenbosch University to pursue doctoral studies under my supervision, on the grounds that my area of educational research connected with her own interests in democracy and citizenship education. Since Nerina is an intelligent, proud and hard-working person, we soon connected and developed a mutually respectful, trustworthy and impeccable professional relationship. The fact that our friendship developed so remarkably over the three years is a profound testimony to how both of us recognised our humanity within ourselves and in association with one another. As further recognition of humanity within her, our institution supported her to attend the Annual Philosophy of Education Society of Great Britain Conference (Oxford) – a visit that exposed her to other philosophies of education students and academics abroad. The conversations at Oxford further and significantly influenced her understanding of and writing on democratic citizenship and cosmopolitan education in relation to Islamic education.

Thus, our friendship was consolidated further, primarily because she felt that I had acknowledged her as a fellow human being. In acknowledging others as human beings worthy of respect, one should simultaneously acknowledge oneself as a person who should exercise respect. This is what I think Cavell (1979, p. 435) has in mind when he claims: '[A]nother may be owed acknowledgement simply on the ground of his humanity, acknowledgement as a human being, for which nothing will do but my revealing myself to him [her] as a human being, unrestrictedly, as his or her sheer other, his or her fellow, his or her *semblable*. – Surely this is, if anything, nothing more than half the moralists whoever wrote have said, that others count, in our moral calculations, simply as persons; or that we have duties to others of a universal kind, duties to them apart from any particular stations we occupy.' I considered myself to be her '*semblable*' who would later invite her to review articles for a journal of which I am the editor. For me, Nerina possesses the analytical and evaluative competence and skills to perform excellent reviews, and I always enjoy her caring and often uncompromising judgements of others' work – that is, her autonomous action in commenting on other people's academic work that is very similar to her authoring of her own doctoral text.

Attachment with a Readiness for Departure

Of course, as supervisors we are responsible to affect changes in the lives of our students, so we teach them to be civil. And this I have done through exposing Nerina to academic writings that aim to cultivate democratic iterations (learning to talk back), citizenship rights and cosmopolitan justice, particularly in relation to the production of dissertations that aim to contribute towards justice in and about (Islamic) education. But this does not mean that we ought to censure students' actions so that we determine in advance what they ought to research in order to connect their work with achieving civility or what consequences they may be faced with if they do not write theses that connect with issues of civility (e.g. having their work rejected by me). Teaching our students to connect with issues of civility, following Cavell, makes us 'open to complete surprise at what we have done' (1979, p. 325). In other words, supervisors and students can be initiated into practices concerning what is morally good for the society but with the possibility that what is perceived as good for the society is always in the making, continuously subjected to modifications and adaptations. For instance, it may be morally good for the society to produce work (theses) about advancing a common understanding of Islamic education – and we may decide this in advance. But when a common understanding of Islamic education is not shared by some Muslim homosexuals (some of Nerina's interviewees), interactions with them may result in moments of excluding the Other and otherness. Nerina's thesis departs from making arguments for excluding otherness, and hence seems to come into a conflict with a common understanding of Islamic education, that is, what seems to be desirable for the broader public good. The point I am making is that my thoughts alone did not influence Nerina's thesis. Her independence of mind and critical insights determined the thoughts that went into the formulation of arguments. Thus, when I supervise students I initiate them into relevant forms of life – that is, by showing them what I say and do and accepting what they say and do as what we say and do. To put it differently: supervisors tell themselves and others (students) how they must go about things without predicting this or that performance. Cavell (1979, p. 179) makes the point that 'the authority one has, or assumes, in expressing statements of initiation ... is related to the authority one has in expressing or declaring one's promises or intentions'. So, when students are supervised they are initiated into a form of life intended by the supervisor. This also implies that students can subvert these forms of life as they wish. They may be transformed by the practice of supervision and may also subvert this practice in order to give themselves other opportunities – such as those unintended actions of the practice. I often found that Nerina produced revised chapters in which the intended, agreed upon outcomes had not been attained at all.

Responsibility to the Other

Cavell's remark, 'we are alone, and we are never alone', is a clear indication that one does belong to a particular group (being alone with others, i.e. 'we') and that, by virtue of being human, one bears an internal relation to all other human beings – especially those who might not belong to the same group as one. This internal relation with my fellow human beings does not ignore my answerability to/responsibility for what happens to them, although I do not belong to the same group as they do. As a member of a particular cultural group in society I cannot just impose my views (albeit religious or political) on others, for that in itself would deny that there are others in different positions (with different cultural orientations) to mine. Doing so would be doing an injustice to others. But being answerable to/responsible for what happens to them means that their views are acknowledged, although I might not be in agreement with them. Rather, one conceives the other from the other's point of view, with which one has to engage afresh (Cavell, 1979, p. 441). Initially, I challenged Nerina's singular understanding of normative Islamic education. Yet I acknowledged her views, although I might have been in stark disagreement with them. In doing so, I did not compromise my relations with her, for that would mean a complete breakdown of professional friendship. From my own vantage point, I might find another person's views repugnant (what Cavell would refer to as 'living my scepticism'), but this does not mean that I view this person as being unworthy of any form of engagement. That would be an abdication of my responsibility. The point I am making is that, as a human being, I can distinguish firmly between my understandings of a practice and the understandings others have of the same practice. But this does not mean that I compromise my humanitarianism to others – a matter of exercising my responsibility to them. For instance, Nerina queried my understanding of a normative conception of Islamic education. I was obliged to find ways to engage with her with the intention of making her understand what I consider as a justifiable conception of the practice or if I find her lack of seeing my viewpoint to be untenable, I should have responsibly made known to her what was seemingly unknown. I am not suggesting that Nerina had to be responsive to my views in an uncritical way. Rather, I challenged her to raise doubts about her own understandings of the Islamic faith and not always to take things for granted, to the extent that she drafted and re-drafted her research in order for herself to see things as they could be otherwise. I did not offer an alternative to her views but encouraged her to question her own views and to raise doubts about her own understandings – a matter of becoming sceptical herself.

In demonstrating one's responsibility towards others, one immediately acknowledges one's capacity for intimacy with others – thereby limiting one's idiosyncratic privacy. It is for this reason that Cavell (1979, p. 463) claims that 'human beings do not necessarily desire isolation and incomprehension, but union or reunion, call it community'. If my privacy remains restricted to me with the intention not to exercise my responsibility to others, my practices would remain unshared and separated from the people with whom I happen to engage. So, my privacy opens a door through which someone else can tap into my thoughts – which might be of benefit to the person concerned or to the society at large. But if my privacy is prompted by narcissism, the possibility that others might gain something valuable for the good of society might be stunted. If I were to reflect more on my academic encounters with Nerina, then I would only be able to refer to two articles I co-authored with her. These works grew out of our doctoral engagement and she is recognised as the first (primary) author. My responsibility towards her as a supervisor was also to contribute towards creating conditions for her self-empowerment – and, when she saw her name linked to mine as the primary author of peer-reviewed journal articles, she smiled. I knew then that my responsibility towards her had taken on a new dimension. Subsequently, I asked her to co-author two more articles and two book chapters. Again, my responsibility towards her took another turn.

In Cavellian fashion, I have learnt that supervisors ought to be responsible human beings with regard to their students. Responsibility towards one's students implies that one has to create opportunities for them to think, argue and write their texts at a doctoral level. Writing is a truly laborious, yet imaginative, exercise. I have taught students to continue writing even though the comments they receive would at times not be as encouraging as they might have expected. Finally, I have realised that student supervision is about building a friendly relationship between the supervisor and the student – one that can bring forth the articulations of both in an atmosphere of mutual trust, respect and responsibility. My three years of working with Nerina can be considered as a sceptical encounter with the Other. This implies that one needs to experience the Other as a culturally situated being, one needs to engage deliberatively – and at times belligerently so – with the Other through reading, authoring, reflecting and presenting and one needs to establish opportunities for the Other to be present in his or her becoming. Of course, my pedagogical encounters with

Nerina have not been without complexities and contradictions – that is, without scepticism. She usually became annoyed with me for sometimes over-zealously commenting on her work. Yet, at times, my rigorous feedback did not discourage her (I think) from completing her work. In a way, her doctoral work has taken seriously the work of argumentation – what a thesis should actually be doing. Many South African doctoral studies (and I have examined a few) focus too much on techniques of educational research instead of applying the techniques while doing a research. That is, generally, too many studies are concerned with letting one know what procedures of research have been applied in education, yet these studies do not always develop consistent argumentation. My connection with Nerina has always privileged the argumentative route, with the result that her study has often been lauded as theoretically rigorous. However, her study did not and should not ignore the technical and professional use of procedures of educational research, but I would advocate that less emphasis should be placed on these techniques and more on the arguments that should emanate as a result of using the techniques. Too often, many students write a chapter on techniques that seem to be unrelated to the arguments that ensue in their theses. In a way, students should work (like Nerina has done) on the techniques with a readiness to depart from their often pedantic use – a matter of becoming sceptical.

IMPLICATIONS OF AUTONOMOUS ACTION (*IJTIHĀD*), DELIBERATIVE ENGAGEMENT (*SHŪRĀ*) AND RECOGNITION OF THE OTHER (*TAʿĀRUF*) FOR LIBERAL EDUCATION AND THE WORK OF MUSLIMS ADVOCATING FOR COSMOPOLITAN ENACTMENTS

Thus far, my argument has been in defence of reading a doctorate through the use of autonomous action, deliberative engagement and recognition of the other. And not many involved with the doctorate would want to argue against their use. I shall now examine their implications for liberal education. In the first place, autonomous action ought to be an important educative practice of a liberal education (and its doctorate), and cannot just be about imposing one's views on others, as the acquisition of mastery (through achieving a formal technical qualification) requires most of the time. Nevertheless, many students still demonstrate an inability to

understand and reflect on, and show inaptitude to change, conflicting situations in their communities. Mastery represents a form of completion, an
end to learning (this does not mean that a qualification in itself should not
be completed procedurally to comply with institutional regulations), and
points towards a position of finality and closure. In contrast, autonomous
action entails engaging with others by offering some justification for one's
reasons. In turn, others should be persuaded or dissuaded by one's reasons.
If others find one's reasons palatable or unpalatable, this could only be on
the basis of the justifications offered to them. An autonomous practice is
the one underpinned by norms of justification through making one's point
clearer to others, who in turn offer an account of their reasons for agreeing
or disagreeing with one's arguments. This kind of discourse ethics makes
education more deliberative as others are afforded opportunities to engage
with or disengage from one's point of view.

Secondly, deliberative engagement requires that liberal education be
considered as the continuous perpetuation of iterative learning communities in which supervisors and students engage in meaningful work, the
subjects studied would generate new understandings and learning would be
mediated through active experimentation (Alexander in Gray, 2006,
p. 320). In fact, students would be encouraged to be reflective about why
their way of thinking is desirable (or not), and these communities would be
engaging in genuine learning as opposed to mechanical learning (Alexander
in Gray, 2006, p. 321). Through deliberative engagement, liberal education
would be understood as a moral activity that seeks to strengthen the moral
agent within, empowering students to make moral choices more intelligently on their own. This may involve some training but should culminate
in understanding and independence that are expressed concretely (Gray,
2006, p. 321).

Thirdly, recognising the other invariable demands that we reconstitute
the place of critique in liberal education. That is, we need to invoke critique
again. The value of critique (as an instance of a means of recognising the
other) finds itself rightfully associated with 'thinking' that is no longer
determined by an obsession with techno-economic performativity – that is,
that kind of activity that encourages 'technicians of learning' to usurp the
right to judge and decide on the performance of their professions without
being subjected to the authority and censorship of the (liberal) university
and its faculties (Derrida, 2004, p. 97). For me, as for Derrida, critique is a
form of dissonance and questioning that is not dominated and intimidated
by the power of performativity. 'This thinking must also unmask – an
infinite task – all the ruses of end-orienting reason, the paths by which

apparently disinterested research can find itself indirectly re-appropriated, reinvested by programs of all sorts' (Derrida, 2004, p. 148). This is basically always asking: 'What is at stake (in technology, the sciences, production and productivity)?' It is a kind of critique that allows us to take more risks, and to deal openly with the radical incommensurability of the language games that constitute our society, and that invites new possibilities to emerge. Critique is a matter of enhancing the possibility of dissent and the diversity of interpretations, of complicating what is taken for granted and pointing to what has been overlooked in establishing identities, and it is an active opening up of your own thought structures that is necessary for other ways to find an entrance (Burik, 2009, pp. 301–304). Put differently, it is pursuing a liberal education because the latter is innately concerned with creating possibilities for dissent and a diversity of interpretations, complicating the taken-for-granted and opening up to the other.

Finally, I offer some remarks on the task of Muslims working in liberal educational contexts advocating for just or responsible action. What I have been arguing for thus far is that being autonomous, deliberative and together with others involves just and/or responsible action – both rationales of Islamic education and democratic citizenship education. These practices offer oneself and others a better opportunity to learn. What such practices have in mind is to create conditions in terms of which genuine learning can take place – one learns to experience the other and that, in turn, rules out the possibility that the other can remain a stranger to one. But then one learns to take responsibility for the other. It is this practice of assuming responsibility for the other through learning (including the practices of Muslims working in liberal educational environments) that I now wish to pursue in order to find out how one's relationship with the other potentially could be enhanced. For this discussion, I again turn to the seminal thoughts of Jacques Derrida.

Derrida (2001) maintains that it is the responsibility of the modern university to be 'unconditional', by which he means that it should have the freedom to assert, question and profess. In other words, for Derrida (2001), the future of the profession of academics is determined by 'the university without conditions'. Put differently, Derrida frames the profession of those academics who work at the university as a responsibility. This responsibility to profess is no longer associated with a profession of faith, a vow or a promise, but rather is an engagement: 'to profess is to offer a guide in the course of engaging one's responsibility' (Derrida, 2001, p. 35). So, an unconditional university is one that enacts its responsibility of engagement. And, if learning is one of the practices associated with a university, learning per se should also be about enacting a responsibility. Derrida connects the idea of responsibility to the university, but I now specifically want to make an argument for learning along the lines of his conception of responsibility. This is not to say that he does not link responsibility to learning but rather that I want to make the argument for responsibility a corollary of learning in a more nuanced way than Derrida seemingly does.

From my reading of Derrida's idea of responsibility, I infer three features that are central to what could underscore learning: responsibility means to engage the other freely, openly and critically, to act responsibly is to hold open a space for non-instrumental thinking and to be responsible is to constantly resist or disrupt practices that move towards completion (Derrida, 2001, pp. 35–36). What are the implications of responsible action for learning? Firstly, a responsible learner (one who has learnt) concerns himself or herself with social problems. Responsible learners endeavour to argue openly, freely and critically with others in an attempt to solve social problems. Such a form of learning provides a sphere in which genuine critical discourse (investigation and debate as against mere textbook transmission) takes place, and at the same time is likely to produce activities of 'value' in addressing societal problems. In this way, students (as learners) are taught to be critically reflective about society and simultaneously can contribute towards the achievement of, say, improved nutrition and health services, more secure livelihoods and security against crime and physical violence. In a way, responsible learners are responsible citizens who are intellectually, culturally and technologically adept and committed to addressing social problems.

Secondly, for a responsible learner to attend to non-instrumental thinking means that such a learner does not merely perform his or her responsibility for the sake of something else, for instance physical needs, reputation and gratitude. Such instrumental actions would render responsibility conditional. The responsible learner is concerned with the intrinsic worth of his or her actions (and not with the convenient applications of his or her research) and is engaged in just, autonomous, non-instrumental activities. Such learners' actions are not rooted in dubious motives and/or interests. Here, I agree with Haverhals (2007, p. 425), who claims that such learners would enhance 'the development of personal autonomy, which also has a public significance'. The public role of such a learner and the educative value of his or her activities are affected by a legitimate concern to act responsibly.

Thirdly, a responsible learner constantly disrupts or resists the possibility that knowledge production has moved towards or attained completion.

Such irresponsible actions would ignore the contingency and unpredictability of actions themselves. A responsible learner always strives to embark on new narratives in the making, or perhaps moves towards some unimagined possibility. And, for this, responsible learners constantly think of themselves as projects in the making – their work cannot attain completion and perfection. There is always something more to learn, which, of course, enhances how one potentially can respond as a responsible learner to the dilemmas that confront communities.

BIOGRAPHICAL NOTE

Yusef Waghid is a distinguished professor of Philosophy of Education at Stellenbosch University in South Africa. His research focuses on philosophy of education, Islamic education, democratic citizenship education, cosmopolitan education and higher education transformation. He is the author of the books *Conceptions of Islamic education: Pedagogical framings* (New York: Peter Lang, 2011), (co-authored) *Citizenship, education and violence: On disrupted potentialities and becoming* (Rotterdam/Boston/Taipei: Sense Publishers, 2013), *African philosophy of education reconsidered: On being human* (London: Routledge, 2014) and *Pedagogy out of bounds: Untamed variations of democratic education* (Rotterdam/Boston/Taipei: Sense Publishers, 2014).

REFERENCES

Al-Attas, M. N. (1991). *The concept of education in Islam*. Kuala Lumpur: The International Institute of Islamic Thought and Civilisation.

Benhabib, S. (2002). *The claims of culture: Equality and diversity in the global era*. Princeton, NJ: Princeton University Press.

Burik, S. (2009). Opening philosophy to the world: Derrida and education in philosophy. *Educational Theory, 59*(3), 297–312.

Callan, E. (1997). *Creating citizens: Political education and liberal democracy*. Oxford: Oxford University Press.

Cavell, S. (1979). *The claim of reason: Wittgenstein, skepticism, morality, and tragedy*. Oxford: Clarendon Press.

Cavell, S. (1997). *The claim of reason: Wittgenstein, skepticism, morality and tragedy*. New York, NY: Oxford University Press.

Derrida, J. (2001). The future of the profession or the unconditional university (thanks to the 'Humanities', what could take place tomorrow. In L. Simmons, & H. Worth (Eds.), *Derrida down-under*. Palmerston North, New Zealand: Dunmore Press.

Derrida, J. (2004). *Eyes of the university: Right to philosophy 2*. In J. Plug (Trans.), Stanford, CA: Stanford University Press.

Gray, K. (2006). Spirituality, critical thinking, and the desire for what is infinite. *Studies in Philosophy and Education, 24*(5), 315–326.

Haverhals, B. (2007). The normative foundations of research-based education: Philosophical notes on the transformation of the modern university idea. *Studies in Philosophy and Education, 26*(5), 419–432.

MacIntyre, A. (1999). *Dependent rational animals: Why human beings need the virtues*. Peru, IL: Open Court.

DEVELOPING NODES IN LEADING NETWORKS OF KNOWLEDGE FOR LEADER AND LEADERSHIP DEVELOPMENT: SOME AFRICAN STUDENTS' PERSPECTIVES ON THEIR EXPERIENCE OF DOCTORAL EDUCATION

Emefa Takyi-Amoako

ABSTRACT

Purpose — *The purpose of this chapter, which is a response to calls to examine students' perspectives of the doctoral experience, is to investigate the notion that doctoral education facilitates developing nodes in leading networks of knowledge for leader and leadership development — a theme that has not been examined.*

Design/methodology/approach — *Using data generated from in-depth interviews embedded with excerpts of personal life stories and the*

Investing in our Education: Leading, Learning, Researching and the Doctorate
International Perspectives on Higher Education Research, Volume 13, 187–211
Copyright © 2014 by Emerald Group Publishing Limited
All rights of reproduction in any form reserved
ISSN: 1479-3628/doi:10.1108/S1479-362820140000013009

questionnaire, this qualitative study analyses the views of some African students about their experiences of doctoral study in the United Kingdom.

Findings — *The study discovered that doctoral education is perceived as: acquisition of knowledge and capabilities for professional leadership trajectories; creator of learning communities, networks and relationship resources; developing nodes in leading knowledge networks; progression from the self to the relational and to the collective; and action learning, all for leader and leadership development.*

Originality/value — *Drawing on the findings, the chapter argues for the novel notion of doctoral education as developing nodes within leading networks of knowledge for leader and leadership development.*

Research limitations/implications — *Although, the research is a qualitative study that focused on a small group of students in one university, and as a result, its findings cannot be generalised, its implication for doctoral agendas worldwide and Africa and its* Agenda 2063, *in particular, need consideration.*

Keywords: Doctoral education; Doctor of Philosophy/PhD/doctorate; African students; developing node; networks of knowledge; leader and leadership development

INTRODUCTION

The chapter argues that exploring the perspectives of African doctoral students on their experiences of the doctorate in the United Kingdom is relevant because it responds to the observation that, by and large, research on students' views of the doctoral experience has been inadequate (Leonard, Metcalfe, Becker, & Evans, 2006). Accordingly, it examines the findings from a study that explored the experiences of 11 African doctoral students at a research intensive UK University from their perspectives. One aim of this qualitative study is to understand what it means for an international student, particularly, one from Africa to obtain a doctorate in the United Kingdom since it has policy, market, pastoral, knowledge economy and training implications.

It was discovered that while all the African students who participated in the study experienced a few challenges, they perceived their doctoral experiences as largely positive, as an opportunity to experience leader and leadership development within expert networks. Using data generated from in-depth interviews embedded with excerpts of personal life stories and the qualitative questionnaire, as well as drawing on relevant leadership and network literature, this chapter analyses the views of 11 African students about their experiences of doctoral study in the United Kingdom. It illustrates how the doctorate effects their investment in their development as leaders and as nodes in a network in their field(s), and creates opportunities for them to develop lifelong networks that enable them to span disciplines within their local, national, regional, continental and global societies which is essential when fusing ideas within systems of governance. How this connects with the African strategy as a continent to build capacity for leadership and high quality decision making for its people at governance level is crucial.

This is a chapter, which focuses on the leadership development aspects of the doctorate, and it is organised into five main parts. First, it contextualises the study by providing a brief background on the doctorate and the prominent position that it occupies in the economic development process of nations, regions and continents globally. Second, it discusses the conceptual framework through relevant literature that connects doctoral studies with leader and leadership development in the context of networks. Third, it outlines the research approach. Fourth, it reports the study's findings, and draws on them and relevant existing literature to demonstrate and argue that the African doctoral student represents a developing node in a leading network of knowledge for leader and leadership development through the doctorate. Finally, the chapter recaps the discussion and illustrates how the findings of the study connect with the African strategy as a continent to build capacity for leadership.

BACKGROUND

The Significance of the Doctorate

Currently, the doctorate occupies a prominent position in higher education and research policies worldwide. In Europe, for instance, doctoral education reforms have been an important element of the Bologna Process and considered crucial to generating "smart, sustainable and inclusive growth", according to the European Commission's *Europe 2020 Strategy* (European

Commission [EC], 2010; Jørgensen, 2012, p. 8). Jørgensen (2012) maintains that emphasis is on doctoral candidates being trained by means of research but competent to pursue any of the wide-ranging professions, so as to render the fields into which they gain admittance more 'knowledge-intensive'. Developing and emerging nations are giving greater consideration to doctoral education policies as their fast growing higher education sectors need more highly qualified staff that possess strong research capability and other relevant expertise. Simultaneously, the character of higher education and research worldwide is shifting. While, formerly, the North Atlantic (US, Europe, Australia and Japan) dominance in delivering graduate education and magnetising international students was unequivocal, now, India, China and Brazil have surfaced as important centres of knowledge and are defying the belief of a 'Northern' supremacy in this sphere – even though they have anything but routed it. Additionally, other developing countries are also spending substantially on graduate education and showing extraordinary progress paths regarding the doctorate and research productivity and an overall ability to draw global talent. Graduate education, Jørgensen (2012) observes, is thus assuming multipolar dimensions with its centre of gravity steadily shifting away from the North Atlantic. In spite of this contest for research expertise, doctoral education is instantaneously turning out to be more collaborative on an international magnitude, as communication, information sharing and physical movement have been hugely enhanced (Jørgensen, 2012).

What appears like a dispersed terrain for the delivery of doctoral training is essentially steered by powerful waves merging, within which similar concerns and occurrences are evident across separate regions. The connection between economic progress and funding of research and development is now virtually a general fact, normally irrespective of national and regional settings (Jørgensen, 2012).

In spite of the distinctions between developed and developing countries, both are stressing the importance of local knowledge in providing solutions to the specific problems of any nation or region. For instance, upgrading credentials and stimulating productivity by spending on doctoral training and then introducing specialists with research expertise into the economy constitutes a regular strategy for ageing societies to tackle the challenge of a contracting labour force. The objective is to increase innovation and create a highly productive and functional but reduced labour force. However, in societies whose populations are largely young, universities find themselves overstretched to provide quality higher education to growing numbers of students, in addition to meeting their goal to thrive as knowledge economies. Upgrading the qualifications of new and extant research and teaching staff by means of doctoral training is seen as a solution (Jørgensen, 2012).

Africa and the Doctorate
Africa's rising young population with a median age of 19 either presents a huge challenge if not managed effectively, or a substantial prospective labour force that can promote progress on the continent (Ata-Asamoah & Severino, 2014). Quality education with relevant skill training for the youth is key to reaping the benefits of a young population. While the demand for pre-tertiary education is high, in chorus, there is a growing demand for higher education among the youth. As a result, African higher education is experiencing "massification", and populating the universities with good quality and highly qualified doctoral degree holders has become even more urgent (Harle, 2013; Teferra, 2013). However, the perennial lack of adequate investment in this sector has undermined the quality and capacity of most higher education institutions on the continent.

Nevertheless, there are designs to increase doctorate production in Africa. This statement by Dr. Dlamini Zuma, Chairperson of the African Union Commission (AUC): "… higher education and PhD production are critical for the development trajectory of Africa", indicates an essential component of the AUC's *Agenda 2063* (Teferra, 2013). In line with this agenda, countries such as Nigeria and Ghana aim to attain targets of 3,500 and 1,500 doctorates respectively, while Ethiopia, has extraordinarily invested in its higher education system, with a bold strategy to generate 5,000 doctorates within a decade. South Africa presently trains some 1,700 doctoral graduates annually and is anticipating a raise to 5,000 by 2030 (Teferra, 2013). The intense demand for doctorates is extending the borders of new traditions, and some even argue that conventional practices of African graduates pursuing their doctoral studies full time over a number of years abroad is unsustainable, if not already out-dated. The solution, it is argued, is to boost national, regional and continental production of doctorates (Teferra, 2013). In this regard, support is being provided by government bodies, development agencies, research funding agencies and others (Harle, 2013).

Despite these improvements and ambitions, there are still substantial access impediments to doctoral studies on the continent, implying that strained capacity of universities in Africa to train enough doctoral students has often led to some African students pursuing their doctoral studies abroad (Harle, 2013; Jørgensen, 2012). While African countries continue to tackle the issue of brain-drain, and intensify efforts to train more doctorate holders locally, various African students, in the meantime, continue to pursue their doctoral studies abroad including destinations such as the United Kingdom, other countries in Europe, the United States, Australia and other parts of the world. Interestingly, it was observed that in recent years, there had been 70 per cent rise in the number of students from Africa undertaking doctorates in the United Kingdom (Mills, Cox, Zhang, Hopwood, & McAlpine, 2010).

Over the years, UK universities have served as academic homes to many doctoral students from different parts of the world including those from Africa. With the advent of the millennium, UK universities have been tasked to reshape doctoral education as research and knowledge generation, which noted earlier, is ever more viewed as crucial to a nation's global economic competitiveness. Consequently, the United Kingdom and other countries such as Australia and New Zealand have been attempting to remould the doctorate more as a training for prospective researchers, than as principally about generating new knowledge or educating the individual (Leonard et al., 2006). Understanding the implications of this for an African doctoral student in the United Kingdom, his or her ambitions and expectations is important. Doctoral degrees are perceived as an essential component of a nation's development, and the statement that "[n]o country can develop without robust knowledge citadels fortified with PhDs" has implication for the leadership role expected from holders of doctorates in national, regional, continental and global development (Teferra, 2013). Addressing challenges in the development process demands leadership, demonstrated through advanced level of innovativeness and expertise, which as previously stated, could be cultivated through doctoral training that builds global knowledge networks.

CONCEPTUAL FRAMEWORK

Leadership and Doctoral Education

A seminal essay, "The Idea of a University," by Newman (1907), published more than a century ago, although an attempt to define the character and purpose of the university in its entirety, still offers a great insight into contemporary expectations from doctoral education. Though often seen as a view that did not promote the research role of universities, Newman's vision of the university as "a place where inquiry is pushed forward, and discoveries verified and perfected, and rashness rendered innocuous, and error exposed, by the collision of mind with mind, and knowledge with knowledge" gains currency for current doctoral training, with a goal to shape leaders of the twenty-first century (as quoted in Deem, Hillyard, & Reed, 2007, p. 81; MacDonald, 2011).

Duval (2003) in her study that explores the role of universities in preparing effective community college leaders, emphasises the relevance of Newman's view to university doctoral programmes, which play an essential role in leadership development. For her, compelling students to think profoundly and to investigate and advance inquiry as well as deliberately creating learning communities and networks for doctoral students will prime them as effective leaders who confront fresh challenges, and ask the difficult questions of these increasingly unpredictable modern and future times.

In the work of Walker and Thompson (2010), obtaining a doctorate is not merely starting and finishing a research, but a process of becoming a scholar, researcher and leader, which entails engaging with a myriad of ideas and issues mediated through the doctoral research. During this process, networks of student peers and supervisors/experts are critical to the development of doctoral students' into confident scholars, researchers, experts and leaders in their fields. The authors perceive the doctoral experience as a process during which students develop knowledge, capabilities and relationship resources to progress with lifetime professional leadership trajectories. An increasing number of people willing to make economic and educational investment are pursuing doctoral degrees not only to become university academics but also to boost their professional credentials in other workplaces in order to develop as leaders and be able to perform leadership functions (Walker & Thompson, 2010). This aligns with MacCauley and Velsor (2004) work, which defines leader development as expanding an individual's capacity to be efficient in leadership functions and practices.

For Marquardt (2000), there is an essential connection between action learning, a powerful tool and effective leader and leadership development for the twenty-first century. He notes that what is progressively evident is that this new century requires new types of leaders with modern techniques as leadership forms and abilities that were effective in the anticipated setting of the last century are unsatisfactory for this modern age of improbability, ambiguity and express transformation, where our abilities to delineate setbacks and discover viable answers are wanting. According to him, while most existing leadership development processes create technologically erudite leaders who have the capability to tackle sophisticated problem-solving models, in effect, most lack the human element that must be considered. While such leaders are technically competent, they possess inadequate skills to manage the social and interpersonal dimensions of institutions. On the contrary, action learning, according to Marquardt (2000), tackles all aspects of leadership development comprehensively and produces a holistic leader.

Subsequently, for Day and Harrison (2007), leadership is multidimensional and complex, and thus cannot be whittled down to a single definition. They emphasise that while the conventional notion of leadership assumes the form of an individual taking charge of and directing a team or group (with members as followers) to achieve a goal, a more evolving and sophisticated notion takes on the character of collaboration with team members. Day and Harrison (2007, pp. 365–366) note that:

> [r]ecent work has suggested that the development of a leader identity is critically important in the ongoing and continuous development of a leader. The more salient and crystallized a leader identity, the more likely that individual is to seek out experiences to enact and develop that aspect of the self. In short, thinking of oneself as a leader is an important motivator for acting as a leader.

This implies the individual sense making of his/her identity, which entails a progression from the notion of the singular self to relational self and collective self (Day & Harrison, 2007; Sedikides & Brewer, 2001). This process of how a person thinks of him/herself as a leader is termed critical because it anchors persons in the knowledge of who they are, their aims, fortes and inadequacies. These culminate in their ability to seek interactions that will expand their singular selves to the relational and the collective and transform them into exceptional leaders that will not only elicit merely competent performance but also inspire extraordinary achievement (Bass, 1985; Bourdieu, 1986; Coleman, 1988; Day, 2001). Thus, the aim of recent leadership scholarship is to meet the growing need to comprehend how leadership might be shaped more collectively and collaboratively in order to be more effective (Bouty, 2000; Brass & Krackhardt, 1999; Burt, 1992; Day, 2001; Day, Gronn, & Salas, 2004; Day & Harrison, 2007; Day, Sin, & Chen, 2004; Pearce & Conger, 2003; Tsai & Ghoshal, 1998). In this collaborative and collective behaviour in leader and leadership development, the notion of networks is relevant (Castells, 2005). A network represents a prescribed configuration with a system of interrelated nodes that point where the curve intersects itself (Castells, 2005; Monge & Contractor, 2004).

The above leader and leadership development insights in relation to doctoral education are relevant to the subject under analysis. I argue that out of the perspectives of the study's participants, which suggest from both fulfilment and challenges can be gleaned the notion that doctoral education facilitates learning networks and generates new knowledge for leader and leadership development. This experience begins to endow the individual with a strong sense of professional leadership identity and leadership qualities, which s/he expects to apply in his/her field of expertise or future professional life. The African doctoral candidate in the United Kingdom, who is classified as an international student, perceives him/herself (as a developing leader in conjunction with his/her research and training) as a developing node in a leading network of knowledge for and in Africa and globally.

Conceptualising the International/African Doctoral Student

The classification, "international students" is not perceived in the context of this study as monolithic. It is a heterogeneous entity, hence the focus on African students, another sub-category, which equally defies homogeneity. These assumptions underlie how the respondents as a group and their experiences are analysed. As a result, in interrogating the tendency to homogenise the classification, "international students", the study focuses on 11 African students, in a particular university, and examines their experiences of pursuing doctoral studies in the United Kingdom from their perspectives.

According to Marshall and Rossman (1999, p. 25), "[i]n a qualitative inquiry, initial curiosities for research often come from real-world observations, emerging from the interplay of the researcher's direct experience, tacit theories, political commitments, interests in practice and growing scholarly interests". This statement holds true for me, because my interest in the experiences of international students, particularly, those from Africa at a research intensive UK University was awakened during my time as a doctoral student at (Name of University). As a student from Ghana, I was classified international and African. My experience during the process of the doctorate, shaped by this identity, was characterised by challenges despite it being extremely rewarding. This shaped a lot of the career choices I made since successfully completing my doctorate, and also led me to wonder what the experiences of other doctoral students from Africa at (Name of University) are or have been. It had led me to yearn to explore the question, "What does the doctorate and its experience in the United Kingdom mean to international students, particularly, those from Africa?"

In tackling issues regarding academic oversimplification of the doctoral experience, there have been studies that have examined the doctoral experiences, academic life stories and career objectives of students from sub-Saharan Africa (Mills et al., 2010). However, what has not been explored is the notion that the African doctoral candidate perceives himself/herself and his/her research and training as leader and leadership development. The question emerges, to what extent does s/he see the doctoral training experience as endowing the individual with a strong sense of professional leadership and leadership qualities, which s/he expects to apply in his/her field of expertise. Also, his/her perception of himself/herself, as a developing node in a leading network of knowledge, needs investigating. Like Day and Harrison (2007), I argue that the very multilevel character of leadership defies one single definition. Consequently, the chapter progresses the view that leader and leadership development is simultaneously individual, relational and collective, all of which take shape in a developing node. Thus, central to the doctoral students' perception of their doctoral experiences as leader and leadership development is the network within which they assume the character of the developing node. This node derives nourishment, nurturing and development from the networks within which it is formed, where it is imbued with the multilevel character of leadership − the individual, relational and collective. The doctoral student only gains her/his individual skills as leader and, develops those individual leadership skills and traits by virtue of the network, which is at once relational and collective. Adopting a qualitative approach, the study examines these within the context of some African students' doctoral experiences at (Name of University).

RESEARCH APPROACH

Methodology

This was a qualitative study with a qualitative survey that contained mostly open-ended questions.

Sampling
Non-probability sampling (Merriam, 1988), which is known as purposive, purposeful or criterion-based sampling was employed. The nature of the research question and the qualitative strategy in this study required a

qualitative or non-probability sampling approach. Sampling was more purposeful than random because the judgement of the researcher was used to
achieve a specific purpose, that is, to gain an in-depth understanding of the
experiences of these African doctoral students at (Name of University)
(Robson, 1993). The doctoral students from Africa or doctoral students
who identified themselves as African were purposefully targeted in the
survey, and for the in-depth interview (Punch, 1998).

Access, the Survey and Interview
An email inviting African doctoral students at (Name of University) to
voluntarily participate in the study led to 12 students completing a survey
and 4 being interviewed. The qualitative survey conducted through Survey
Monkey was distributed through the (Name of University) Africa Society,
a student society at (Name of University) with a membership of students
from Africa and those who considered themselves African. One of the 12
students doing the Doctorate of Philosophy, or more commonly known as
the PhD skipped all questions thus there were 11 respondents whose
responses were analysed. Those who completed the survey came from
Ghana, Nigeria, Uganda and South Africa, and seven of them were male
students and the rest, four were female students. The doctoral programme
they were pursuing ranged from International Development, Health care
Innovation, Biomedical Engineering, Law, Public Health, Politics and
International Relations. While eight respondents answered the question to
do with the stage at which a student is in his/her programme, four skipped.
While four were in their second year, two each were in their first and third
years. In-depth interviews were conducted with two male and two female
students out of the 12 that responded to the survey. Both the survey and
interview questions were shaped from themes that had to do with the stage
and structure of the student's doctoral programme; his/her reasons for
studying for a doctorate, why in the United Kingdom and in this particular
case, why (Name of University); what does obtaining the doctorate mean
to the student, the advantages and challenges; and a general description of
his/her doctoral experience.

In-depth interviewing, a method used extensively by qualitative researchers was employed in this study (Marshall & Rossman, 1999). The interview
sessions were much more like "conversation[s] with a purpose" than "formal events with predetermined response categories" (Kahn & Cannell,
1957, p. 149; Marshall & Rossman, 1999, p. 108). This implies that during
interview sessions, I enquired into some broad themes to assist in revealing
the interviewee's perspectives but otherwise respected how s/he shaped and

configured the answers (Marshall & Rossman, 1999). For example, a general question like – "How would you describe your doctoral experience?" was asked of the interviewees, while in the survey this open-ended question had this phrase added: "Please, elaborate and give some specific examples". This is because qualitative research basically assumes that the "participant's perspective on the phenomenon of interest should unfold as the participant views it, not as the researcher views it" (Marshall & Rossman, 1999, p. 108). This gave me the opportunity to ask probing questions formulated from the interviewee's account during the interview session and also by the help of an interview guide.

Data Analysis
Data were analysed by listening repeatedly to the audio-recorded interviews and reading transcripts using existing categories I had reviewed, and generating a few new ones indigenously (using phrases or words employed by the interviewees). The themes from the findings developed recursively through interactions between the literature review that addressed the study's objectives, and the analysis of the findings.

Trustworthiness Features and Limitations of the Study
The qualitative study does not generate generalisable findings. Rather its aim is to gain an in-depth understanding of a phenomenon through thick descriptions (Geertz, 1973). The study's trustworthiness is grounded within the four constructs of Lincoln and Guba (1985): credibility, transferability, dependability and confirmability. The in-depth interviews create an opportunity to emerge with credible rich descriptions of the participants' doctoral experiences and to explore in more depth the survey responses from four of the respondents. Using multiple perceptions to clarify what the doctoral experiences mean for the participants through the interviews, the survey responses and the literature provides an element of dependability to the findings. Themes that developed from the findings have the potential of transferability. While this transfer may be problematic, it is mitigated by the explicit statement of the conceptual and theoretical boundaries of the study (Marshall & Rossman, 1999). Attempts were made to ensure the confirmability of the study's findings by drawing on the strengths of qualitative methodology which were the rationale for its choice and high ecological validity ensured by the data generated through in-depth interviews in the natural settings of the participants. Indeed, the trustworthiness of a study will be incomplete without reference to its ethical implications.

Ethical Considerations

In accordance with ethical principles, the interviewees were given assurance about the study's commitment to anonymity and confidentiality with emphasis on the voluntary nature of the exercise and the interviewee's freedom to withdraw at any point if s/he wanted to. This assurance was given in the survey questionnaire and right at the beginning of every interview. Permission then to record the interview was sought from the interviewee. Most of the interviews lasted between two and three hours. Before the end of every interview, the interviewee was asked if the right questions were being posed, and if not, she/he was asked for suggestions. This was an attempt to build into the study respondent validation in order to enhance its authenticity. I normally would then conclude the interview with an expression of gratitude to the interviewee. The University is anonymised, however, it does have a perceived unique character and acclaimed status nationally and globally which constituted one reason why the participants in this study perceived themselves as potential leaders. These findings are examined in next.

FINDINGS

The African students' doctoral experience – developing nodes in leading networks of knowledge for leader and leadership development

In this section, I argue that out of the perspectives of the participants with regard to their doctoral experiences, which suggest, mainly, fulfilment albeit a few challenges, can be gleaned the notion that doctoral education facilitates (or is expected to facilitate) learning networks, action learning and generates new knowledge for leader and leadership development. It begins to endow the individual with a strong sense of professional leadership and leadership qualities, which s/he expects to apply and further develop in his/her field of expertise. I argue that the African doctoral student perceives him/herself and his/her research as a developing node in leading networks of knowledge in Africa and globally. S/he views the self or his or her identity as a potential leader undergoing a process of leader and leadership development.

Thus, the findings suggest: first, doctoral education as acquisition of knowledge and capabilities for professional leadership trajectories; second, doctoral education as creator of learning communities, networks and relationship resources for leadership development; third, the doctoral student as a developing node in leading knowledge networks; fourth, doctoral education as progression from the self to the relational and to the collective for leader and leadership development; and finally, doctoral education as action learning for leader and leadership development. These themes, which shaped recursively from the engagement between the literature and findings, are exemplified by the participants' experiences from their perspectives. Before examining these, I consider the structure of the doctoral programme at Oxford University.

The Structure of the Doctoral Programme at Oxford University

The doctoral programme at Name of University is structured with three different stages of assessment through which students must progress. A student enroled on the Doctor of Philosophy programme begins as a Probationer Research Student (PRS), who after the first academic year writes a comprehensive doctoral research thesis proposal (also called the Transfer Paper), which s/he must defend orally before two assessors. If the student emerges successfully from this process, s/he is officially transferred to the Doctor of Philosophy status, which implies that the student is no longer PRS but a full Doctor of Philosophy candidate. At the next stage, the Confirmation process, the student again presents and orally defends a progress report and a number of chapters of his/her thesis including preliminary results/findings chapter to two examiners. If s/he qualifies, then his/her status as a Doctor of Philosophy student is confirmed. Then the third stage, the confirmed Doctor of Philosophy candidate, finally, submits and orally defends his/her completed doctoral thesis before two examiners during a *Viva Voce*. If the candidate is successful, then s/he is awarded the doctorate. Participants in this study were at all three stages. Their perspectives are examined next.

Doctoral Education as Acquisition of Knowledge and Capabilities for Professional Leadership Trajectories

First, one particular reason given by all 11 respondents and 4 interviewees who participated in the study for pursuing a doctorate in the United Kingdom and at (Name of University) was that, they perceived doctoral education as leader development, through the expansion of an individual's capacity to be efficient in leadership. In other words, it was seen as a process that would enable them to acquire knowledge and capabilities for professional leadership trajectories. To them, the opportunity to gain good quality education and relevant skills training, as well as be stimulated intellectually in preparation for careers, which will enable them to lead and contribute to the fulfilment of the developmental needs of their countries was important. The reputation of (Name of University) as a world class institution with various departments regarded as outstanding and at the cutting edge of knowledge and research was central. Below are some examples:

> I find the Doctor of Philosophy intellectually stimulating and it's the training I require for an academic profession. In my opinion, (Name of University) and the UK were the best options I found while looking. (Survey Respondent)

> I chose to study for the doctorate for four reasons namely, to study my subject at an elevated and the highest critical level, to acquire an advanced degree to help the development needs of my country, to research and generate reform ideas for my country's financial sector, and to position myself to work internationally. I chose to study in the UK and at the (Name of University) to access the very best of education and research that this country and the university are known for. (Survey Respondent)

Eight of the respondents and all four interviewees also made references to the first class reputation of their departments and the university globally as well as the opportunity to develop the requisite skills as reasons for undertaking the doctorate. The two quotes below are more examples:

> My inspiration to study here came from (Name of University) being one of the best in Europe and the world. (Interviewee)

> The nature of the programme and the reputation of the department brought me to (Name of University). You have a year to come up to speed with skills, academic skills; how to write or read academic papers. (Interviewee)

For another interviewee, it had always been a life-long vision and logical process in her academic life because she knew since her undergraduate days that she would pursue doctoral studies. According to her, her ambition had always been to work in the development sector where getting jobs had been very competitive. After she applied for so many of such jobs and secured none, she decided to enrol on a doctoral programme. At the same time, she had come up with a research idea related to development politics that she felt passionate about, and consequently, felt inspired and believed that it was the appropriate time to pursue it. For her, the merit of (Name of University) was not only that it was a top university with limitless opportunities but also a university known all over the world:

> You can go to a remote village in Africa and they probably know what it is compared to say a university like Yale, which is a very good university but barely known outside

North America and Europe. A few people really know the value of Yale University. Being in (Name of University) is definitely a plus and doing a doctorate at (Name of University) is wonderful. It opens up so many opportunities for you – so many plat-forms to do a lot of things. Sometimes I just get so positively overwhelmed with socie-ties, clubs and activities in the department and other mini-projects that you can be part of. This is very very rewarding. The key to (Name of University) is just to know what you want, and think about what resources to tap into to achieve your goals. (Interviewee)

Another interviewee also perceived the Doctor of Philosophy as a dream and passion that he had always had because 'I thought that my education wouldn't have been complete without a Doctor of Philosophy. I think the Doctor of Philosophy provides me with the opportunity to apply all that I learnt into a socially relevant issue by way of research'. While he empha-sised that it enabled the broadening of knowledge horizons, an opportunity to gain deeper insight into phenomena, and the prospect of coming up with something that was ground-breaking by way of research and be innovative, he also believed that it represented an achievement that earned one respect in society:

There's a world out there that takes you more seriously when you have a 'Dr' attached to your name. For me the Doctor of Philosophy gains me an acceptance from the wider community generally. (Interviewee)

For all of the participants, despite a few challenges, the doctoral experi-ence had been largely positive, which included academic fulfilment, acquisi-tion of relevant skills, and the renowned reputation of (Name of University). Other advantages were positive college experience, effective supervisor-student relationship, forming and enrichment of professional and social networks, and the opportunity to engage with the top experts in the different fields. These are explored next.

Doctoral Education as Creator of Learning Communities, Networks and Relationship Resources for Leadership Development

Second, doctoral education is also perceived as creator of learning commu-nities, networks and relationship resources for leadership development. All participants felt that their doctoral experiences were worthwhile. They all believed that doctoral training or obtaining a doctorate, particularly, at (Name of University) would not only equip them with the requisite skills and shape them as leaders in their fields or future professions, but also position them in a manner that entrenched them within professional and social networks that would provide them with the social capital and enable them to perform their leadership functions more effectively in their home countries or in their fields of study in general. This was made clear even by those who suggested the improvement of some aspects of the doctoral experience.

Forming and enriching one's professional and social networks and the opportunity to engage with the top experts in the world was seen as a component of the doctoral training. All the four interviewees expressed the view that the cosmopolitan nature of (Name of University) and its world class status definitely made it possible to meet people from all over the world, some of whom were already well recognised experts and were doing great things in the world. They, therefore, viewed the Oxford doctorate as a plus (and not only as a degree to obtain) because it served as a platform from which to create other experiences and access social and cultural capitals and networks, which they stressed were significant and highly beneficial to the doctoral student undergoing leader and leadership development. All the interviewees declared:

> My supervisor gets me connected to some of the top scholars and these other experts around the world. He helps to expand my networks, giving me the opportunity to meet these people. These are top scholars around the world. It becomes easier because I'm in (Name of University). (Interviewee)

> (Name of University) is where people have connections in the world; a place where you can make contacts. These lecturers are the people whose works challenge the narratives. If I didn't come here I don't think I'd have had the opportunity to meet these gurus in my field. (Interviewee)

> (Name of University) is a place to meet the global experts and establish contacts with top scholars whose works you read in seminal books. In (Name of University) there is 99 percent chance that you will meet these people. There is a mega seminar happening in my college and all these top experts in my field from all over the world will attend. It means a great deal, to be able to meet these people. It makes it all the better because you get the opportunity to engage with your intellectual heroes- an opportunity to tell them what I am doing and that for me is special. (Interviewee)

> You have read these people whose works shape your ideas. Meeting them and engaging them is special and unique – they can give guidance and direction. These are people who have "wowed" you with their writing and intellectual engagements. (Interviewee)

The significance of these networks to these participants is crucially linked to the development of their selves and individual identities as well as their positioning within them.

The Doctoral Student as a Developing Node in Leading Knowledge Networks

Consequently, the doctoral student perceived him/herself as what could be described as a developing node in networks for leader and leadership development – a self that increases through collaboration and networks. For one interviewee, an experience of a "telethon" she had raising funds for her college through its alumni, inspired her to want to facilitate a similar initiative in the future to help her former university to raise funds to employ more qualified lecturers in order to reduce class sizes. She mentioned how she would like to help reduce class sizes at the undergraduate level in her former university where she hoped to become a lecturer after obtaining the doctorate. She believed that her main role as a lecturer in the future would not be effective if she could not assist in the reduction of class sizes for undergraduate students. According to her, the undergraduate years were formative years for students, 'and it was so sad that because we were so many in a class, we could not engage with our lecturers productively'. She wanted to see herself in the position of encouraging others to challenge themselves intellectually. However, she believed this could only be done in smaller class sizes, and not in large classes of nearly 1,000 students per class. This is because, in her case, it was when she enroled on a Master's programme and the classes were smaller, that her lecturers got to know her capabilities and encouraged and advised her accordingly. She was convinced that some of her undergraduate colleagues, who did not return to pursue graduate studies, perhaps, had potentials that were missed and not encouraged, and, therefore, might have missed out due to the large class sizes. She stressed:

> The telethon experience gives me an idea about how to deal with the alumni office of my former university. The training that was given was useful. We have an alumni office in my former university but I don't know what they do. You only go there when you are about to graduate and I haven't been contacted since I finished my study. One way alumni should help is by raising funds. We need to make use of our alumni by encouraging them to make a donation to the university. It was terrible when I was an undergraduate because classes were so large. What we learnt during the telethon was the importance of giving and how to encourage people to give. This could be an avenue to raise funds from alumni in order to employ qualified lecturers to reduce class sizes. (Interviewee)

His/her development as a leader in her field is not only seen in terms of developing human capital, that is, the individual acquiring knowledge, skills and abilities linked to official leadership roles that enable the individual to think and act in innovative ways (Coleman, 1988; Day, 2001). It is also perceived as leadership development, a process in which the function of human capital is entrenched within work connections that assume the form of social capital, which is shaped from networked associations among persons that improve collaboration and resource trading in generating institutional worth (Bouty, 2000; Brass & Krackhardt, 1999; Burt, 1992; Day, 2001; Tsai & Ghoshal, 1998). Although a leader develops by virtue of focused investment in human capital, leadership is a process that involves an intricate interaction between the chosen leader and the ecology of the social and the organisation (Day, 2001; Day & Harrison, 2007). There is therefore constant interaction between the leader's human capital and social capital rooted in associations, generated through interpersonal connections (Bourdieu, 1986). What is important in this experience was that the participant's proposed solution to large class sizes in her former university did not only emerge from her human capital, but also from her interaction with the network of which she was a part of − her college, the groups engaged in the telethon and the alumni with whom she was communicating, which represented her social capital. In this context, she, her doctoral experience and her interactions represent the node in the network. A network, in this case, is a formal structure with a system with interconnected nodes and, she represents a node because she becomes a connection point (Castells, 2005; Monge & Contractor, 2004). This connection point or intersection, which is the node, is a space within the network where her human capital (leader development) interacts with her social capital (leadership development) to generate new knowledge in leading and managing knowledge that mediates varying contexts of power and privilege. Thus, this participant asserted that if this solution becomes a reality, then chances that class sizes would reduce and some undergraduates would now be privileged to experience an education that empowers and enables them to unlock and develop their potential to the fullest would be higher. In this vein, I examine further doctoral education as progression from the self to the relational and to the collective for leader and leadership development.

Doctoral Education as Progression from the Self to the Relational and to the Collective for Leader and Leadership Development

Furthermore, thinking of oneself as a leader is an essential motivator for acting as a leader, according to Day and Harrison (2007). The constant interaction between the doctoral student's human capital, also, referred to as the self/identity and social capital, known as the relational/collective in his/her doctoral training was eloquently outlined by another interviewee. For instance, academic and research networks in departments were seen as crucial and intimately linked to shaping the doctoral student as a node in a leading network of knowledge, in other words, the self, collaborating and interacting with these networks, expanded to become the relational and collective:

> For instance, for those who are studying courses related to migration at the department, there is the Institute of Migration, and so, for them there's that network structure within which they operate. They fall on the faculty (lecturers) and do research for them and they use that as a starting point for their own research. (Interviewee)

According to this participant, apart from the official supervisor support, the doctoral process deliberately created spaces for enhanced structural support in departments such as academic and research networks on which students could draw. Departmental networks developed into a hub of research, and also, a place which integrated different approaches and the work of more people exploring similar subjects into one place for doctoral students to draw from that pool and networks of expertise and resources. Thus, for them, the doctoral experience facilitated learning networks on the basis of which doctoral students generated new knowledge for future professional leadership. In this context, the doctoral student, the self and his/her work represented a developing node in leading network of knowledge, and simultaneously, the self, interacting with associations and networks, expands to assume the relational and collective for leader and leadership development.

Two interviewees also emphasised the fact that they were pursuing a doctorate, and more so, at (Name of University) which they had assumed offered them an elevated status in the eyes of their former colleagues, who expected them to assume leadership roles. Consequently, expectations had been high, and although there had been huge pressures, they felt excited and challenged to do better and excel in their studies, since this would enable them to play the leadership role that their knowledge and professional communities expected from them. However, they maintained that they would not be able to assume these leadership roles without the networks of world class experts with whom they engaged as part of their doctoral experiences. In other words, their positioning as a developing node (the individual self) in leading networks of knowledge would be crucial in facilitating learning networks and generating new knowledge for leadership. This perception, by these two interviewees, aligns with the view of Day and Harrison (2007), who argue that leadership development is multilevel to which individual leader development is fundamental. In this case, leadership is conceptualised from an individual, relational and collective perspective, and within this context the role of the 'self' is crucial. Indeed, a particular conceptualisation of leadership and leader development that is being accorded rising recognition is that through the perspective of the self-concept or identity, which is multidimensional, is as a result of self-perceptions and a person's experiences (Baltes & Carstensen, 1991; Day & Harrison, 2007).

According to another interviewee, because he is keenly aware of the value of knowledge networks to the success of his doctoral training for leadership, his supervisor's plan to facilitate a study fellowship for him in Norway to enable him to engage with networks of knowledge experts in his field of study was, particularly, a special offer that he welcomed wholeheartedly. He believed that such an association with a network of experts in a different country and institution would definitely enhance his doctoral training. He also perceived this opportunity as a doctoral experience that would facilitate his engagement with other learning networks and support him in generating new knowledge through his research and for his professional and leadership development. This implies the student's sense making of his identity, which entails a progression from the notion of the singular self to the relational self and the collective self (Day & Harrison, 2007; Sedikides & Brewer, 2001).

Doctoral Education as Action Learning for Leader and Leadership Development

Finally, the doctoral experiences of two interviewees suggest action learning for leader and leadership development. The extent of the significance of these networks to the doctoral training of students was expressed when another participant demanded more structural support of academic and research networks. He took the initiative to participate in relevant seminars and knowledge networks that were external to his department. He was of the view that there should be conscious efforts to create these networks of experts as visible structural support for doctoral students. He was convinced that these seminar series' constituted the platform on which he would usually engage with networks of experts. They enabled him to discuss topics that were directly or indirectly connected to his research, which according to him was useful to his doctoral experience. They facilitated his access to learning networks from which he could generate new knowledge for his doctoral studies and develop leadership skills and as a leader in his field.

He recommended that more support structures and networks could start from the scope of supervision being broadened and not limited to one's supervisor alone. It should be broadened to include two or more lecturers playing the role of mentors and co-supervisors with a wider network of interests and knowledge networks that would support the doctoral student's research and development as a leader. Here, this interviewee's doctoral experience exemplifies action learning for leader and leadership development.

Similarly, according to another interviewee, such knowledge networks were so crucial to the success of their studies, professional and leadership development that he and some of his colleagues exploring similar topics had planned to make a working group proposal to their supervisors. This participant maintained that there were many students and lecturers, who individually were exploring topics that connected to their areas of focus. Nevertheless, since there was no readymade unifying platform around which much information and research on different aspects of their research focus could coalesce for them to access, he was leading his colleagues to facilitate the process of creating more of these knowledge networks. He was of the view that these expert networks were immensely beneficial because they would nurture them as doctoral students with their research as developing nodes within them (networks) for leader and leadership development. Marquardt (2000) stresses that the mainstay of this type of action learning is that, the content and process of leadership development cannot be disconnected since what an individual learns is shaped by how s/he learns. This type of learning process promotes knowledge that leaders of the twenty-first century ought to acquire through the vital process of action learning in order to cultivate these qualities and competences. Seven main roles underscore the competences: a systems thinker, change agent, innovator, servant, polychronic coordinator (multitasker), teacher-mentor and visionary. Central to how action learning develops each of these key leadership abilities are: the combining forces of actual difficulties; fellow potential/leaders in the action learning group; a reflective inquiry procedure; dedication to action; and concentration on learning (Marquardt, 2000). Certainly, these two interviewees' doctoral experiences suggest action learning for leader and leadership development.

The above analysis suggests that the doctoral experience was perceived by the participants as an opportunity to facilitate learning networks within which doctoral students and their engagements assume the position of a developing node in order to expand the self to the relational and the collective as well as generate new knowledge for leader and leadership development.

CONCLUDING REMARKS

Overall, this study has illustrated through doctoral experiences of 11 African students at (Name of University) that the doctorate represented a medium by which students expected their academic, professional and social network to expand their selves for leadership. They perceived these knowledge networks as having the ability to shape and nurture them into independent confident leaders in their fields nationally and globally. Simultaneously, they viewed themselves as active constituents or developing nodes of these networks which they expected to stimulate their creativity and innovativeness for their professional leadership ambitions. In this context, the doctoral experience facilitating learning networks that would enable the generation of new knowledge for leader and leadership development had become paramount.

Africa, through its AUC *Agenda 2063* (AUC, 2014), increasingly regards the doctorate as critical for capacity building in support of the development trajectory of the continent. There is no doubt that more African doctorate holders: who have relevant knowledge and skills; and can create learning communities, networks and relationship resources; and, thus, continue developing as nodes in leading knowledge networks; in order to iteratively progress from the self to the relational and to the collective; and regularly engage in action learning; will be able to lead the national and continental development of African countries and Africa respectively.

According to Jørgensen (2012), doctoral students generate a significant chunk of universities' research work through teams or individual contributions, and also constitute a group that is highly mobile, and therefore, could form the mainstay of research cooperation. Indeed, the crucial role of doctoral education in providing solution to national and continental problems cannot be underestimated. While these are problems with national roots, there are challenges that emerge from the global arena, which transcends national, regional and continental boundaries. Addressing these global challenges demands an advanced level of innovativeness and expertise, which could be cultivated in young researchers through doctoral training that builds global collaborations, amalgamates resources, and delivers active and sensitive research training (Jørgensen, 2012). Thus, the participants in this study viewed being actively part of various knowledge networks at different national, regional, continental and global levels, during and after doctoral education as crucial to the leadership role of one who holds the doctorate. This is because these networks expose error "by the collision of mind with mind, and knowledge with knowledge", and continue to prime doctorate holders as exceptional leaders that will not only elicit merely competent performance but also inspire extraordinary achievement – indeed, develop effective leaders who confront fresh challenges, and ask the difficult questions of these increasingly unpredictable modern and future times.

REFERENCES

African Union Commission. (2014). *African union agenda 2063*. Washington, DC: The Info Shop. Retrieved from http://agenda2063.au.int/en/vision. Accessed on May 26, 2014.

Ata-Asamoah, A., & Severino, J. (2014). Head-to-head: Is Africa's young population a risk or an asset? *BBC*. Retrieved from http://www.bbc.co.uk/news/world-africa-25869838. Accessed on April 4, 2014.

Baltes, M. M., & Carstensen, L. L. (1991). Commentary. *Human Development, 34*, 256–260.

Bass, B. M. (1985). *Leadership and performance beyond expectations*. New York, NY: Free Press.

Bourdieu, P. (1986). The forms of capital. In J. G. Richardson (Ed.), *Handbook of theory and research for the sociology of education* (pp. 241–258). New York, NY: Greenwood.

Bouty, I. (2000). Interpersonal and interaction influences on informal resource exchanges between R and D researchers across organizational boundaries. *Academy of Management Journal, 43*, 50–65.

Brass, D. J., & Krackhardt, D. (1999). The social capital of twenty-first century leaders. In J. G. Hunt, G. E. Dodge, & L. Wong (Eds.), *Out-of-the-box leadership: Transforming the twenty-first-century army and other top-performing organizations* (pp. 179–194). Stamford, CT: JAI Press.

Burt, R. S. (1992). *Structural holes: The social structure of competition*. Cambridge, MA: Harvard University Press.

Castells, M. (2005). The network society: From knowledge to policy. In M. Castells & G. Cardoso (Eds.), *The network society: From knowledge to policy*. Washington, DC: Johns Hopkins Center for Transatlantic Relations.

Coleman, J. S. (1988). Social capital in the creation of human capital. *American Journal of Sociology, 94*, S95–S120.

Day, D. V. (2001). Leadership development: A review in context. *Leadership Quarterly, 11*(4), 581–613.

Day, D. V., Gronn, P., & Salas, E. (2004). Leadership capacity in teams. *Leadership Quarterly, 15*, 857–880.

Day, D. V., & Harrison, M. M. (2007). A multilevel, identity-based approach to leadership development. *Human Resource Management Review, 17*, 360–373.

Day, D. V., Sin, H. P., & Chen, T. T. (2004). Assessing the burdens of leadership: Effects of formal leadership roles on individual performance over time. *Personnel Psychology, 57*, 573–605.

Deem, R., Hillyard, S., & Reed, M. (2007). *Knowledge, higher education and the new managerialism: The changing management of new universities*. Oxford: Oxford University Press.

Duval, B. (2003). Role of universities in leadership development. *New Directions for Community Colleges, 123*, 63–71.

European Commission. (2010). *Europe 2020. A European strategy for smart, sustainable and inclusive growth.*

Geertz, C. (1973). Thick description: Toward an interpretive theory of culture. In C. Geertz (Ed.), *The interpretation of cultures: Selected essays* (pp. 3–30). New York, NY: Basic Books.

Harle, J. (2013). *Doctoral education in Africa: A review of doctoral student needs and existing initiatives to support doctoral training and research development. A needs analysis undertaken as part of DocLinks project.* London: The Association of Commonwealth Universities.

Jørgensen, T. E. (2012). CODOC – Cooperation on doctoral education between Africa, Asia, Latin America and Europe. Brussels: European University Association.

Kahn, R., & Cannell, C. (1957). *The dynamics of interviewing.* New York, NY: Wiley.

Leonard, D., Metcalfe, J., Becker, R., & Evans, J. (2006). *Review of literature on the impact of working context and support on the postgraduate research student learning experience.* UK: The Higher Education Academy.

Lincoln, Y., & Guba, E. (1985). *Naturalistic inquiry.* Beverly Hills, CA: Sage.

MacCauley, C. D., & Velsor, E. V. (2004). *The center for creative leadership handbook of leadership development.* San Francisco, CA: Jossey-Bass.

MacDonald, A. (2011). Ideas of the university, and of education. In *The nineteenth century: Selected readings* (A draft). Campion College, University of Regina.

Marquardt, M. J. (2000). Action learning and leadership. *The Learning Organization, 7*(5), 233–240.

Marshall, C., & Rossman, G. B. (1999). *Designing qualitative research* (3rd ed.). London: Sage.

Merriam, S. B. (1988). *Case study research in education: A qualitative approach.* San Francisco, CA: Jossey-Bass.

Mills, D., Cox, M., Zhang, J., Hopwood, N., & McAlpine, L. (2010, June). *Internationalisation and the next generation of social scientists: Experiences of early career academics from sub-Saharan Africa.* Oxford CETL Network Research Project.

Monge, P., & Contractor, N. (2004). *A theory of communication networks.* New York, NY: Routledge.

Newman, J. H. (1907). *The idea of a university: Defined and illustrated.* London: Longmans, Green, and Co. (Revised by Newman Reader, 2007).

Pearce, C. L., & Conger, J. A. (Eds.). (2003). *Shared leadership: Reframing the hows and whys of leadership.* Thousand Oaks, CA: Sage.

Punch, K. F. (1998). *Introduction to social research: Quantitative and qualitative approaches.* London: Sage.

Robson, C. (1993). *Real world research.* Oxford: Blackwell.

Sedikides, C., & Brewer, M. B. (Eds.). (2001). *Individual self, relational self, collective self.* Philadelphia, PA: Psychology Press.

Teferra, D. (2013). *The African quest for nurturing doctoral education.* Center for International Higher Education. Retrieved from http://www.insidehighered.com/blogs/world-view/african-quest-nurturing-doctoral-education. Accessed on March 4, 2014.

Tsai, W., & Ghoshal, S. (1998). Social capital and value creation: The role of intrafirm networks. *Academy of Management Journal, 41*, 464–476.

Walker, M., & Thompson, P. (2010). *The Routledge doctoral supervisor's companion: Supporting effective research in education and the social sciences.* Oxon: Routledge.

INVESTING IN OUR EDUCATION? LEADING, LEARNING, RESEARCHING AND THE DOCTORATE

Annette Thomas-Gregory and Justine Mercer

ABSTRACT

Purpose – *This chapter explores how different aspects of middle manager identity relate to knowledge, research and practice. It argues that effective leadership depends more upon the person than the role.*

Methodology/approach – *Semi-structured interviews were conducted with 14 middle managers at a single school of healthcare in a research-intensive, chartered UK university.*

Findings – *The middle managers revealed both core and situated identities. Their core selves included various personality traits such as curiosity, a competitive streak, optimism, sociability and a sense of humour. Their situated selves were shaped by socialization, life history, critical people, and incidents and chance. In a symbiotic relationship with these core and situated components was a complex, tri-partite professional identity, as a healthcare professional, a higher education (HE) academic, and an*

Investing in our Education: Leading, Learning, Researching and the Doctorate
International Perspectives on Higher Education Research, Volume 13, 213–232
Copyright © 2014 by Emerald Group Publishing Limited
ISSN: 1479-3628/doi:10.1108/S1479-362820140000013010

education manager. All the participants greatly valued professional development and ongoing academic study.

Social implications − *This chapter illustrates how the best postgraduate courses develop exemplary education managers/leaders. They do this not by giving students role-specific skills but by developing their analytical and critical thinking skills. Through a process of deep learning and experience, individuals undertaking a doctorate are able to develop into reflexive and reflective practitioners who can act with personal integrity.*

Originality/value − *Little has been published about the relationships between the career background, the identity and the role of a university middle manager, and virtually nothing from the field of healthcare. The figure presented in this chapter offers a new framework for understanding the relationship between self, professional identity and role.*

Keywords: Identity; management; knowledge; research; practice

INTRODUCTION

In recent years, modernization practices introduced by successive UK governments and university funding bodies have converged to bring about a much larger and more diverse student body. In the current higher education (HE) climate, increased bureaucracy, marketization and changes in government accountability have contributed to a growing perception that the pressures associated with being an HE middle manager outweigh any potential rewards. Paradoxically, while the role itself has been explored in great depth, the identities of the individuals who perform it have received relatively little attention.

This chapter explores the interrelationships between the different aspects of the middle manager's identity and how these relate to knowledge, research and practice. It argues that performance within any given role is intrinsically dependent upon the essential integrity of the individual. In other words, effective leadership and management is more about the person than the role. The chapter explores the role of the middle manager within a context of extensive reform and re-organization within UK HE. This restructuring has led to the emergence of 'new managerialism' with increased focus upon efficiency, economy and effectiveness and, arguably, an erosion of academic freedom. Being a successful leader and manager within this context requires a certain degree of personal authenticity, something that can only be acquired via a lengthy process of deep learning and experience. The chapter proposes that doctoral study offers middle leaders the chance to engage with critical analysis and to become reflective and reflexive practitioners who are comfortable with the discomfiture that has become synonymous with the role of the middle manager. By focusing on the role within a university department of healthcare, it also brings into sharp relief the complementary changes that have taken place within the National Health Service (NHS), in general, and within the training of healthcare professionals, in particular.

The chapter is organized into four sections: in the first section, changes within non-medical healthcare education and within HE more generally are explained, in order to show how the research being presented fits into a wider policy agenda and chronology; in the second section, the literature on HE middle managers is explored and the concepts of 'identity', 'self' and 'role' are interrogated; in the third section, Annette (the primary author of this chapter) presents the findings of her own doctoral study of 14 middle managers within a single school of healthcare; in the final section, we reflect upon the impact that doctoral study can have upon those who undertake it.

MOVING NON-MEDICAL HEALTHCARE EDUCATION OUT OF THE NHS AND INTO HIGHER EDUCATION

For much of the twentieth century, nurse education was managed by regional or district Health Authorities on behalf of the NHS. In the 1990s, however, in a process commonly referred to as Project 2000, nurse education followed in the footsteps of other non-medical healthcare education and gradually relocated financially, legally and structurally out of the NHS and into HE (Watson & Thompson, 2004). This represented a massive organizational and cultural shift whose ramifications are still being felt 20 years later by those HE academics who work in this field.

Throughout the process (which lasted for years), the central government failed to state unequivocally whether, from their point of view, integrating nurse education into HE was wanted or intended. Thus, it remains a moot point whether the move was planned, a historical inevitability, an academic/professional necessity, or an accidental outcome of the creation of the internal market in the NHS (Burke, 2003). Between 1999 and 2000, the NHS spent £703 million on pre-registration training places and student bursaries for some 50,000 nursing and midwifery students. Training for these students was provided through approximately 100 NHS pre-registration contracts, held by just over 70 HE institutions (NAO, 2001). Clearly, non-medical healthcare education, at that time, represented a potentially lucrative and expanding market, which HE providers were understandably keen to exploit, even though it also entailed huge changes in identity, environment and management. The changes just described in non-medical healthcare education ran ahead of and then alongside wider changes within the HE sector, as a whole, further details of which are presented in the next section.

THE RISE OF NEW MANAGERIALISM WITHIN HIGHER EDUCATION

Massification of HE; the emergence of the knowledge society; the unprecedented development of information technology; the marketization of HE and the turbulence of globalization have brought radical changes to the university's mission and purposes (Sotirakou, 2004). HE institutions face dynamic changes in their environment, most of which stem from the adoption of 'New Public Management' or 'new managerialism' (Clarke & Newman, 1997). Within the United Kingdom, new managerialism is underpinned by three core assumptions:

- There must be increased emphasis upon the 'three Es': Economy, Efficiency and Effectiveness (Metcalfe & Richards, 1987; Rhodes, 1994);
- Good management did not exist prior to the election of a Conservative government in 1979 (Major, 1989);
- Good management was found in the private sector, and privatization and marketization of public sector institutions would improve the 3Es (Kirkpatrick & Martinez Lucio, 1995).

Proponents of new managerialism argue that universities are business concerns as well as moral and intellectual institutions, and that if business methods are not applied to their management, they will break down (Draper, 1906 in Bok, 2003, p. 2). An open market in education is to be encouraged because profit is an intrinsically beneficial motive, whatever the sector (Tooley, 1996, 1998, 1999). If educational organizations do not provide a quality service, they deserve to go out of business (Tooley, 2000).

In contrast, critics lament the way in which bureaucratic management now takes precedence over all other activities, and professional values are ignored because of their alleged under-efficiency (Bottery, 2000). In his seminal and highly damning article, '*The teacher's soul and the terrors of performativity*', Stephen Ball (1998) draws attention to the way in which client 'need' and professional judgement have been replaced by commercial decision-making, to the huge detriment of both teachers and learners. This is because:

> *The policy technologies of market, management and performativity leave no space of [sic] an autonomous or collective ethical self.* (Ball, 1998, p. 226)

THE ROLE OF THE MIDDLE MANAGER

Although the role of the middle manager has always been important (Dopson, Risk, & Stewart, 1996; Middlehurst, 1993; Smith, 2002), the rise of new managerialism has greatly increased its significance (Hellawell & Hancock, 2001). Middle managers play a vital, even pivotal, role in the implementation and delivery of organizational goals (King, Fowler, & Zeithaml, 2001). They are 'the disturbance handlers, resource allocators and negotiators' (Crouch, 1979, p. 37). Their primary purpose is to reconcile the vision and expectations of top-level leaders with the concerns and aspirations of those working below them, and to alleviate the tensions that inevitably arise when different layers of a 'loosely coupled' (Weick, 2001) hierarchy have to function as one.

As befits their crucial importance, HE middle managers have been the subject of a growing body of literature. Some of the more major studies we discuss in detail below; others (Clegg & McAuley, 2005; Floyd, 2012; Floyd and Dimmock (2011); Mercer, 2009; Smith, 2005), we have space to reference only in passing.

In her much-cited, multi-disciplinary research project, Rosemary Deem (Deem, 1998, 2000) examined perceptions of how new managerialism had been adopted by UK universities, focusing, in particular, upon academic-managers. The research, which generated a plethora of publications (Deem, 2001, 2002, 2003a, 2003b, 2004; Deem, Hillyard, & Reed, 2007; Deem & Johnson, 2000; Johnson & Deem, 2003), involved focus group discussions with academics from different disciplines alongside interviews with 135 academic-managers (from heads of department to vice chancellors) and 29 senior administrators in 12 chartered (pre-1992) and statutory (post-1992) universities. The findings revealed that only a third of the total sample had received any formal training for their management role. Moreover, their working lives involved long hours packed with meetings, mountains of paperwork and a constant search for additional resources.

A follow-up study by Bolden, Petrov, and Gosling (2008a, 2008b) for the Leadership Foundation revealed some changes. They interviewed 152 senior and middle leaders from 12 institutions, comprising both academics and professional administrators. More training was now available, and at an earlier (pre-appointment) stage. In addition, middle level leadership was increasingly seen by both the incumbent and their role set as strategic rather than operational or administrative. This was especially true for those Heads of Department or Heads of Faculty who controlled multi-million pound budgets.

MIDDLE MANAGERS WITHIN NON-MEDICAL HEALTHCARE EDUCATION

It is not clear precisely which departments Bolden, Petrov & Gosling studied, but the picture within non-medical healthcare education may be rather different. Annette (the primary author of this chapter) used to be a senior lecturer at a statutory (post-1992) school of healthcare. In her department, leadership remained largely operational and administrative rather than strategic. The need for students to achieve professional accreditation seemed to limit the scope for inspirational and innovative leadership. The demand for 'product uniformity over time' necessitated a certain degree of rationalization and bureaucracy. Indeed, the department displayed many of the features of Weber's Model of Bureaucracy, namely, division of labour, specialization, a hierarchy of authority, rules, regulations and career orientation. Moreover, despite the integration of non-medical healthcare education into HE, the prevailing culture, at least in Annette's experience, felt more akin to Machiavelli's large power distance than More's Utopia.

It was clear to Annette that the middle managers within her school played a vital role in relieving the tensions associated with curriculum planning, delivery and implementation. However, recruitment to the position appeared to be haphazard, and the role description seemed broad and idealistic. Colleagues who had taken on the role complained of enormous pressures outweighing any perceived rewards. Within this particular school of healthcare, though the middle managers had varying clinical specialisms, they all had a background in nursing. Their academic portfolios were very varied and their career pathways were rarely linear. Many had Bachelors and Masters degrees, but only a small minority had doctorates. Informal conversations with those without doctorates revealed how insecure they felt, given the increasing emphasis upon research and publication, as defined by quality-related research (QR) funding and the Research Assessment Exercise (RAE) and its successor, the Research Excellence Framework (REF). Yet, these middle managers also spoke of the impossibility of pursuing doctoral studies while still in post. This made Annette even more convinced of the pivotal role of this group of middle managers but equally despairing of the approach being taken towards their recruitment, support and professional development. This motivated her to embark upon the doctoral research described below.

We argued in the introduction that performance within any given role is intrinsically dependent upon the essential integrity of the individual. This means that to understand the full meaning and significance of any particular 'role', one must first grapple with the even thornier concepts of 'identify' and 'the self'.

IDENTITY AND THE CONCEPT OF SELF

At its most basic level, identity means 'being recognized as a certain kind of person, in a given context' (Gee, 2001, p. 99). Because it is context-specific, identify is highly unstable and ambiguous. Indeed, a single individual may well have multiple identities. Some of these, they will have chosen themselves, but others will have been assigned to them by external actors. According to Gee (2001), society has a habit of sorting people into different categories, and these labels may be influenced by particular times and contexts. Furthermore, identity cannot be viewed without some form of 'interpretive system' (Taylor, 1994). This system may be based upon historical or cultural views of human nature; it may also be associated with concepts of normality (norms), traditions or rules of an organization. This means that the identity traits of an individual are not just context-variable at the level of the individual; they are also influenced by the interpretive systems of the observers. In other words, how observers interpret and react to an individual's 'ways of being' can reinforce that individual's thinking and/or behaviour. But, equally, the observers' interpretations and reactions can exert pressure on the individual to change or adapt in order to conform better to established norms.

Bradby's (1990) work is particularly pertinent here because she considers socialization and adaptation of identity on entry into nursing. Although her study was conducted before the radical changes in nurse education, it highlights the process of 'divestiture' that often occurs within a highly conformist organization. Bradby defines 'divestiture' as the:

> attempt of the organisation to strip the individual of his or her identity in order that conformity with the institution's needs will occur. (Bradby, 1990, p. 1222)

Though this type of conditioning has become less favoured, there remain subtle yet powerful forms of the process in many organizations, particularly the armed forces (Hockey, 1981). The prevailing consensus is that despite pressure to adapt to organizational (or other) circumstances and situations, the individual only alters what Ball (1972) calls their 'situated identity', leaving their 'substantive identity' or 'core identity' (Gee, 2001) intact. The situated identity is presented as malleable whereas the core identity is stable.

Although many authors continue to distinguish between a core and a situated identity, Fulcher and Scott (2007, p. 119) write, instead, of a social and a personal identity. Social identity is an individual's perspective upon the type of person they are, which may influence how they behave or how others expect them to behave. It is affected by presumptions and stereotypes, such as the preconceptions many people hold about what constitutes appropriate behaviour for a doctor or lawyer. By contrast, personal identity is a sense of individuality, how people see themselves and how others see them. Taking this distinction a step further, Jenkins (2004) suggests that individual and collective identity are interlinked, and, therefore, it becomes impossible to separate individual identity from its social construct and the socialization processes contained therein.

ROLE DISTANCE AND ROLE AMBIGUITY

No discussion of role theory can be complete without some reference to 'role distance', as theorized by Goffman (1959). He argues that life is like a play in which people act out different roles depending on the situations in which they find themselves. As they do so, they continually monitor and then modify the impressions they are giving to others. As Goffman (1959, p. 30) puts it:

> It is probably no mere historical accident that the word person, in its first meaning, is a mask. It is rather recognition of the fact that everyone is always and everywhere, more

or less consciously, playing a role .... It is in these roles that we know each other; it is
in these roles that we know ourselves. (Goffman, 1959, p. 30)

'Role distance' then becomes the difference between an individual's
perception of themselves and their perception of their role. The greater the
distance between the two, the more potential there is for disillusionment
and stress. Goffman's (1959) notion of role distance makes it obvious that
the large-scale changes described above (both to HE, in general, and to
non-medical healthcare education, in particular) will have an emotional
impact upon some, if not all, university staff. Moreover, because educational leaders invest so much of themselves in their work, interweaving
their personal and professional qualities in pursuit of a moral purpose
(West-Burnham, 2009), they are more likely to find role distance detrimental to their self-identity and sense of self-worth. With this in mind, we now
turn to the results of the case study that formed Annette's doctoral study.

A CASE STUDY OF HE MIDDLE MANAGERS IN A SCHOOL OF HEALTHCARE

Annette's study explored the professional identities of 14 middle managers,
not at her own statutory (post-1992) institution, but at another school of
healthcare located within a research-intensive chartered (pre-1992) UK university (Thomas-Gregory, 2012, 2014). The study adopted an interpretive
paradigm, in line with social constructivism, exploring the respondents'
beliefs, feelings and perceptions with regard to their career background, identities and role. The participants had diverse clinical backgrounds and had
accumulated a wealth of experience, skills and knowledge. They claimed
legitimacy as leaders in healthcare education because of their credentials not
just as educators and managers, but as practitioners who knew and understood the field of healthcare. Their careers had been influenced by primary
socialization into healthcare and secondary socialization into academia. As
already noted, their career pathways ran parallel to some dramatic changes
to the UK National Health Service during the 1980s and 1990s. The interviewees reflected upon the impact of business management models during
the 1980s and how this had led to their own moves into NHS management
roles. They argued that their considerable experience of NHS management
had equipped them for education management, and that, therefore, the
university-run management training programmes were of limited value. By
the time, they decided to move to an educational organization, the

participants had already performed a multitude of different roles, in different contexts. The decision to move out of clinical practice into education was usually explained in terms of personal development and/or academic aspiration, and seemed to be a turning point in their concept of self.

Hodkinson and Sparkes (1997) argue that in real-life, the concepts of social, cultural, economic and symbolic 'capital' developed by Bourdieu in 1986 are blended with personal choices, preferences and opportunities in a way that incorporates serendipity (Hodkinson and Sparkes 1997, p.32). This certainly seemed to be the case with the 14 interviewees. As they spoke about their clinical experiences, there were many references to the processes by which they decided which specialism or field of healthcare they would work within. They often mentioned people, critical incidents or particular experiences that helped them make these choices. Their career pathways were not necessarily as predictable, gradual or methodical as the terms 'career ladder' or 'career trajectory' might suggest. Indeed, the interviewees described career pathways pitted with turning points and epiphanies (Antikainen, Houtsonen, Kauppila, & Huotelin, 1996; Denzin, 1989; Hodkinson & Sparkes, 1997; Strauss, 1962). They presented themselves as individuals who had outgrown their original identity as a consequence of many different turning points. These included developing self-knowledge; seeing new opportunities; interacting with key players, and networking. They also included changes in *habitus,* which means the predisposition acquired by members of a particular social group to think, feel and act in certain ways (Bourdieu, 1997).

THE RELATIONSHIP BETWEEN SELF, PROFESSIONAL IDENTITY AND ROLE

Fig. 1 is an attempt to depict the multifaceted relationships between self, professional identity and role that emerged from the 14 interviews. It uses concentric rings (the so-called 'onion' approach) since this device is frequently utilized in psychology and social psychology as a way of representing self and social identity (Hofstede, 1991; Hofstede & Hofstede, 2005; Hsu, 1985; Trompenaars, 1994).

Identity and the Concept of Self

At the centre is the most static and least malleable aspect of self; the core self, sometimes called the nuclear self (Donner, 2010; Suler, 1995). It is hard

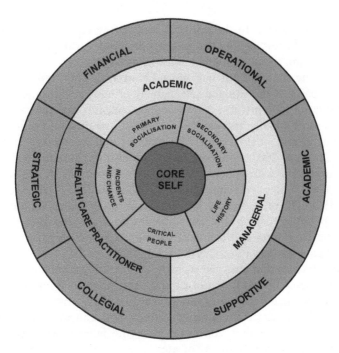

 CORE SELF:
Encompasses: traits such as curiosity, optimism, sociability, sense of humour, neuroticism, extraversion, openness and conscientiousness (Goldberg 1990).

SITUATED SELF:
Corresponds with Bourdieu's (1984) concepts of cultural and social capital.

PROFESSIONAL IDENTITY:
Corresponds with Bourdieu's concept of symbolic capital.

ROLE:
Corresponds with Bourdieu's (1984) concept of economic capital.

Fig. 1. Concentric Diagram Depicting the Relationships Between Self, Professional Identity and Role in a Group of Middle Managers in the Case Study School of Healthcare.

to access (Ball, 1972; Gee, 2001), especially in a small-scale study. Goldberg (1990) used a longitudinal approach to elicit core personality traits from the participants in his study. Judge, Higgins, Thoresen, and Barrick (1999) explored the relationship between the 'big five' personality traits, namely: neuroticism, extraversion, openness to experience, agreeableness and conscientiousness. In the doctoral study being reported here, the core personality traits revealed by the participants were: curiosity, a competitive streak, optimism, sociability, and a sense of humour.

Surrounding the core self is a second concentric ring, representing five different aspects of the situated self, namely primary socialization; secondary socialization; life history; critical people; incidents and chance. Situated identity is more pliable and can be significantly shaped and influenced by personal development (Erikson, 1959), primary and secondary socialization (Fulcher & Scott, 2007; Giddens, 2006), life history (Inman, 2007; Olesen, 2001), interaction with others (Gronn, 1999; Mead, 1934; Parker, 2004; Turner, 1994) and environment (Ball, 1972; Bradby, 1990; Gee, 2001; Taylor, 1989). If an individual has both a core self and a situated self, it becomes possible to reconcile the apparent contradiction that the self is both stable over time and significantly shaped by development (Erikson, 1959) and environment (Gee, 2001; Taylor, 1989).

The five themes that emerged from Annette's study resonate with two of Pierre Bourdieu's (1984) forms of capital. According to Bourdieu, cultural capital is concerned with the advantages acquired via primary and secondary socialization, especially through family and educational experience. Similarly, social capital is concerned with the advantages derived from social networks of friends and associates.

Professional Identity

The third concentric ring illustrates the three elements of professional identity (healthcare practitioner, education manager and HE academic) that were presented by the participants. This layer reveals the unique tensions faced by middle managers within a university school of healthcare, as they juggle the 'expanding and proliferating hybrid identities' (Clegg, 2008, p. 343) that are necessary to perform the role. The respondents had well-defined identities as healthcare practitioners based upon their broad clinical experience. They also presented as confident leaders and managers with a solid track record of managing within the NHS (Ferlie & Pettigrew, 1996). All had Masters qualifications and, unlike at Annette's own institution, 11 of the 14 had doctorates. These aspects of their professional identity had evolved over long periods of time. They were important not just to the middle managers, themselves, but also to their role set because of the way in which they shaped what such people came to expect of them (Goodson & Cole, 1994; Volkmann & Anderson, 1998). Again, there are resonances with

Bourdieu's work on symbolic capital and the processes by which an individual develops credibility within a particular field. Gunter (2001) draws upon Bourdieu's (1990) theory of practice to argue that qualifications such as a PhD furnish individuals with a universally approved perspective within a field, and are therefore good 'currency' within the market place.

That said, Annette's own experience of doctoral study indicates that, for some people, the qualification represents far more than an entry ticket into a particular field. This is because those who undertake postgraduate research become better-placed to engage with issues of power. Doing a doctorate developed not only Annette's knowledge base, but also her confidence, something she acknowledged herself, but something that was also evident to Justine, her supervisor. As a result, she had a better understanding of both her own position within certain power relationships and of the legislative, historical, political, economic and social constraints that may have underpinned the decisions being made by others around her. Central to this process is knowledge of self. Doctoral study helps managers and leaders not only to critique and evaluate the work of others, but also to appreciate the complexities of their own situation. It allows them to go beyond mere tick boxes and bureaucratic approaches, enabling them to manage with personal authenticity, integrity, and a deep appreciation of the need to continue learning from others, despite the lack of time and space.

Role

The outermost concentric ring represents aspects of role identified by the participants. Once again, the layer is divided according to the key themes that emerged from the data, namely: strategic, financial, operational, collegial, supportive and academic. There are resonances, too, with Bourdieu's (1984) notion of economic capital, which, in this case, comprised the salaries being paid to the interviewees by their university employer. At the case study university, as elsewhere, if an academic-manager's performance was deemed effective by the central university, it could result in movement up the salary scale. The middle manager's role was moulded at all levels by the strategic direction of the particular university in question. It was clear that any divergence from the university's core values was incompatible with the middle manager's role and, therefore, with salaried employment at that level of the university hierarchy.

As previously mentioned, the university considered itself to be research-intensive and its strategic vision was an extremely powerful influence upon the professional identities and roles of the participants. The middle managers in this study claimed they needed to demonstrate a strong academic identity in order to survive. Even though some had left school without any formal qualifications, all had a Masters degree and, as previously noted, 11 of the 14 had doctorates. Those without doctorates still spoke of the need for further development opportunities and time to pursue ongoing academic study. Those with doctorates saw the qualification as a minimum requirement, something that needed to be augmented with publications and/or research grants.

Moreover, all of the interviewees were now expected to develop a culture of research excellence within their respective departments, something that had not previously been a high priority within the field of healthcare. To them, the challenge to publish or perish was a very real threat, and one which placed limits upon their own and their colleagues' academic freedom and autonomy. Some participants embraced this cultural shift towards research excellence, whilst others felt alienated by it because of the role distance it created between their perceptions of their identity and their role.

In contrast to the above, at many, less high-ranking universities, research-led teaching remains inadequately resourced and, therefore, entirely unrealistic aspiration, despite what it might say on their websites and promotional material. In many schools of health and social care, only a small proportion of staff have the kind of high-level research training that would allow them to mentor more junior colleagues (Girot, 2010; Orme & Powell, 2008; Segrott, McIver, & Green, 2006). Moreover, staff are often so overburdened with teaching and administrative responsibilities that there is no time left for research. Tackling this mismatch between rhetoric and reality requires the recruitment of appropriately qualified and research-committed leaders and managers, of course, but it also requires the provision of adequate, ring-fenced research time.

CONCLUSIONS

The middle managers within Annette's study revealed identities that comprised a complex interplay between self and role. Their core selves included a range of personality traits such as curiosity, a competitive streak, optimism, sociability, and a sense of humour. Surrounding this core self was a situated identity that had been shaped by primary and secondary socialization, life history, critical people, and incidents and chance. In a symbiotic relationship with these two elements was a complex professional identity, as a healthcare professional, a HE academic and an education manager. In combination, these three facets of their professional identity allowed the middle managers to make appropriate and credible decisions within their field of educational practice. Their professional identities had evolved in a myriad of different ways over time, being shaped not only by their own career pathways but also by changes in the profession itself. As Bourdieu (1986, p. 46) notes, 'the social world is accumulated history' and cannot be reduced to a discontinuous series of agents and events. The middle managers' career pathways were certainly not predictable, gradual or methodical, but neither were they entirely random. Similarly, although some parts of each interviewee's life history had been influenced by unique personal encounters with other people and/or critical events, other parts were the result of systemic changes on a national scale, including the importation into the NHS of business models and the movement of initial nurse education out of hospitals and into HE. This had led, in some cases, to a 're-washing' of an interviewee's perception of their professional identity at several points during their career to date.

Traditionally, a doctorate was seen as a gateway into academia. It indicated to others that the recipient had acquired a substantive body of knowledge in a particular field; made an original contribution to that field, and mastered a set of specific research skills. This view of the doctorate has shifted somewhat in recent years, driven, in part, by the addition to the traditional PhD of professional doctorates such as the EdD. As Taysum (2012, p. 57) notes, engaging in postgraduate and postdoctoral research now has the potential to develop educational leaders and managers for a complex and rapidly changing educational system located within an equally challenging international context. As Annette's own experience shows, doctoral study can help academic-managers not only to critique and evaluate the work of others, but also to appreciate the complexities of their own situation. It allows them to go beyond mere tick boxes and bureaucratic approaches, enabling them to manage with personal authenticity, integrity, and a deep appreciation of the need to continue learning from others, despite the lack of time and space.

The real value of postgraduate research lies in its ability to develop education managers and leaders who can exercise evidence-informed, ethical leadership. It gives them the ability to make informed judgements on complex issues, and to design innovative approaches to solving problems. If discussions about middle managers centre solely on role, rather than identity, we will fail to exploit the human resources of these individuals.

Simultaneously, we will fail to develop them as leaders who can utilize their own extensive knowledge and experience to support teaching, learning and research, and to contribute to policy formulation. To avoid these pitfalls, we must re-conceptualize our understanding of what being an academic middle manager means. It is not the mere performance of a role, or even multiple roles; rather, it is the development of a unique individual into an analytical, reflective and reflexive practitioner who has personal integrity and is comfortable with discomforture (Taysum, 2012, p. 91). This kind of growth requires a lengthy process of deep learning and experience which, we would argue, doctoral study is extremely well-placed to facilitate.

> If you want to be a leader, you have to be a real human being. You must recognise the true meaning of life before you can become a great leader. You must understand yourself first (Senge, Scharmer, Jaworski, & Flowers, 2004, p. 186).

REFERENCES

Antikainen, A., Houtsonen, J., Kauppila, J., & Huotelin, H. (1996). *Living in a learning society: Life histories, identities and education.* London: Falmer.

Ball, S. (1972). Self and identity in the context of deviance: The case of criminal abortion. In R. Scott & J. Douglas (Eds.), *Theoretical perspectives on deviance.* New York, NY: Basic Books.

Ball, S. (1998). Performativity and fragmentation in postmodern schooling. In J. Carter (Ed.), *Postmodernity and the fragmentation of welfare.* London: Routledge.

Bok, D. (2003). *Universities in the marketplace: The commercialisation of higher education.* Princeton & Oxford: Princeton University Press.

Bolden, R., Petrov, G., & Gosling, J. (2008a). Tensions in higher education leadership: Towards a multi-level model of leadership practice. *Higher Education Quarterly, 62*(4), 358–376.

Bolden, R., Petrov, G., & Gosling, J. (2008b). *Developing Collective Leadership in Higher Education: Final report*, Leadership Foundation for Higher Education.

Bottery, M. (2000). *Education, policy and ethics.* New York, NY: Continuum.

Bourdieu, P. (1984). *Distinction – A social critique of the judgement of taste.* Abingdon, Oxon: Routledge.

Bourdieu, P. (1986). The forms of capital. In J. E. Richardson (Ed.), *Handbook of theory of research for the sociology of education.* Santa Barbara, CA: Greenwood Press.

Bourdieu, P. (1990). *In other words: Essays towards a reflexive sociology.* In M. Adamson (Trans.), Cambridge: Polity Press in association with Blackwell.

Bourdieu, P. (1997). *Outline of a theory of practice.* Cambridge: Cambridge University Press.

Bradby, M. (1990). Status passage into nursing: Another view of the process of socialisation into nursing. *Journal of Advanced Nursing, 15*, 1220–1225.

Burke, L. (2003). Integration into higher education: Key implementers' views on why nurse education moved into higher education. *Journal of Advanced Nursing, 42*(4), 382–389.

Clarke, J., & Newman, J. (1997). *The managerial state: Power, politics and ideology in the remaining of the social welfare*. London: Sage Publications.

Clegg, S. (2008). Academic identities under threat? *British Educational Research Journal, 34*(3), 329–345.

Clegg, S., & McAuley, J. (2005). Conceptualising middle management in higher education: A multifaceted discourse. *Journal of Higher Education Policy and Management, 27*(1), 19–34.

Crouch, P. (1979). Learning to be a middle manager. *Business Horizons, 22*(1), (February), 33–41.

Deem, R. (1998). 'New managerialism' and higher education: The management of performances and cultures in UK universities. *International Studies in Sociology of Education, 8*(1), 47–70.

Deem, R. (2000). *'New Managerialism' and the Management of UK Universities*. End of Award Report on the Findings of an Economic and Social Research Council Funded Project. October 1998–November 2000. ESRC award number R000 237661. Lancaster University.

Deem, R. (2001). Globalisation, new managerialism, academic capitalism and entrepreneurialism in universities: Is the local dimension still important? *Comparative Education, 37*(1), 7–20.

Deem, R. (2002). Talking to manager-academics: Methodological dilemmas and feminist research strategies. *Sociology, 36*(4), 835–855.

Deem, R. (2003a). Gender, organisational cultures and the practices of manager-academics in UK universities. *Gender, Work and Organisation, 10*(2), 239–259.

Deem, R. (2003b). Managing to exclude? Manager-academic and staff communities in contemporary UK universities. In M. Tight (Ed.), *International perspectives on higher education research: Access and inclusion*. Boston: Elsevier Science/JAI.

Deem, R. (2004). The knowledge worker, the manager – Academic and the contemporary UK university: New and old forms of public management? *Financial Accountability & Management, 20*(2), 107–128.

Deem, R., Hillyard, S., & Reed, M. (2007). *Knowledge, higher education, and the new managerialism: The changing management of UK universities*. Oxford: Oxford University Press.

Deem, R., & Johnson, R. (2000). Managerialism and university managers: Building new academic communities or disrupting old ones? In I. McNay (Ed.), *Higher education and its communities*. Buckingham: Open University Press.

Denzin, N. (1989). *Interpretive biography*. Qualitative Research Methods Series (Vol. 17). London: Sage Publications.

Donner, S. (2010). Self or no self: Views from self psychology and Buddhism in a postmodern context. *Smith College Studies in Social Work, 80*(2), 215–227.

Dopson, S., Risk, A., & Stewart, R. (1996). The changing role of the middle manager in the United Kingdom. *International Studies of Management and Organisation, 22*, 40–53.

Draper, A. (1906). The University Presidency. *Atlantic Monthly*, 97.

Erikson, E. (1959). *Identity and the life cycle*. New York, NY: International Universities Press.

Ferlie, E., & Pettigrew, A. (1996). Managing through networks: Some issues and implications for the NHS. *British Journal of Management, 7*(1), 81–99.

Floyd, A. (2012). 'Turning points': The personal and professional circumstances that lead academics to become middle managers. *Educational Management Administration & Leadership, 40*(2), 272–284.

Floyd, A., & Dimmock, C. (2011). 'Jugglers', 'copers' and 'strugglers': Academics' perceptions of being a head of department in a post-1992 UK university and how it influences their future careers. *Journal of Higher Education Policy and Management, 33*(4), 387–399.

Fulcher, J., & Scott, J. (2007). *Sociology* (3rd ed.). Oxford: Oxford University Press.

Gee, J. (2001). Identity as an analytic lens for research in education. In W. Secada (Ed.), *Review of research in education* (Vol. 25, pp. 99–125). Washington, D.C.: American Educational Research Association (AERA).

Giddens, A. (2006). *Sociology* (5th ed.). Cambridge: Polity Press.

Girot, E. A. (2010). The challenges facing healthcare lecturers and professors to lead and promote a research-based culture in practice. *Journal of Research in Nursing, 15*(3), 245–257.

Goffman, E. (1959). *The presentation of self in everyday life*. London: Penguin Publications.

Goldberg, L. (1990). An alternative description of personality. The big five factor structure. *Journal of Personality and Social Psychology, 59,* 1216–1229.

Goodson, I., & Cole, A. (1994). Exploring the teacher's professional knowledge: Constructing identity and community. *Teacher Education Quarterly, 21*(1), 85–105.

Gronn, P. (1999). Substituting for leadership: The neglected role of the leadership couple. *Leadership Quarterly, 10*(1), 41–62.

Gunter, H. (2001). *Leaders and leadership in education*. London: Sage Publications.

Hellawell, D., & Hancock, N. (2001). A case study of the changing role of the academic middle manager in higher education: Between hierarchal control and collegiality? *Research Papers in Education, 16*(2), 183–197.

Hockey, J. (1981). *Squaddies patterns of conflict and cooperation amongst private soldiers.* PhD thesis, University of Lancaster, Lancaster.

Hodkinson, P., & Sparkes, A. (1997). Careership: A sociological theory of career decision making. *British Journal of Sociology of Education, 18*(1), 29–44.

Hofstede, G. (1991). *Culture's and organisations: Software of the mind.* New York, NY: McGraw-Hill.

Hofstede, G., & Hofstede, G. J. (2005). *Culture's and organisations: Software of the mind.* New York, NY: McGraw-Hill.

Hsu, F. (1985). The self in cross-cultural perspective. In A. Marsella et al. (Eds.), *Culture and self: Asian and western perspectives.* London: Tavistock Publications.

Inman, M. (2007). *The journey to leadership: A study of how leader-academics in higher education learn to lead.* PhD thesis, University of Birmingham.

Jenkins, R. (2004). *Social identity* (2nd ed.). Key Ideas. Abingdon, Oxon: Routledge.

Johnson, R., & Deem, R. (2003). Talking of students: Tensions and contradictions for the manager-academic and the university in contemporary higher education. In *Higher education* (Vol. 46, pp. 289–314). Netherlands: Kluwer Academic Publishers.

Judge, T., Higgins, C., Thoresen, C., & Barrick, M. (1999). The big five personality traits, general mental ability, and career success across the life span. *Personnel Psychology, 52,* 621–652.

King, A., Fowler, S., & Zeithaml, C. (2001). Managing organisational competencies for competitive advantage: The middle management edge. *Academy of Management Executive, 15,* 95–106.

Kirkpatrick, I., & Martinez Lucio, M. (Eds.). (1995). *The politics of quality: Management of change in the UK public sector.* London: Routledge.

Major, J. (1989). *Public service management: The revolution in progress*. London: London Audit Commission.

Mead, G. H. (1934). *Mind, self, and society: From the standpoint of a social behaviorist*. Chicago, IL: The University of Chicago Press Ltd.

Mercer, J. (2009). Junior academic-manager in higher education: An untold story? *International Journal of Educational Management, 23*(4), 348–359.

Metcalfe, L., & Richards, S. (1987). *Improving public management*. London: Sage Publications.

Middlehurst, R. (1993). *Leading academics*. Buckingham: Society for Research in Higher Education and Open University Press.

National Audit Office (NAO). (2001). *Education and training the future health professional workforce for England*. 01.03.2001. ISBN: 0102840016.

Olesen, H. (2001). Professional identity as learning processes in life history. *Journal of Workplace Learning, 13*(7/8), 290–297.

Orme, J., & Powell, J. (2008). Building research capacity in social work: Process and issues. *British Journal of Social Work, 38*, 988–1008.

Parker, M. (2004). Becoming manager or the werewolf looks anxiously in the mirror, checking for unusual facial hair. *Management Learning, 35*(1), 45–59.

Rhodes, R. (1994). The hollowingout of the state – The changing nature of the public service in Britain. *Political Quarterly, 65*, 138–151.

Segrott, J., McIver, M., & Green, B. (2006). Challenges and strategies in developing nursing research capacity: A review of the literature. *International Journal of Nursing Studies, 43*(2006), 637–651.

Senge, P., Scharmer, C., Jaworski, J., & Flowers, B. (2004). *Presence*. Cambridge, MA: Sol.

Smith, R. (2002). The role of the university head of department – A survey of two British universities. *Educational Management & Administration, 30*(3), 293–312.

Smith, R. (2005). Departmental leadership and management in chartered and statutory universities: A case of diversity. *Educational Management, Administration & Leadership, 33*(4), 449–464.

Sotirakou, T. (2004). Coping with conflict within the entrepreneurial university: Threat or challenge for heads of departments in the UK higher education context. *International Review of Administrative Sciences, 70*(2), 345–372.

Strauss, A. (1962). Transformations of identity. In A. Rose (Ed.), *Human behaviour and social processes: An interactionist approach*. London: Routledge & Kegan Paul.

Suler, J. (1995). In search of the self: Zen Buddhism and psychoanalysis. *The Psychoanalytical Review, 82*(3), 407–426.

Taylor, C. (1989). *Sources of the self: The making of the modern identity*. Cambridge: Cambridge University Press.

Taylor, C. (1994). The politics of recognition. In C. Taylor, K. Appiah, S. Rockefeller, M. Waltzer, & S. Wolf (Eds.), *Multiculturalism: Examining the politics of recognition* (pp. 25–73). Princeton, NJ: Princeton University Press.

Taysum, A. (2012). *Evidence informed leadership in education*. London: Continuum International Publishing Group.

Thomas-Gregory, A. (2012). *A case study exploring the professional identities of a group of middle managers in a school of healthcare*. EdD thesis, University of Leicester.

Thomas-Gregory, A. (2014). Professional identities of middle managers: A case study in the faculty of health and social care. *Educational Leadership, Management and Administration, i-first* (February). doi:10.1177/1741143213513186

Tooley, J. (1996). *Education without the state*. London: Institute of Economic Affairs.
Tooley, J. (1998). The 'neo-liberal' critique of state intervention in education: A reply to Winch. *Journal of Philosophy of Education, 32*(2), 267–281.
Tooley, J. (1999). *Should the private sector profit from education? The seven virtues of highly effective markets* (Educational Notes No. 31). London: Libertarian Alliance.
Tooley, J. (2000). *Reclaiming education*. London: Cassell.
Trompenaars, F. (1994). *Riding the waves of culture: Understanding diversity in global business.* Chicago: Irwin.
Turner, J. (1994). *Sociology – Concepts and uses*. New York, NY: McGraw-Hill.
Volkmann, M., & Anderson, M. (1998). Creating professional identity: Dilemmas and metaphors of a first year chemistry teacher. *Science Education, 82*(3), 293–310.
Watson, R., & Thompson, D. (2004). The Trojan horse of nurse education. *Nurse Education Today, 24*, 73–75.
Weick, K. (2001). *Making sense of the organisation*. Oxford: Blackwell Publishers Ltd.
West-Burnham, J. (2009). *Rethinking educational leadership: From improvement to transformation*. London: Continuum Books.

CONCLUSIONS: THE DOCTORAL DIVIDEND; LEADING, LEARNING, RESEARCHING

Stephen Rayner and Alison Taysum

ABSTRACT

Purpose − *The purpose of this chapter is to consider a doctoral dividend in regard to leading, learning and researching.*

Methodology − *Our methodology is to analyse the chapters here presented and argue for key findings of the doctorate as an educational dividend. The doctorate yields a distinctive dividend in three important ways. First, it provides a strategic approach to purposes, processes and practices embedded in professional learning that is required for a profession committed to self-improving education systems to provide high quality learning opportunities for students in their local and globalized contexts culturally, economically and politically. Second, because it provides a valuable contribution to the knowledge economy and role models the discovery approach to knowledge generation. Third, it enables the profession to develop the knowledge, skills and experience required to engage with what counts for evidence when making decisions.*

Investing in our Education: Leading, Learning, Researching and the Doctorate
International Perspectives on Higher Education Research, Volume 13, 233−247
ISSN: 1479-3628/doi:10.1108/S1479-362820140000013011

Findings – *The profession can share these ways of thinking and doing with all stakeholders in communities of practice which move beyond students and staff within education systems.*

Originality/value – *The social implications are that the doctorate enables capacity building for professional, organizational and participant learning communities and networks, thus creating new and effective directions for knowledge creation, transformative learning and an understanding of quality in a local, national and international context.*

Keywords: Professional; research; capacity building; learning communities; self-improving; quality

Why would an educational practitioner find time, resource and commitment to pursue a doctorate in professional learning? Should a university be concerned and involved with offering such provision? And is there any purpose, relevance or meaning in such a pursuit or provision for the wider field of Education, in terms of its leadership, direction, future and the substance of what we will call here the 'educative endeavour'? These questions form a basis for revisiting the nature of educational leadership, management and policy that has implications for the declared purposes, provision and practice of and in Education, and more particularly, the university (see Delanty, 2001; Green & Powell, 2005), across a range of contexts that are local, regional and ultimately global. The answer to any and most of these questions, we suggest, is revealed in different ways as a combined outcome in the collection of chapters in this book. It represents a dividend that when imagined as a result or pay-off is in fact a rich mix of learning experience, new knowledge and a process that embodies a continuing investment in both professional and practitioner 'learning leadership'.

The notion of a doctoral dividend, however, as encompassing a set of distinctive qualities that mark out a meaningful engagement with professional learning, and which at the same time is a continuing creation of new knowledge is not new. The criteria for fulfilling the requirements of a doctoral degree are marked by a close examination of originality and a new contribution to the field. In this way, we would contend that involvement in the doctoral learning experience represents a form of scholarship that is both an apprenticeship as well as a further formation of educational expertise and understanding. Moreover, in this sense, doctoral students in education learn leadership as they become 'stewards of the discipline' and a source of new insights and direction for developments in pedagogy as described by Golde and Walker (2006). The researching professional is therefore a student who as a learner and scholar, in turn, actively contributes to the propagation of a 'doctoral dividend', that is, the assurance of originality, significance and rigour in an opportunity to further engage with a learning journey as well as contribute to the activity of a practitioner community in the educational profession.

EDUCATING EDUCATORS: NOW PAROCHIAL, GOING SYSTEMIC OR STAYING PERSONAL?

Existing provision for continuing professional development (CPD) in the English educational system across all phases is increasingly site-centred, inward directed and technical (frequently based upon a particular form or kind of evidence-based data linked to performance management and badged as training), with the implication that there is often little critical reflection, or higher order learning involved in a model of professional development. The approach is in essence parochial. There are not only worries for institutions about the removal of previously established government funding for provision in CPD as a result of this policy trend, which once upon a time ensured 'beyond the classroom walls' activity and a wider engagement with knowledge creation/acquisition, but also about the destruction of systems of education recognized as an imperative for safeguarding and assuring quality in a profession.

In what might seem an unexpected development, the Medical Profession offers an early example of what has been the 'new wave' introduction of more formalized systems for knowledge management in the organizational context, with concurrent positioning of research as evidence-based or clinical practice, and personal/professional education obligations required and purchased by the individual practitioner (Fraser et al., 2007; Mowatt, Grimshaw, Davis, & Mazmanian, 2001; Thomas, Hicks, Martin, & Cressey, 2008). In passing, and perhaps also as a significant under-tow effect of this development, the import of this approach is a re-casting or even removal of professional boundaries, and more crucially, professional identities, functions and knowledge within the profession. It is a trend contingent to more obvious movements in the re-shaping of a functional and performative model of leadership and management informing actual practice (in the working contexts of hospitals and clinical practice this embraces new paraprofessional boundaries and roles for practitioners).

In the public sector more widely, and Education in particular, this same new approach to workforce training is now marked by a deepening establishment of a managerial and administrative provision for site-based leadership in education, set in the context of a full range of practices associated with 'new managerialism' and a 'modernizing reform' of workforce in all phases of the educational system (Eva & Lingard, 2008). For an easy rejoinder, with a focus upon higher education, the headlined article in the *Times Higher Educational Supplement* (Grove, 2012) entitled, *'University manager numbers rising "twice as fast as academics"'* another insight is offered into this same changing priority. There is an apparent convergence of new governance and public reform, evidenced in the expansion of the 'quality branded' management of organizations by 'professional' administrators, and reflected in the profile of a changing academic workforce.

Perhaps ironically, much of this earlier development of provision for professional learning in Medicine has involved close collaboration on several fronts in recent years in England between University Schools of Education and NHS Trusts, with the further developing of online and portfolio-based training embedded in a medical practitioner working practice (Davis et al., 2003; Fraser et al., 2007). This is explored in Thomas-Gregory and Mercer's chapter in this volume where they conclude the kind of growth middle managers in a single school of healthcare require is a lengthy process of deep learning and experience which, we would argue, doctoral study is extremely well-placed to facilitate.

In part, and again perhaps reflecting an unintended direction and certainly one increasingly taken, the recognition of research as a key aspect in change management and assuring of quality in practitioner expertise has seen the UK University typically commit to the doctoral degree as a *bona fide* contribution to the 'knowledge economy' (Usher, 2002). It is also branded as an opportunity for extending range and quality in CPD. For example, the number of professional doctorates available in the United Kingdom, and internationally, has grown significantly albeit unevenly during the first decade of this century (Neumann, 2005; Usher, 2002; Wikeley & Muschamp, 2004). Amoaka has argued in her chapter in this volume that the contribution to knowledge can also develop governance systems. African students have come to the United Kingdom to do a doctorate and this connects with the African Unified Commission Agenda 2063 which regards the doctorate as critical for capacity building in Africa.

The African full-time doctoral students' learning journeys enable them to develop as nodes in leading international networks of knowledge that are sustainable. However, part-time doctoral study increasingly affords students similar opportunities through blended learning. Courses with blended learning include face-to-face and distance learning elements. Increasingly doctoral courses are offered as purely distance learning courses, but these can offer opportunities for a short period of campus-based learning for writing up a thesis, to develop multicultural dispositions and in some cases to enhance language skills if the doctorate is provided through a medium that is an additional language for the doctoral student.

The opportunity to progress with part-time personal study as a foundation in professional development, however, appears to be fading fast as a standard route of progression structuring practitioner education. Sabbaticals, secondments and study leave of an unconditional kind are a financial luxury only now associated with halcyon days gone by and in many English universities, the hazy memory of academic folklore. Twilight report writing sessions, in-house training days and on-the-job performance management have disrupted the space previously filled by accredited degree programmes of study provided by HEIs, and this despite HEI attempts to re-engage with an in-service education and training (INSET) market, by redesigning and offering modular programmes which are flexible and accessible to teachers studying part-time. To a greater extent, as previously inferred, this is further reinforced with fast moving changes and take-up in technologies associated with information management and communication. Yet the value and place of doctoral study as knowledge mediation, and thereby a bridging and integrating force in professional and personal development is considerable. This is critical to ensure that CPD remains relevant and is personal and of good quality. This assurance, in part is reflective of Shulman's original contention that those who understand knowledge growth will teach more successfully and that teachers need to develop deeper notions of professionalism and membership of an academic guild (Shulman, 1986).

MOBILIZING KNOWLEDGE MANAGEMENT: TECHNOLOGIES, TURNABOUTS AND TRADE

Part of an answer to the questions raised at the start of this chapter, furthermore, has to do with lifting 'horizons of thinking' and 'professional dialogue' for practising educationists. This might in one way be described as creating, mobilizing and establishing application of knowledge in a learning exchange. Or to adopt an alternative way of saying the same thing: it is about harnessing new technologies and understandings in theory and practice to foster learning communities of practice as a means of sustaining a 'stewardship of the discipline'. It is not difficult when taking this view to see advantages in an expectation that involves exchanges, taking turnabouts, new thinking, different directions and establishing a trade in partnership compacts which play a leading role in the advancement of research and development. Such work is aimed at epistemological change, personal education and professional development, and in other words, with a focus upon the educative endeavour, learning to critically analyse and reflect for emancipation (Taysum, 2012).

An example of this kind of thinking is found in the approach to establishing research interest groups described in Rayner (2011), and also instrumental in developing the focused research strategy underpinning the more recent approach at BELMAS in the past five years. The BELMAS Doctoral Research Interest Group, which led to running a seminar series and the generation of this book, are further examples of the same approach. As explained in the example of developing research focusing upon educational psychology and cognitive styles (Rayner, 2011, 2013), meaningful advancement arguably requires a need for establishing a concerted paradigmatic shift in the field. The contemporary research agenda failed in looking beyond a single prevailing research paradigm to consider what Storberg-Walker (2006) identifies as the potential of a theory-building research process, and realizing deeper understandings of the phenomenon under investigation.

As argued in the same approach to research and developing theory and practice in the research of cognitive style, educational policy, and leadership, management and administration, and in anticipation of a RIG initiative, the analogy of a 'constellation' of RIGs being orchestrated as a project was deemed helpful. Such a project was expected to share common purpose or agreed intention. It should also deliberately avoid adopting a specific differences model but certainly seek to establish a more coherent account of differences in human principles, values, habits and behaviours. In many ways, this approach is about domain-general theory (see Sternberg, 2008), and knowledge reconstruction facilitated by researchers involved in what we would like to propose is a grounded process of critical reflection, reflexion, revision and renewal. The aim for a RIG project is therefore one of facilitating a stepwise paradigm shift that will enable establishing:

- an inclusive research rubric;
- a theory-building research methodology;
- an integration of theory and re-connection with a common conceptual framework reflecting interdisciplinary knowledge, and multicultural dispositions that Taysum and Slater identify in their chapter in this book, located within an epistemological presence (Sockett, 2012);
- production of a quality-warranted collection of quantitative analyses to address the 'what' questions with qualitative analyses to examine the 'how' and 'why' questions of articulated objectives and underlying principles of particular systems for use in research and practice;
- production of practice and theory (praxis) based evidence for further developing knowledge creation, exchange, transfer and management.

Unsurprisingly, in work completed in the past 15 years, doctoral students and study played a central part in establishing the RIG idea in the European Learning Styles and Individual Differences Network (see: http://www.elsinnetwork.com/home-2014.html). Researching practitioners were often represented as a majority in this initiative forming a distinctive learning community. A second distinguishing feature of the same community was the consensual engagement with a process of professional learning that embodied the same research action of critical inquiry, reflection, reflexion, revision and renewal.

In this way, adopting the structure of a network reinforces a specific approach to doctoral work, and quite possibly, a re-forming of key conceptions in doctoral pedagogy and the planning of student experience. It is a way forward in bridging and/or mediating the theory-practice dichotomy, and frees up the constraints of simply imagining the interplay of research and learning as a continuum reflecting pure to applied work. As Rayner (2007, p. 116) has argued, 'types of network are increasingly important to how and what is exchanged as a form of professional knowledge'. The purpose and intended outcome in such work are both pivotal to the generation and delivery of good knowledge management. Professional learning ideally should always be about both developing an individual and collective *praxis* (Bernstein, 1983). A blending of theoretical and practical knowledge is an essential ingredient in any transformative learning that is by definition the 'stuff' of leadership for learning (Rayner, 2009).

All of this, moreover, is further reinforced by a constant and seemingly insatiable press in contemporary society for more connected ways of working and living using information technology. Developments over the past few years do not seem to be slowing at all and the changing implications for education, business management and workplace continue to grow apace. Coincident to this is a wave of new approaches to managing performance and expectations for life-long learning, knowledge management and organizational leadership in the working context. One such approach, which not only explains but also accurately describes the kind of changes occurring in our working lives [across the public, private and third sector settings], is the sociological construct of *heterarchy*. As Stephenson (2009) explains, heterarchy is a complex construct describing a 'mega-state of networked or connected hierarchies ...' which is most usefully represented as a series of autonomous but linked entities serving some common purpose.

This structural arrangement has been adopted across the British public sector, and by the UK government, partly as a consequence of market-driven approaches to efficiency and profit, which for example are characterized by outsourcing work previously completed by the single institution. Crucially too, however, the same approach has been used deliberately to restructure bureaucracy across the same workplace. As further explained by Stephenson (2009), the concept is central to understanding how a bureaucracy can be changed to allegedly become more fit for purpose by aligning its work so that a collective good can be realized in a way that previous hierarchies invariably fail to achieve. As Pring in his chapter in this book identifies, the collective good is thereby achieved within this system through open invitation into flat decision-making structures in a spirit of democratic participation, or coercion into forced hierarchical mechanisms as a means to an end, or some point between these two. The moral imperative is therefore crucial within the different parts and levels of a system when working for cultural alignment in order to exist via collaboration and/or coercion, and thereby agreement. The point of mentioning this changing structure as a device for organizing work here is that the same thinking seems to have influenced approaches to massive and continuing changes in the English educational system. It is now the case, arguably, that ways of learning are being restructured as a consequence of the heterarchy not only in terms of provision but also in terms of pedagogy and the status of epistemic frameworks underpinning the doctoral programme.

Ball (2009a, 2009b) writes persuasively about some of the implications of such changes in the English educational system, but for present purposes we should be clear that the important concept of networking, associated with new technologies and the heterarchy, is about how these changes both affect and offer opportunity for new forms of collaborative community building, professional learning, organizational leadership and doctoral study. Certainly, personal experience in leading research interest groups as one aspect of this approach, and indeed evidenced in the collection of work in this book, reflects an effort to generate both doctoral and post-doctoral study associated with professional and organizational learning linked to practitioner enquiry, new knowledge creation and mobilization (see Rayner, 2011).

DIGGING FOR THE DOCTORAL DIVIDEND – PROSPECTING FOR KNOWLEDGE

The dividend or pay-off for commitment to a doctorate exists at both the personal level of the individual, and for the workplace or organizational context. The dividend, as previously stated, is in fact a rich mix of learning experience, new knowledge and a process that embodies a continuing investment in both professional and practitioner 'learning leadership'. For Educationists, the Doctor of Education (EdD) is described by Scott, Brown, Lunt, and Thorne (2004) as a professionally focused doctorate allowing the development of research skills, reflection on practice and the undertaking of a substantial piece of research. Whilst previous research into professional doctorates offers comparisons between types of doctoral award (Maxwell & Shanahan, 1997), there is, with the exception of Lunt (2002) and Wikely and Muschamp (2004) who have looked at learning in virtual learning environments (VLEs), relatively little research specifically on learning, pedagogies or curricula associated with the EdD or Doctor of Business Administration (DBA) in the United Kingdom. Wellington and Sikes (2006) have considered motivation and choices made by participants following an EdD in the United Kingdom. Taysum (2007a, 2007b, 2012, 2013a, 2013b) and Taysum and Gunter (2008) have also researched how the EdD has facilitated development of educationists as knowledge users, and producers who impact upon the professional context.

Bowden, Bourner, and Laing (2002) identify the role professional doctorates contribute to a further generation of perspectival synthesis and transformative learning, which may be linked in turn to a theory of organizational management focusing upon conceived modes of knowledge production (Johnson, Lee, & Green, 2000). Further, working definitions in the doctorate arena are still being sought with regard to what counts as professional knowledge, in the effort to secure and assure relevance for an integrated approach to theory and practice in research methodologies employed in the professional doctorate (Lunt, 2002; Wikeley & Muschamp, 2004). The EdD to date also ostensibly offers a collaborative form of learning, and a professional-practitioner community as context for learning, which is different from the traditional independent learning offered by the more research-focused PhD.

The concept of the professional or taught doctorate, however, is an approach to CPD that irrespective of continuing wider changes in policy and provision remains work in progress. It presents, in its own right as problematic: this is because doctorates (professional, taught and (traditional) research-focused) are awarded according to criteria that largely remain and reside in the academic definition and interpretation of scholarship as one of contributing to new knowledge (Quality Assurance Agency [QAA], 2001). This leads in particular to an ongoing gap, for example, between research endeavour and knowledge generation in course-work components of professional doctorates, and the intellectual synthesis of theory and practice (see Manathunga, Smith, & Bath, 2004). This, and other related issues of defining and creating knowledge, learning and professional development, re-cast in the doctoral forum of studies in educational leadership and management, represent a key challenge for the future of CPD (its nature, function, place and value) in education over the next decade. As Waghid in his chapter in this book identifies, re-defining of pertinent forms of knowledge, and how they are created is important, as well as ways and means of exchanging, transferring and managing new knowledge. These aspects therefore remain both vital and relevant to both doctoral pedagogy, pedagogical relationships, and practitioner learning/expertise employed in the workplace. Equally importantly, doctoral programmes as a major plank in educational CPD will by definition underwrite continuing concern for good levels of *originality*, *significance* and *rigour* in approaches to educational research.

RE-ENVISIONING THE DOCTORATE AND PROFESSIONAL LEARNING

The development of evolving forms of CPD pedagogy/andragogy is an issue of serious concern in all forms of doctorate study (Scott et al., 2004;

Wellington & Sikes, 2006). As Samier identifies in her chapter in this book, crossing boundaries as an international scholar there is much importing and exporting of cultural knowledge where some forms are privileged over others, and important knowledge may be lost (Stuart Mills, 1859). While an emerging policy inertia in CPD provision is not desirable, and as previously argued a cause for concern, it is an indication for the need to re-think the construction of knowledge creation as a doctoral process, as well as the participatory basis of scholarship in an applied discipline within often polarized global understandings and misunderstandings of East and West. In effect, as Andrews in his chapter in this book identifies, this brings us around to re-examining how the curriculum, pedagogy, examination and accreditation of the doctoral degree should be further refined, with a view to closing the 'relevance gap' between basic and applied research (Aram & Salipante, 2003; Eva & Lingard, 2008; Flessa, 2007; Manathunga et al., 2004; Shulman, Golde, Bueschel, & Garabedian, 2006; Starkey & Madan, 2001). These, in turn, should ideally further deepen our intention to ensure these elements interrelate within a doctoral curriculum, to form a major vehicle for CPD, and we suggest, this is an overdue debate that should be shared between providers and users (participants/beneficiaries) of doctoral education.

A first part in such a debate might ideally focus upon issues of purpose, quality and outcome in an effort to re-evaluate what is worthwhile in doctoral study. These three sets of qualities are essentially the framework for informing the learning and teaching criteria in the process of completing doctoral study (Flessa, 2007; Taysum, 2007b). A form of criterion-referencing sits closely by similar debates focusing upon practitioner standards and ideas of 'quality' (Taysum, 2012c) occurring in a number of sites across research and social science, as it is applied to particular fields such as those of public health services, education, and business management. Critiques have addressed a range of key issues from the fundamental purpose of management research (Tranfield & Starkey, 1998) and the relevance gap with regard to practitioners (Starkey & Madan, 2001), as well as to issues of strategic significance such as the researcher capability in the workplace, where research informed practice is a hallmark of a forward thinking profession (see Cassell, 2006; Eva & Lingard, 2008; Pettigrew, 2001; Sahlberg, 2012), and in education (see Furlong & Oancea, 2005).

A second consideration in this proposed debate would focus upon issues of quality in research and teaching (also essential aspects in the work of any postgraduate research (PGR Study)), running to and with the realization of knowledge creation, exchange, transfer and management.

A consideration for such work might examine the requirements for advancing both applied and theoretical research in the areas of a widening of CPD policy development, teacher professionalism and pedagogy, educational leadership and knowledge management (Bulterman-Bos, 2008; Cassell, 2006; Shulman et al., 2006).

Lastly, a third crucial aspect to any debate of this kind must be a re-examination of the import and implications developing doctoral CPD has for a leadership of learning, and the management of educational policy. An interesting feature of current EdD cohorts is the diversity of public sector workers (leaders) making up the student group. This is particularly the case in EdD programmes which are generic, or those which contain a specific leaders and leadership strand. Students come from social care, public healthcare, local government and indeed from smaller agencies created as the result of recent reform. The benefits for leaders in acquiring the learning experiences associated with a vibrant EdD are rich, and complement the previously traditional route of a PhD. The impact for professional practice and workplace are considered by others (see Garrick & Rhodes, 2000; Powell & Green, 2007; Rhodes & Garrick, 2002) but arguably these impacts are clearly felt and generally perceived to be worthwhile (Wellington & Sikes, 2006), from the 'doctoral dividend' both as a personal and professional benefit, a benefit to a particular professional body, and thereby a public good.

It is vital, in conclusion, that such a debate is joined, and in our view, that it is both led and managed in a way that will lead to new and shared understandings in four key areas of policy, leadership, management and administration in education. Firstly, an intervention in the world of CPD for educationists that reflects a more clearly thought through strategic approach to purposes, processes and practices of embedded professional learning is needed. As Morrison identifies in her chapter in this book such strategic approaches may begin to address 'wicked problems' present within systems, their drivers and their mechanisms. Academic and professional communities/networks have a crucial part to play in helping to make this happen. Secondly, a clearer positioning and valuing of the EdD is required, with particular linkage to the traditional PhD, as doctoral education that is also professional learning, and as such offers a valuable contribution to the knowledge economy. Thirdly, it is necessary to consider a sector-wide effort in generating new warrants of quality for professional forms of knowledge creation, exchange, transfer and management, with information technologies and professional learning in the forum of PGR study. Finally, the identification of specific opportunities for outcomes and benefits of doctoral work could be further taken up as an embedded feature in professional, organizational and participant learning communities and networks, thus creating new and effective directions for quality provision in CPD in the new world of an educationally reformed leadership for learning and management of educational provision.

REFERENCES

Aram, J. D., & Salipante, P. (2003). Bridging scholarship in management: Epistemological reflections. *British Journal of Management, 14*, 189–205.

Ball, S. J. (2009a). Privatizing education, privatizing education policy, privatizing educational research: Network governance and the 'competition state'. *Journal of Education Policy, 24*(1), 83–100.

Ball, S. J. (2009b). Academies in context: Politics, business and philanthropy and heterarchical governance. *Management in Education, 23*(3), 100–103.

Bernstein, R. J. (1983). *Beyond objectivism and relativism*. Oxford: Blackwell.

Bowden, R., Bourner, T., & Laing, S. (2002). Professional doctorates in England and Australia: Not a world of difference. *Higher Education Review, 35*(1), 2–23.

Bulterman-Bos, J. A. (2008). Will a clinical approach make education research more relevant for practice? *Educational Researcher, 37*(7), 412–420.

Cassell, C. M. (2006). Advancing research in the business and management field. ESRC. Manchester Business School, University of Manchester.

Davis, D., Evans, M., Jadad, A., Perrier, L., Rath, D., Ryan, D., ... Zwarenstein, M. (2003). The case for knowledge translation: Shortening the journey from evidence to effect. *British Medical Journal, 327*, 33–35.

Delanty, G. (2001). *Challenging knowledge: The university in the knowledge society*. Buckingham: SRHE and Open University Press.

Eva, K. W., & Lingard, L. (2008). What's next? A guiding question for educators engaged in educational research. *Medical Education, 42*(8), 752–754.

Flessa, J. (2007). The trouble with the EdD. *Leadership and Policy in Schools, 6*, 197–208.

Fraser, A., Thomas, H., Deighan, M., Davison, I., Bedward, J., Field, S., & Kelly, S. (2007). Directions for change: A national survey of general practice training in the United Kingdom. *Education for Primary Care, 18*(1), 22–34.

Furlong, J., & Oancea, A. (2005). *Assessing quality in applied and practice-based educational research: A framework for discussion*. Oxford: Oxford University.

Garrick, J. & Rhodes, C. (Eds.). (2000). *Research and knowledge at work: Perspectives, case-studies and innovative studies*. London: Routledge.

Golde, C. M. & Walker, G. E. (Eds.). (2006). *Envisioning the future of doctoral education preparing stewards of the discipline*. Stanford: Jossey-Bass.

Green, H., & Powell, S. (2005). *Doctoral study in contemporary higher education*. Maidenhead: Open University Press and McGraw-Hill.

Grove, J. (2012). University manager numbers rising 'twice as fast as academics'. *Times Higher Educational Supplement*. Retrieved from http://www.timeshighereducation.co.uk/story. asp?sectioncode=26&storycode=419229&c=1. Accessed on March 05, 2012.

Johnson, L., Lee, A., & Green, B. (2000). The PhD and the autonomous self: Gender, rationality and postgraduate pedagogy. *Studies in Higher Education, 25*(2), 135–147.

Lunt, I. (2002). *Professional doctorates in education, state of the art paper commissioned by ESCalate*. Retrieved from www.escalte.ac.uk

Manathunga, C., Smith, C., & Bath, D. (2004). Developing and evaluating authentic integration between research and coursework in professional doctorate programs. *Teaching in Higher Education, 9*(2), 235–246.

Maxwell, T. W., & Shanahan, P. J. (1997). Towards a reconceptualisation of the doctorate. *Studies in Higher Education, 22*(2), 133–150.

Mills, J. S. (1859). On liberty. In M. Warnock (Ed.), *Utilitarianism*. London: Collins.

Mowatt, G., Grimshaw, J. M., Davis, D. A., & Mazmanian, P. E. (2001). Getting evidence into practice: The work of the Cochrane Effective Practice and Organization of Care Group (EPOC). *Continuing Educational Health Professional, 21*, 55–60.

Neumann, R. (2005). Doctoral differences: Professional doctorates and PhDs compared. *Journal of Higher Education Policy and Management, 27*(2), 173–188.

Pettigrew, A. M. (2001). Management research after modernism. *British Journal of Management, 12*, 61–70.

Powell, S., & Green, H. (2007). *The doctorate worldwide*. Maidenhead: Open University Press and McGraw-Hill.

Quality Assurance Agency. (2001). *The framework for higher education qualifications in England, Wales and Northern Ireland*. Retrieved from http://www.qaa.ac.uk. Accessed on March 5, 2012.

Rayner, S. (2007). *Managing special and inclusive education*. London: Sage.

Rayner, S. (2009). Educational diversity and learning leadership: A proposition, some principles and a model of inclusive leadership? *Educational Review, 61*(4), 433–447.

Rayner, S. (2011). Researching style: Epistemology, paradigm shifts and research interest groups. *Learning and Individual Differences, 21*(2), 255–262.

Rayner, S. G. (2013). Problematizing style differences theory and professional learning in educational psychology. *The Australian Educational and Developmental Psychologist, 30*(1), 13–35.

Rhodes, C., & Garrick, J. (2002). Economic metaphors and working knowledge: Enter the cogito-economic subject. *Human Resource Development International, 5*(1), 87–97.

Sahlberg, P. (2012). *Finnish lessons. What can the world learn from educational change in Finland?* New York, NY: Teachers College Press.

Scott, D., Brown, A., Lunt, I., & Thorne, L. (2004). *Professional doctorates: Integrating professional and academic knowledge*. Berkshire: The Open University Press.

Shulman, L. S. (1986). Those who understand: Knowledge growth in teaching. *Educational Researcher, 15*(2), 4–14.

Shulman, L. S., Golde, C. M., Bueschel, A. C., & Garabedian, K. J. (2006). Reclaiming education's doctorates: A critique and a proposal. *Educational Researcher, 35*, 25–32.

Sockett, H. (2012). *Knowledge and virtue in teaching and learning*. London: Routledge.

Starkey, K., & Madan, P. (2001). Bridging the relevance gap: Aligning stakeholders in future management research. *British Journal of Management, 12*, 53.

Stephenson, K. (2009). Neither hierarchy nor network: An argument for heterarchy. *Perspectives: Point/Counterpoint, 3*(2), 4–13.

Sternberg, R. (2008). Applying psychological theories to educational practice. *American Educational Research Journal, 45*, 150–165.

Storberg-Walker, J. (2006). From imagination to application: Making the case for the general method of theory-building research in applied disciplines. *Human Resource Development International, 9,* 227–259.

Taysum, A. (2007a). The distinctiveness of the EdD in producing and transforming knowledge. *Journal of Education, Administration and History, 39*(3), 285–296.

Taysum, A. (2007b). EdD research; does it have a future in developing educational leaders? *New Zealand Journal of Educational Leadership, 22*(2), 22–36.

Taysum, A. (2012). *Evidence informed leadership in education.* London: Continuum.

Taysum, A. (2013a). Educational leaders' doctoral research that informed strategies to steer their organizations towards cultural alignment. *Educational Management, Administration, and Leadership* (first published on October 1). doi:10.1177/174114321 3496660

Taysum, A. (2013b). The impact of doctoral study on educational leaders' work for students' participation in education systems and society. *Educational Review, 65*(4), 432–446.

Taysum, A., & Gunter, H. (2008). A critical approach to researching social justice and school leadership in England. *Education, Citizenship and Social Justice, 3*(2), 183–199.

Thomas, H., Hicks, J., Martin, G., & Cressey, G. (2008). Induction and transition in the national health service for four professional groups. *Learning in Health and Social Care, 7*(1), 27–36.

Tranfield, D., & Starkey, K. (1998). The nature, social organization and promotion of management research. *British Journal of Management, 9,* 341–353.

Usher, R. (2002). A diversity of doctorates: Fitness for the knowledge economy? *Higher Education Research and Development, 21*(2), 143–153.

Wellington, J., & Sikes, P. (2006). A doctorate in a tight compartment: Why do students choose a professional doctorate and what impact does it have on their personal and professional lives? *Studies in Higher Education, 31*(6), 723–734.

Wikely, F., & Muschamp, Y. (2004). Pedagogical implications of working with doctoral students at a distance. *25*(1), 125–142.

ABOUT THE AUTHORS

Richard Andrews is Professor and Deputy Vice-Chancellor for Research at Anglia Ruskin University in Cambridge. Until recently, he was Professor in English and Dean at the Institute of Education, University of London, and has held professorships at Middlesex, Hull and York universities. He has also been a visiting professor at New York University and a visiting research fellow at The University of Illinois at Urbana-Champaign. Prior to his work in higher education, he taught English and Drama in schools in London, Bedfordshire, York and Hong Kong. He holds a degree in English Language and Literature from the University of Oxford and a doctorate from the University of Hull. He was also awarded a double distinction for his PGCE at The University of Leeds, and won the Edwin Hopkins prize in Chicago in 1996 for an article on argument and democracy in education. His research interests are in argumentation at school and higher education levels; e-learning research methodologies; writing development; and contemporary rhetoric and poetics. He is the author or editor of the following recent publications: Re-Framing Literacy: Teaching and Learning in English and the Language Arts, Routledge, 2010, 240 pp.; E-Learning Theory and Practice (with Caroline Haythornthwaite), Sage, 2011, 262 pp.; Developing Writers: Teaching and Learning in the Digital Age (with Anna Smith), Open University Press/McGraw-Hill, 2011, 210 pp.; Rebirth of Rhetoric: Essays in Language, Culture and Education (Ed.), Routledge, 1992, 239 pp. (re-issued in Routledge Library Editions: Education, 2012); The Sage Handbook of Digital Dissertations and Theses (Ed., with Erik Borg, Stephen Boyd Davis, Myrrh Domingo and Jude England), Sage, 2012, 544 pp.; A Theory of Contemporary Rhetoric, Routledge, 2014, 204 pp. (ISBN 978-0-41550-355-6); Hamlet (Ed.), Cambridge University Press, 2014 (3rd ed.), 284 pp.; The Sage Handbook of E-Learning Research (2nd ed., with Caroline Haythornthwaite, Michelle Kazmer and Jude Fransman), Sage, in preparation for publication in 2015, 544 pp. He is preparing a book for Routledge, New York, on a prosody of free verse. He has published 50 research articles in peer-reviewed journals. Richard is on a number of editorial boards of journals, including: *Argumentation* (US/The Netherlands); *Learning, Media & Technology*

(UK); *Informal Logic* (Canada); *English in Australia* (Australia); *Educational Research Review* (Europe/Belgium); *Changing English* (UK); *International Journal of Computer Assisted Language Learning* (China).

Justine Mercer, is an Associate Professor of Educational Leadership at the University of Warwick. In an international career spanning nearly two decades, she worked as a British Council project manager, Ministry of Education advisor, school inspector, and Higher Education lecturer in Thailand, Turkey, China, Hungary, Oman and the United Arab Emirates. In March 2005, she returned to the United Kingdom to take up a lectureship at the Centre for Educational Leadership and Management at the University of Leicester. Five years later, she moved to the University of Warwick, as an associate professor, and now works at the Centre for Education Studies. She convenes the Educational Leadership Academic Group within the department. She is also responsible for an MA in Educational Leadership taken by teachers working in areas of socioeconomic disadvantage and recruited by the charity, TeachFirst. The MA programme enrols over 100 part-time students each year. Not surprisingly, given her international experience, she is particularly interested in cross-cultural understanding of educational leadership. Her own doctorate looked at the system of faculty appraisal at two universities in the United Arab Emirates (UAE). Since then, she has supported doctoral students doing studies in the UAE, Oman, Saudi Arabia, Kenya, Malaysia and Barbados. Whilst at the University of Leicester, she led a two-year collaboration with Herzen State Pedagogical University of Russia under the auspices of the British Degrees in Russia (BRIDGE) programme. This was funded by the Department for Industry, Universities and Skills. She has also been the recipient of research funding from the British Educational Research Association (BERA), the Society for Research into Higher Education (SRHE), the Leadership Foundation for Higher Education, the National College for School Leadership (NCSL) and the British Educational Leadership, Administration and Management Society (BELMAS). Her research interests include human resource management (HRM) within the higher education sector, the evolution of academic identity, and the influence of gender. This has led to a co-authored book on HRM and to peer-reviewed journal articles on international partnerships, junior academic-managers, women early career researchers and university heads of department. She has just completed a research project looking at the academic leadership offered by professors and is half-way through a similar study looking at the leadership preparation experienced by Further Education college principals. She is an elected council member for BELMAS.

Marlene Morrison is Emeritus Professor of Education at Oxford Brookes University, UK. A sociologist of education, her career spans nearly three decades in research and teaching, with an expansive publication record that reflects her professional, substantive and methodological interests. An educational ethnographer of long standing, her research interests are in leadership and in learning for social inclusion, most recently as a critical analyst of recent trends in education administration and research, and in applied ethnography. She has directed research and evaluations in all education sectors, including schools, further, adult and post-compulsory education, as well as in other public services, where recent interests include interprofessional education and collaborative practice. She was Research Director at the Oxford Brookes University and formerly an active member of three university-located research institutes, namely the Centre for Educational Development Appraisal and Research (University of Warwick), the International Institute of Educational Leadership (University of Lincoln), and the Centre for Citizenship Studies in Education (University of Leicester). She is an experienced external examiner of advanced studies, having examined the MA and EdD programmes of four UK universities in recent years. She has a long standing and consistent record as doctoral supervisor, internal and external examiner of PhD and EdD theses in the United Kingdom, and internationally. An experienced leader of undergraduate, Masters and PhD/EdD programmes, she has directed EdD programmes in several UK universities, including Oxford Brookes University School of Education, where she retains an active role and interest in research methods for doctoral studies, and education leadership and management.

Richard Pring, PhL (Gregorian University Rome; BA Hons University of London; PhD London; MA Oxon; Hon Doctorate, University of Kent; Bene Merenti medal Pope Pius XII; Award of Distinction Aga Khan University). Currently Professor of Education, University of Winchester; appointed as the first Professor of Educational Studies at Oxford University in 1989, and was Director of the Department from 1989 to 2003. From 2003 to 2009 he led the Nuffield Review of 14-19 Education and Training for England and Wales, a £1 million research funded by the Nuffield Foundation, published in 2009 by Routledge as 'Education for All'. Prior to Oxford, he was Professor of Education at Exeter University and Dean of the faculty, Lecturer in Curriculum Studies at the University of London Institute of Education, Lecturer at Goldsmiths College, teacher in London comprehensive schools, and Assistant Principal at the then Ministry of Education. Books publications since 2000: Philosophy of Educational Research, 2000, London: Continuum (2nd edition 2004, 3rd edition with considerable new material 2014 – being printed); Philosophy of Education: Aims, Values, Common Sense and Theory, 2004, Continuum; John Dewey: The Philosopher of Education for the 21st Century, 2007, Continuum; The Life and Death of Secondary Education for all, 2013, Routledge; Paperback edition of John Dewey: The Philosopher of Education for the 21st Century, 2014, Bloomsbury. Editorial Board of Oxford Review of Education. Previously Editor of British Journal of Educational Studies for 14 years. President of the Socialist Education Society of Great Britain. Hon. Fellow of Green Templeton College Oxford.

Stephen Rayner, Dean, School of Education, Newman University, holds both a first-class honours BA in American Studies, a PGCE with Distinction in English and History, and MEd from the University of Nottingham as well as a PhD from the University of Birmingham. He is the recipient of an Adjunct Professorship at the Faculty of Education, Monash University, in Melbourne, Australia. Stephen was previously Professor of Education and Research Lead in the School of Education at Oxford Brookes University, UK. He was while at Oxford also the Humanities and Social Sciences Faculty Lead for Postgraduate Research Degrees. Before this, he has over time taught in a secondary school, special schools and university. He was for five years head teacher of Penwithen School, Dorchester; then worked in the School of Education at Birmingham University, where he was Lead for several CPD programmes in Teacher Education as well as more latterly, the Director of Programme for PGR Studies. Stephen has served on several academic journal editorial boards including Educational and Behavioural Difficulties, Educational Psychology, Educational Review, Educational Administration and History, and Management in Education. He has in addition acted as a peer reviewer for many more academic journals in the related fields of Education, Psychology of Education, and Business Management. He has also been an active member of several professional associations, was the co-founder and for 15 years, President of a research interest group entitled ELSIN (see http://www.elsinnetwork.com), and served for five years as the Research Coordinator on Council for BELMAS (see http://www.belmas.org.uk).

Stephen has participated in a wide range of research projects with over 115 publications reflecting a long-standing interest in the study of style differences in teaching, learning and educational leadership, the management of inclusion and diversity in education, academic leadership and doctoral scholarship in higher education. Recent research has included work on professional learning in educational settings, intellectual and academic leadership in the professoriate, and research into University reform in England.

Eugenie A. Samier is Associate Professor of Educational Administration and Leadership at the British University in Dubai, United Arab Emirates. She is editor of and contributor to a number of books with Routledge on Ethics, Aesthetics, Politics, Emotions, and Trust and Betrayal, and is author of the recently released Secrecy and Tradecraft in Educational Administration: The Covert Side of Educational Life (Routledge). She has also contributed to a number of handbooks in the field and a number of journals internationally, and has been guest lecturer at universities in Canada, Germany, Russia, Estonia, Finland, Lithuania, Norway and the United Arab Emirates. She is currently working on the societal and cultural security dimensions of globalised education in developing countries, and leadership and administrative aspects of the Islamic tradition.

David Scott is currently Professor of Curriculum, Pedagogy and Assessment, Institute of Education, University of London. Previously he was Acting Dean of Teaching and Learning, Acting Head of the Centre for Higher Education Teaching and Learning, Director of the International Institute for Education Leadership and Professor of Educational Leadership and Learning, University of Lincoln. His most recent research projects include: Facilitating Transitions to Masters-level Learning through Improving Formative Assessment and Feedback, Higher Education Academy; Evaluating Teacher Development, CAPES, Brazil; Assessment for Learning (with the Hong Kong Institute of Education), Hong Kong Funding Council; Curriculum Structures 14-18 in a Mexican State (with C. Posner, C. Martin and E. Guzmann), Mexican Ministry of Education; National Curriculum Standards and Structures in Mexico (with C. Posner, C. Martin and E. Guzmann), Mexican Ministry of Education; India Capacity Building to the Elementary Education Programme (with G. Kingdon, G. Stobart, et al.), Department of International Development, in conjunction with Cambridge Education (Principal Investigator); Roles and Responsibilities of School Business Managers (with F. O'Sullivan and E. Wood), National College for School Leadership; How Teams Make a Difference: The Impact of Team Working (with T. Bush, M. Morrison and D. Middlewood), National College for School Leadership; and Professional Doctorates and Professional Development in Education (with I. Lunt, A. Brown and L. Thorne), ESRC. He has published widely in the fields of curriculum, educational assessment, comparative education and learning theory. His most recent books include: Scott, D. (2014) Bhaskar and Education, Springer; Scott, D. (2014) Curriculum, Pedagogy and Assessment, Springer; Mota, R. and Scott, D. (2014) Educating for Innovation: A Guide to Independent Learning in Brazil and England, Elsevier; Scott, D., Posner, C., Martin, C. and Guzman, E. (2014) Interventions in Education Systems: Reform Processes and Capacity Development, Bloomsbury; Scott, D., Evans, C., Hughes, G., Walter, C., Burke, P-J. and Watson, D. (2013) Transitions in Higher Education, Palgrave Macmillan; Scott, D. and Usher, R. (2011) Researching Education, Continuum; Scott, D. (2010) Education, Epistemology and Critical Realism, Routledge; Scott, D. (2008) Critical Essays on Major Curriculum Theorists, RoutledgeFalmer; Scott, D. and Morrison, M. (2005) Key Ideas in Educational Research, London: Continuum; Scott, D., Lunt, I., Thorne, L. and Brown, A. (2004) Professional Doctorates: Integrating Professional and Academic Knowledge, Open University Press; Scott, D. (2000) Reading Educational Research and Policy, RoutledgeFalmer.

Carolyn M. Shields is professor of educational leadership in the College of Education at Wayne State University, in downtown Detroit, Michigan, as well as being past president of the Canadian Association for Studies in Educational Administration and former Canadian representative to the Board of the Commonwealth Council for Educational Administration and Management. Her teaching is in the area of transformative leadership and ethics, deep democracy, equitable policy, social justice and research methodology. She is a recipient of several awards including the Leadership for Social Justice Special Interest Group's 'Teaching for Social Justice Award' in 2011. Her research focuses on how educational leaders can create learning environments that are deeply democratic, socially just, inclusive of all students' lived experiences, and that prepare students for excellence and citizenship in our global society. These interests are reflected in her presentations and publications – over 100 articles and 12 books – the most recent of which is Transformative Leadership in Education: Equitable Change in an Uncertain and Complex World. She has also received recognition for her career contributions to the field of educational leadership.

Charles L. Slater is Professor of Educational Leadership at California State University Long Beach (CSULB). He previously served as professor at Texas State University San Marcos and was superintendent of schools in Texas and Massachusetts. He received his PhD from the University of Wisconsin-Madison, his MAT from Occidental College-Los Angeles, and his BA from the University of Minnesota. He came to CSULB after serving as the Director of Doctoral Programs at Texas State University and at the University of the Incarnate Word. With this experience, he led the writing of the EdD Proposal at CSULB and guided it through the approval process. He now coordinates internal assessment for the Educational Administration Program and has served on numerous College and Department Committees. He teaches and conducts research in educational administration in Latin America and recently served as visiting professor at the University of Barcelona. He taught in the doctoral programme at la Universidad del Valle de Mexico for five years and has collaborated with colleagues to publish comparative studies of the United States and Korea. He has conducted research on social justice leadership in Costa Rica as part of the International Study of Leadership Development Network (ISLDN), jointly sponsored by the British Educational Leadership Management and Administration Society (BELMAS) and the University Council for Educational Administration (UCEA). The first line of research has focused on leadership with attention to cultural differences. These studies explore different requirements for successful leadership and the commonalities and differences in what people look for in a good leader. The second line of research has looked at the challenges of school directors around the world to determine what the experience of directors suggests for educational administration preparation. This work has been conducted with the International Study of Principal Preparation (ISPP), a collaboration of researchers in 13 countries. He recently edited a book summarising the experiences of this project. He has published numerous articles on educational leadership in journals including: *Educational Administration Quarterly, School Management and Leadership, Journal of Educational Administration, International Journal of Servant Leadership, Educational Forum, Journal of School Leadership, International Journal of Leadership in Education* and *Journal of Adult Development*.

His career in teaching, administration and research has been international in scope and focused on the development of students to become scholars of integrity, teachers of compassion and challenge and leaders who will advocate for social justice.

Emefa Takyi-Amoako is an Education, Gender and Research Consultant with a Doctorate from Oxford University. She is the CEO of ATP Global Educate Ltd and Executive Director of Oxford ATP International Education, which provides mentoring support to under/graduate and school students from a wide range of backgrounds to unlock and develop their intellectual and professional potential to the highest level for the benefit of not only themselves but also society in general. After her Bachelor of Arts Degree in English (Language and Literature) and a Diploma in Education from UCC, Ghana, Emefa went on to obtain a Master of Studies in Women's Studies from Wadham College, Master of Science in Educational Research Methodology and Doctor of Philosophy in International Education from St Anne's College, Oxford. Her interests are education policy, youth development, foreign aid partnerships, globalisation and power studies, African studies, gender and feminist theories, and postcolonial theories. She is an expert on education policy analysis, skills/training and youth development in the United Kingdom and countries in Africa. She has a rich experience in educational systems, and published works and authored a number of reports on education. She develops and implements educational enrichment programmes for the youth and taught in the educational systems of both the United Kingdom and Ghana. She taught on the Post Graduate Certificate of Education (PGCE) course and provided dissertation support for PGCE students in the Oxford University Department of Education. She also taught graduate level seminars on the Master of Science in Comparative and International Education Course, and was a study group mentor in the same Department. She was a Visiting Lecturer at Bath Spa University and a Guest Lecturer at other institutions. Emefa was a Visiting Fellow at the Centre for Cross-Cultural Research on Women (CCCRW now the International Gender Studies Centre) at Queen Elizabeth House, Oxford University. Emefa is, currently, involved in initiatives that aim to provide various support to students, and, also, editing a book on education in 18 African countries.

Alison Taysum began her working life as an industrial production manager before becoming a primary school teacher and School Governor. After becoming a mother, she moved into Higher Education in 2001 and taught on undergraduate courses at the University of Wolverhampton. Alison joined the University of Leicester in 2005 pursuing a research agenda with international partners to understand how post graduate research and research conducted in schools and colleges in partnership with Higher Education Institutions equip educational leaders and professional educationals to work as agents of change within policy frameworks to facilitate students' full cultural, economic and political engagement in their globalised societies. Alison has worked on funded Inter-University collaborations between the University of Leicester and Herzen State Pedagogical University of Russia. She was commissioned to do research on 'rethinking global trends of education reforms in England' by The Japanese Educational Administration Society and the Korean Society for Educational Management, and by the Japanese Education Forum on 'English Policies for Early years children and their implications for primary education provision and economic returns on investment'. The Japanese Ministry of Education, Culture, Sport and Technology and the National Education Policy Research Institute also commissioned a lecture she presented at the Ministerial Offices, Tokyo, on the training of the school leader through policy and structural reforms. She serves on the editorial board and reviews for international peer-reviewed journals, book publishers, and has reviewed for the UK Research Council. She is Treasurer for BELMAS. Alison's teaching at The University of Leicester is informed by her research agenda, which in turn informs her teaching. Alison was a Primary PGCE tutor and helped introduce Masters level to the Primary PGCE programme. She has served as external examiner for a Masters programme in England, and served on two Masters Programme validation panels in Scotland, and Northern Ireland. She was the programme leader of a large International EdD for three years 2009–2012. She currently supervises PhD and EdD students, contributes to doctoral substantive and methodological teaching at school and college level, and has served as external examiner for Doctoral programmes at Kings College, London and Lincoln University. She has examined doctoral theses for Universities in Pakistan, Dublin, London and Lincoln. In her local community, she is Secretary to Arden Parents' Teachers' Association, sings in a church choir, plays trumpet for Meridian Winds and is a former gym instructor and active gym member.

Annette Thomas-Gregory, Having trained as a nurse in the early 1980s at St Bartholomew's Hospital, London, Annette specialised in oncology, initially working as a haematology specialist nurse at St Bartholomew's and the Royal London Hospitals. During the early 1990s her focus shifted from acute haematology and oncology, towards palliative care, and she worked as a Macmillan nurse in North London. An opportunity arose to develop Cancer and Palliative care education within Cambridgeshire and this led to a further shift from clinical nursing to education and training.

Initially Annette took up post as a Senior Lecturer in Cancer care and was heavily involved in the development of Cancer and Palliative care programmes throughout East Anglia. In 2007 she was project lead for a partnership development of a Masters level course for Breast Care practitioners in response to a Department of Health call to action. Annette also broadened her interests to assume an active role in the development and delivery of pre-registration nursing programmes. More recently, as Course Group Leader, Annette's role has encompassed managerial and leadership responsibility for a broad spectrum of courses, including midwifery, public health palliative care and community care. Within this role she has led teams towards validation, and achieved success in a number of internal and external quality reviews. Her role has included the management of the department in relation to curriculum planning, delivery and review, effective communication with teams, action planning, teaching reviews and appraisal of staff. Since working within Higher Education Annette has completed a Master's degree in Nurse Education at the Southbank University and an Educational Doctorate in Education Leadership and Management at Leicester University. She believes that these exceptional educational experiences have given her role-specific skills, but more importantly developed her confidence and ability to think critically, be reflexive and exercise evidence informed, ethical leadership. In addition the combination of these opportunities and more recent experience as Course group leader have furnished her with an ability to make informed judgements on complex issues and design innovative approaches towards educational leadership and management.

Yusef Waghid is currently Distinguished Professor of Education in the Department of Education Policy Studies at Stellenbosch University. His most recent books that accentuate his research foci, include Conceptions of Islamic Education: Pedagogical Framings (New York: Peter Lang, 2011); (co-authored) Citizenship, Education and Violence: On Disrupted Potentialities and Becoming (Rotterdam/Boston/Taipei: Sense Publishers, 2013); African Philosophy of Education Reconsidered: On Being Human (London: Routledge, 2014); and Pedagogy Out of Bounds: Untamed Variations of Democratic Education (Rotterdam/Boston/Taipei: Sense Publishers, 2014).

INDEX